JESUS IN LATIN AMERICA

Jon Sobrino

JESUS IN LATIN AMERICA

ORBIS BOOKS

Maryknoll, New York 10545

Second Printing, June 1988

The Catholic Foreign Mission Society of America (Maryknoll) recruits and trains people for overseas missionary service. Through Orbis Books Maryknoll aims to foster the international dialogue that is essential to mission. The books published, however, reflect the opinions of their authors and are not meant to represent the official position of the society.

Originally published as *Jesús en América Latina: Su significado para la fe y la cristología*, © 1982 by UCA/Editores, Universidad Centroamericana, San Salvador and © 1982 by Editorial: SAL TERRAE, Santander

English translation © 1987 by Orbis Books, Maryknoll, NY 10545

Manuscript editor: Mary J. Heffron

Scripture quotations in chapters 1–4 and 7 are from *The New American Bible;* those in chapters 5, 6, and 8 are from *The Jerusalem Bible.*

Library of Congress Cataloging-in-Publication Data

Sobrino, Jon.
  Jesus in Latin America.

  Translation of : Jésus en América Latina.
  Includes index.
    1. Jesus Christ—History of doctrines—20th century.
  2. Theology, Doctrinal—Latin America—History—20th century.   I. Title.
  BT198.S6313   1987   232'.098   86-23489
  ISBN 0-88344-412-7 (pbk.)

FOR FATHER PEDRO ARRUPE

Contents

PART III
JESUS AND THE CHRISTIAN LIFE

Foreword

This book consists of a series of articles written by Jon Sobrino between 1978 and 1982. The first two chapters, and especially the first, are the most important and most theological. One can easily see how seriously the author has considered and developed them. They constitute a careful, complete presentation of his christological thought. As he says himself chapter 1 "seeks to remove doubts and answer questions addressed . . . to my *Christology at the Crossroads.*"[1]

Sobrino repeatedly expresses his intent to clarify certain difficulties that his earlier book has stirred up and thus respond to the demands of Puebla in its call for the totality of the truth about Jesus Christ.[2] He analyzes Puebla's christology objectively, both in its descending aspect (from a point of departure in the Incarnation) and its ascending aspect (starting with the historical, pre-Easter Jesus). He quotes Puebla's precise formulary, "It is our duty to proclaim clearly the mystery of the Incarnation, leaving no room for doubt or equivocation" (no. 175).

With a remarkable self-critical sense, Sobrino recognizes the "possible dangers" and misunderstandings occasioned by some of the texts of his earlier book, which "may be the fruit of limitation, precipitancy, or imprecision in [their] formulations." He realizes—and expressly acknowledges—the danger that Latin American christology may fall into the mistake of basing its faith in Christ the Liberator only on aspects relevant for intrahistorical liberation, thus omitting transcendent, metahistorical liberation, and that the ultimate criteria for liberation be taken not only from Christ the Liberator but from other sources too.

All of this demonstrates that Sobrino is fully aware of the risks that threaten the christological endeavor, and that he is being careful to avoid all reductionism or adulteration of it. He clearly affirms the transcendent dimension of Christian eschatology (the full, definitive salvation of the human being after death and the resurrection); nor is his view of the Christian practice of liberation inspired in any ideology alien to Christian faith, but rather in the praxis and message of Jesus.

This foreword is an edited translation of "Análisis del libra 'Jesús en América Latina' de Jon Sobrino," which was first published in *Revista Latinoamericana de Teología*, 1984. The translation is by Robert R. Barr.

THEOLOGICAL PROCESS

The author designates his own thought "Latin American christology" in order to qualify it as springing from Christian faith as lived in the historical situation of the Latin American people, and thus to express that the christology he develops is conditioned by that faith and situation. This formula obviously designates his own personal christological reflection.

The reflexive process of Sobrino's christology is easy to follow. It begins with what the gospels, especially the Synoptics, have handed down to us concerning the history of Jesus, his praxis and his message, the why and the how of his death, then moves to the basic fact of his resurrection, and from there to the faith of the infant church expressed in the transcendent (divine) titles of Lord, Messiah, and Son of God, as contained and explained in the so-called christological hymns of the New Testament (Phil. 2:5–9; Col. 1:15–19; Rom. 1:1–2; Gal. 4:4; Heb. 1:2–3; John 1:1–19) and culminating in the letters of Paul and the fourth gospel, which explicitly assert the divinity of Jesus, the crucified-and-raised one. Sobrino rightly claims that this procedure faithfully reproduces the route followed by the New Testament itself, which gradually moves to the revelation of Jesus' divinity—from the prophet of Nazareth to the preexistent Christ.

As transcendent aspects of the historical Jesus, the author points to Jesus' unique personal relationship to God, and to the kingdom; the definitive coming of the kingdom (the definitive, gratuitous salvific act of the father) in the person of Jesus; the demands of Jesus' "discipleship" for entry into the kingdom; Jesus' fidelity, obedience, and trust where the Father is concerned, even unto death on the cross; his person, praxis, and message as mediation of definitive salvation; his resurrection as confirmation (on God's part, who, in raising him, does him justice) of the ultimate truth of Jesus' person. The unitary whole of these data constitutes what various Catholic theologians today (Karl Rahner, Walter Kasper, and others) term "implicit christology," which of its very nature calls for "explicitation" in an express affirmation of the divinity of Jesus.

Sobrino doggedly insists on the deep christological meaning of the praxic "discipleship" of Jesus. Anyone in quest of unconditional attachment to the person of Jesus, to the point of making praxis the ultimate norm of his or her life, is implicitly professing, with a real and effective (praxis) faith, Jesus' divine transcendence: The personal surrender to Jesus in life and death is already an assertion (in the deep meaning of one's actions) of the divinity of Jesus.

An analysis of this work leads us to important conclusions. I shall divide these into two groups: those bearing on the orthodoxy of Sobrino's faith, and those bearing on his theology, his christology.

Sobrino's Orthodoxy

First, Sobrino expressly and repeatedly asserts his faith in the divinity (the divine filiation) of Christ. Second, he acknowledges his belief in the normative, binding character of the christological dogmas, as defined by the magisterium of the church in the ecumenical councils. Third, Sobrino asserts his faith in Christian eschatology, an end-time already initiated in the historical present of today as the anticipation of its metahistorical fullness to come after death.

Finally, Sobrino professes his faith in Christian liberation as "integral liberation"—that is, as human beings' total salvation, in their interiority and corporeality, in their relation to God, to others, to death, and to the world.

These four truths of Christian faith are basic for any christology. Sobrino asserts them without any ambiguity.

Sobrino's Christology

The process Sobrino follows in his christology can only be characterized as completely legitimate, as it corresponds to the progressive revelation of the divinity of Jesus in the writings of the New Testament. It is not an exaggeration to say that current exegesis unanimously acknowledges this progressive character of Christian revelation. It implies the divine element in Jesus' person (in his actions and message) from the outset, and culminates in the explicit profession of his divinity. Sobrino's christological process is complete, as it embraces the two indispensable aspects, the ascending and the descending, conjointly: It proceeds from the historical Jesus to the incarnation of the Logos, and vice versa. One might wish that Sobrino had sought to illuminate the profound meaning of the historical Jesus in his "poverty" and "pro-existence" (his existence-for-others) from the incarnation, as impoverishment and "emptying," since the ascending and descending (from the incarnation) phases of christology each shed their own light on the other and so fuse into a single christological process.

Sobrino himself remarks deficiencies of expression in his earlier work, *Christology at the Crossroads*. He has achieved the purpose of this sequel: to present, in conformity with the document of the Latin American Bishops Conference in Puebla, "the whole truth about Jesus Christ," explaining, precisely and without ambiguity, what it is that constitutes the basic kernel of the Christian faith, the nucleus that any and every christology must take up and endeavor to understand: that *Jesus is the Son of God*.

In presenting the figure of the historical Jesus, Sobrino emphasizes his praxis. Surely one may not overlook the special importance of Jesus' praxis in the synoptics (cf. Acts 1:1; 10:38). Here, however, we might ask whether Sobrino has sufficiently underscored the correspondence, the complementarity, and the mutual explanation in Jesus' praxis and message. Is not the kingdom precisely the center of Jesus' praxis and message alike? How can they be considered in isolation? Here we must recall the position of the Second Vatican Council on revelation as constituted "by deeds and words having an inner unity," and on the culmination of Christ's revelation "through His words and deeds" (*Dei Verbum* 2, 4: cf. 17).[3]

There is nothing novel in proposing Christian praxis as the "following" or "discipleship" of Jesus, as unconditional attachment to Jesus' person and the assimilation of his praxis. Neither is there anything new in seeing, in this normativity and ultimate motivation of Jesus with respect to Christian praxis, the implicit affirmation of his divinity (taking "implicit" in the profound sense of an unconditional option for Jesus and his praxis). But this merely implicit affirmation is insufficient for Christian faith. In Sobrino's own words, "the explicit assertion of Christ's divinity is indispensable."

Obviously, we are facing the problem of the pluridimensionality of faith here and of the relationship between orthodoxy and orthopraxis. The confessional, decisional, and praxis aspects of faith are united with one another, and only their unity constitutes the fullness of faith. The same is true regarding the connection between orthodoxy and orthopraxis. Accordingly, although the theological understanding of faith has need of distinguishing these aspects, the "indispensability" precisely of each of them and of their unity must be set in relief in order to have an authentic and fully Christian faith. To be sure, neither of these aspects of Christian faith is absent in Sobrino's book; still, it could be wished that a more express emphasis had been laid on their unity.

Sobrino correctly notes that Jesus has joined together the commandments of love of God and love of neighbor (love fulfilled in works: Mark 12:29-31; Matt. 22:38-40; Luke 10:25-37). But it should be observed that Jesus did not identify them either in his personal attitude toward God or in his message, where he maintained the absolute primacy of the relationship of the human being to God.

Sobrino presents, altogether clearly, both the personal and the social aspects of conversion to Jesus' gospel: a radical interior change, from a situation of sin (self-sufficiency with regard to God and selfishness with regard to neighbor) to a filial attitude toward God and brotherly/sisterly attitude toward human beings and a praxis commitment to justice—that is, today, a commitment to improvement and transformation of socio-economico-political structures in favor of the "poor" (the needy and oppressed). Only thus, in the unity of interior conversion and Christian commitment to new structures of justice, would the kingdom of God, as reconciliation, peace, and love, be reality in the world.

In his reflection on the situation of the Latin American people, Sobrino never resorts to the Marxist analysis of society, nor does he ever draw his inspiration from any ideology alien to Christianity. His reflection is always developed within that which is Christian.

There remains one point to be clarified. In his analysis and enumeration of the conditions required for a *Christian* praxis of liberation, as discipleship of Jesus, Sobrino stresses the need to proceed according to the spirit of the Beatitudes.

The follower of Jesus must have bowels of mercy, even in the struggle necessary for justice . . . must work for peace, must see to it that peacemaking be an ingredient of the struggle for justice, even though the struggle for justice, by the time it is over, justly involves some considerable form of violence, *which in extreme cases can even include legitimate armed struggle* [emphasis mine—J.A.].

I confess that this last clause perplexed me. My first thought was that Sobrino would have done better not to write it: it seems difficult to reconcile it with the praxis and message of Jesus and in our days we see that armed struggle does not bring true peace but provokes new violence and oppression. Then I recalled the words of Pope Paul VI in the encyclical *Populorum Progressio*, and we must of course take account of them:

> There are certainly situations whose injustice cries to heaven. When whole populations destitute of necessities live in a state of dependence barring them from all initiative and responsibility, and all opportunity to advance culturally and share in social and political life, recourse to violence, as a means to right these wrongs to human dignity, is a grave temptation.
>
> We know, however, that a revolutionary uprising—*save where there is manifest, long-standing tyranny which would do great damage to fundamental personal rights and dangerous harm to the common good of the country*—produces new injustices, throws more elements out of balance and brings on new disasters. A real evil should not be fought against at the cost of greater misery [nos. 30–31; italics added].[4]

I leave it to the reader to pass judgment as to similarity of content between Paul VI's expression, and that of Sobrino. I shall only observe that in both passages it is the extreme case that is in question.

JUAN ALFARO

Preface

This book is a collection of articles written between 1978 and 1982. With the exception of chapter 2, each of the articles has been previously published. The central theme of all of them is Jesus of Nazareth and his relevance to faith and the Christian life in Latin America. The first two articles have an additional theoretical finality: The first seeks to remove doubts and answer questions addressed to Latin American christology and to my *Christology at the Crossroads* (Maryknoll, N.Y.: Orbis, 1978). The second is an attempt to offer a more precise theoretical explanation of the meaning of the historical Jesus for christology.

In rereading these articles for publication I have noted certain shortcomings and I should like to share them with my readers so that they may read my book with greater profit and critical vision. I think that what is basic to the book—Jesus, the kingdom of God, the God of life, the poor, persecution, crucifixion—is already common property, at least theoretically, to much of theology and Christian life in Latin America and elsewhere. To repeat all this once more—and to repeat this central kernel in each of the articles in this book—may appear unnecessary and superfluous. Time does not allow me to eliminate certain unnecessary repetition. I trust the reader will forgive this.

In spite of these difficulties, I have decided to publish this book. My only apologia is that I think it can be of service. I am constantly reminded, as I reread these articles, that they were all written at the request of others, and that, in all of the different requests, with their different shadings and nuances, what is really being asked for is always the same: Tell us what is basic about Jesus. This indicates to me that Jesus' presentation—and repeated presentation—continues to be important for christology and certainly for the actual life of Christians. Curiously, all but one of these articles were requested in Europe. This indicates to me that the figure of Jesus as sketched in Latin American christology is of genuine help to the faith of Christians there, and perhaps to their christologies as well, although the latter are formally so much more complete than our fragmentary reflections on Christ.

All of this inclines me to think that the figure of a Jesus of the poor, who defends their cause and takes up their lot, who enters the world's conflict and dies at the hands of the mighty, and who thus proclaims and is good news is still fundamentally and eternally new. This is why I keep writing and publishing about Jesus, occasionally making theoretical advances and occasionally "repeating the same thing."

We do not easily become accustomed to what is "always the same," and we shall never become absolutely accustomed to it. One who approaches Jesus only as a student of christology can rather quickly assimilate—if this is what is desired—the theoretical novelty Jesus represents for christology. But for one for whom Jesus is good news and an eternal call to conversion and discipleship, this everlasting return to the figure of Jesus is a strict necessity.

This last fact does not, of course, in itself justify the publication of another book about Jesus, nor does it imply that the abundant theological literature on Jesus need not be judged on its own merits. But it does explain the intent behind this book. It may be that the reader will find here some theoretical advance: a stronger emphasis on relating Jesus not only to the kingdom of God but also to the God of the kingdom, a new effort to root faith in Jesus in the faith of the church in Christ. This certainly is my aim. But my aim has been above all to foster clear vision and bold courage in Christians who follow Jesus, who seek conversion, who battle for justice by struggling with oppression, who defend the cause of the poor and the oppressed, who suffer persecution, and who—sometimes—end on the cross. If these writings help these Christians a little, they will have more than fulfilled their purpose.

I should like to dedicate this book to Father Arrupe. This dedication has nothing routine about it. It is not being made because this is the style today—although it does not seem to me that this is a meaningless style, either, if it indicates that the theologian is not thinking or writing alone, but is relying on the professional and "testimonial" help of many others. I could have dedicated this book to any of a great number of Christians, living or dead, who remind me of Jesus and whose faith causes me to go back again to Jesus-who-is-the-Christ. I dedicate it to Father Arrupe by reason of the need I have to express my gratitude to him for all that he has done—amid great difficulties, tension, and suffering—to help the Society of Jesus be a little more like Jesus and follow him a little better. I do not know whether Father Arrupe will identify with the explicit theology of this book. For that matter, this is incidental. What is certain is that his example, his insistence on the *sensus Christi,* his discipleship of Jesus *in actu,* has been an inspiration to me. For this, I simply thank him.

PART I

BASIC THEMES FOR CHRISTOLOGY

1

The Truth about Jesus Christ

All through the history of the church, explicitly or implicitly, we hear the question Jesus himself put to his disciples: "Who do you say that I am?" (Mark 8:29). There has always been an answer in the real faith of individuals and community groups, arising out of theological reflection, liturgical celebration, pastoral ministry, and on special occasions, authoritative formulation by the church in its dogmatic declarations.

Jesus' question echoes down through the centuries, even though it has already been answered, because it is a question asked by Jesus himself—the one proclaimed in the answer to be the Christ, the Lord who died and rose again and who is still present in history with his questions and challenges.

The answer Christians give to this everlastingly historical question is always a historical one, since believers are themselves historical. In some eras the answer has come serenely and obviously. In others, however, earlier answers have had to be reexamined, either to be rejected, as has sometimes happened, or to be enriched by the signs of the times in which the Spirit of Christ has been made present.

In this article I shall attempt to anwer Jesus' question once more. I shall state the answer and attempt to show why it is the truth. The answer will be, as in the passage in Mark, that Jesus is the Christ. Most especially, I shall attempt to show that the Christ, the Messiah, the Son of God—is none other than Jesus.

To this purpose, I shall gather the fundamental data of the New Testament and the magisterium of the universal church, the data afforded by the reality of

This article, written in 1981 and translated by Robert R. Barr, was first published in Jon Sobrino, *Jesús en América Latina* (Santander, Spain: Sal Terrae; San Salvador, El Salvador: Universidad Centroamericana, 1982). It is intended as a response to the variety of reactions provoked by Latin American christology, in the form of gratitude and support, as well as doubts, questions, and attacks. Its purpose, then, is to clarify reasonable doubts, to defend Latin American christology— enriching and deepening that christology through a more explicit referral to church tradition and dogma—and to enrich the christological tradition of the church through any contributions Latin American christology may be able to make.

faith in Christ as found in the Christians of Latin America, theological reflection on this reality, and the pronouncements of the Latin American magisterium concerning Jesus Christ.

Accordingly, I propose to divide this article into the following parts: (1) The new situation in christological reflection; (2) The figure of Jesus Christ in Latin American christology; (3) Jesus Christ, true God: divine transcendence; (4) Jesus Christ, true human being: human transcendence; (5) The mystery of Jesus Christ: christological transcendence; and (6) Faith in Jesus Christ.

THE NEW SITUATION IN CHRISTOLOGICAL REFLECTION

The recent and current history of the church shows one of those ages in which Jesus' question again rings out mightily, one of those ages in which earlier answers are restated.[1] In order to give its answer, the church relies on the New Testament, tradition (especially its conciliar dogmatic statements) and on a new historical and cultural situation and a manifestation of the Spirit in the signs of the times.

This new situation surfaced clearly in the 1979 meeting of the International Theological Commission on *Quaestiones Selectae de Christologia*, "Special Questions in Christology."[2] The commission's document is a serene analysis of the enormous body of christological literature produced over the last twenty years, especially in Europe, and an attempt to harmonize the truth about Jesus Christ handed down by the New Testament and the christological dogmas of the church with the present situation, which is characterized by a novel emphasis on Christ's humanity and its salvific character. And so the document acknowledges that "theological dogma can be presented in current perspective without any detriment to its original meaning."[3] At the same time it demands that christology "take up in some way, and integrate, human beings' current view of themselves and of history."[4]

The situation described in the International Theological Commission's document has its analogy in Latin America as well. Let me briefly sketch the Latin American situation.

On our continent, faith in Christ has been maintained for centuries without any special christological discussion. We have accepted the dogmatic statements underscoring the divinity of Christ rather than those stressing his humanity, and those emphasizing the individual and transcendent rather than the historical, salvific significance of this divinity. Meanwhile, popular piety has reinterpreted Christ's divinity in its own fashion—as power in the face of the people's helplessness—and has sought its own ways to recover his humanity, especially in the suffering Christ.

Here, as in other areas of theology, Medellín recognized a change taking place in Christian milieus and expressed some of the elements of this change in a manner calculated to afford direction for a new pastoral and theological understanding of Christ. Medellín did not produce a document on Christ or sketch a christology. But it did make a number of statements with unquestionable implications for the understanding of Christ and for the subsequent development of christologies in Latin America.

Medellín presented the mystery of Christ most of all in its *salvific aspect*. Further, Medellín introduced a consideration of historical salvation into soteriology. The basic theme of the incarnation is considered as the way in which God's salvific design is realized.

> It is the same God who, in the fullness of time, sends his Son in the flesh, so that He might come to liberate all men from the slavery to which sin has subjected them (cf. John 8:32–35): hunger, misery, oppression and ignorance, in a word, that injustice and hatred which have their origin in human selfishness [Medellín, Justice, no. 3].

Christ is presented as *true human being*, and not only by means of a general acknowledgment of his humanity, but by a focus on a point on which the gospel narratives focus, and a point particularly well suited to a presentation of his humanity in today's Latin America: his relationship with the poor and poverty, a relationship shaping his person at the level of his interior disposition, the level of his actual manner of life and practice.

> Christ, our Savior, not only loved the poor, but rather "being rich He became poor," He lived in poverty. His mission centered on advising the poor of their liberation and He founded His Church as the sign of that poverty among men [and women] [Medellín, Poverty, no. 7].

Christ's *transcendent reality*, which precludes all reductionism, is stated from a point of departure in his transcendent relationship with God as "the image of the invisible God" (Medellín, Education, no. 9, citing Col. 1:15)—but in the context of liberation, of which Christ is judgment, norm, and goal, both with respect to the liberation process and with respect to the new human being to be achieved by that process, as the process is to be furthered by the new human being. In this context, Christ is said to "be manifested in human beings themselves" (Medellín, Introduction, no. 1); that he is "the goal established by God's design for the human being's development" (Medellín, Education, no. 9); and that "any enhancement of our humanity moves us nearer to the reproduction of the image of the Son" (ibid.).

Finally, Medellín develops the theme of *real access to Christ*, by which one knows not only who Christ is, but also how to believe in him, and how to recognize the historical loci of the concrete realization of what is now known of him noetically. Christ is encountered where he is. Thus his presence is repeated in the liturgy (see Medellín, Liturgy, no. 2), and in the witnessing faith communities (see Medellín, Lay Movements, no. 12). But Medellín adds something new: two other places of access to Christ. The first is history:

> Actively present in our history, Christ anticipates his eschatological deed not only in human beings' impatient longing for their total redemption,

but also in those conquests that "produce" the human being through an activity carried out in love. [Thus these partial conquests are] as signs of the future [Medellín, Introduction, no. 5].

The second is the presence of Christ in the poor. The theme is treated indirectly, more as Christ's negation in poverty than as poverty as a locus of positive access to him. The document is forthright: Where the poor are sinned against, marginalized, and oppressed, "there will we find the rejection of the peace of the Lord, and a rejection of the Lord Himself" (Matt. 25:31–46). The biblical basis brought forward is the celebrated passage from Matthew 25 in which we learn where Christ is ultimately and really to be encountered.

Beyond any doubt, these statements concerning Christ, while obviously "remaining ever faithful to the revealed word" (Medellín, Religious Education, no. 15), have had a powerful influence on the fashioning of a new image of Christ in pastoral ministry as well as on the appearance of what has come to be called Latin American christology or the christology of liberation.[5]

Unlike Medellín, Puebla devoted a chapter of its document to an express consideration of Christ: "The Truth about Jesus Christ, the Savior We Proclaim." Christ is also expressly referred to in other chapters. In what we might call Puebla's christology, various approaches to "the truth about Jesus Christ" coexist.[6] We find a "descending christology," presenting Christ from a point of departure in the incarnation of the Son (see Puebla, Final Document, nos. 188–89), and we have a christology of the historical Jesus, citing his proclamation of his kingdom, his words and works, the invitation to his discipleship, his proclamation of the Beatitudes and the Sermon on the Mount as the new law of the kingdom, his own interior life, including his willingness to suffer rejection at the hands of his fellow human beings and his susceptibility to temptation, his being delivered over to death as Servant of Yahweh, and his resurrection (see nos. 190–95). Other parts of the document, too, contain christological statements. We find the characteristics of the historical Jesus, especially his poverty (no. 1141), the example he sets for the ministry as Good Shepherd (nos. 682–84), and his function and nature as liberator (nos. 1183, 1194).

We find in the Puebla Document coexisting perspectives of salvation history and of the ongoing presence of Christ. The first means that Christ is seen from the viewpoint of God's plan from creation onward: with the coming of Christ, the fullness of time has arrived (see nos. 182–88). The second means that Christ is still present in history, and that therefore there are "places" where access can be had to him.

The exalted Jesus Christ has not forsaken us. He lives within his Church, chiefly in the Holy Eucharist and in the proclamation of his Word. He is present among those who gather together in his name (Matt. 18:20), and he is present in the person of the pastors he has sent out (Matt. 10:40; 28:19ff.). And with particular tenderness he chose to identify himself with those who are poorest and weakest (Matt. 25:40) [Puebla, Final Document, no. 196].

Finally, we find the coexistence of a pastoral and a doctrinal viewpoint. On the one side Puebla acknowledges and approves a "search for the ever new face of Christ, who is the answer to . . . legitimate yearning for integral liberation" on the part of God's people (no. 173). But we are warned that this search must safeguard and rest on the authentic doctrine of the church concerning Christ. The Puebla Conference recalls the cautions put forward by John Paul II in his Opening Address (see I, 2–I, 5) and solemnly states: "We are going to proclaim once again the truth of faith about Jesus Christ" (Puebla, Final Document, no. 180).

Puebla seeks to emphasize, from the teaching of the church, the totality of Christ: his human and divine reality, which means that the Conference considers that it has the "duty to proclaim clearly the mystery of the Incarnation, leaving no room for doubt or equivocation" (no. 175), and that it "cannot distort, factionalize, or ideologize the person of Jesus Christ . . . by turning him into a politician, a leader, a revolutionary, or a simple prophet" (no. 178). Of course, Puebla also seeks to maintain Christ's human and historical dimension (nos. 190–94), and warns against reducing him to the area of the purely private (no. 178). Of this there can be no doubt. But the doctrinal emphasis is primarily on the twin danger lurking in a kind of reductionism: the reduction of his divinity to his humanity, and the reduction of his humanity to the mere sociopolitical, through " 're-readings' of the Gospel" (John Paul II, Opening Address, I, 4; see also Final Document, no. 199).

Thus it is true that Puebla's christology takes in several different elements in its effort to maintain a needed variety of viewpoints and even includes elements of "liberation christology," moving beyond Medellín's formulations. Still, during and after Puebla, various members of the Latin American hierarchy have repeated the warnings we have just quoted, sometimes pointing the accusing finger at liberation christology in general and even citing particular authors.

This is the determinate context in which this work has been written. There is no ignoring the fact of a Latin American christology, or at least the basic outline of one, even though what is actually presented focuses on the life of Jesus and is not structured along the lines of traditional tractates on christology.[7] This Latin American christology has had pastoral consequences, in large part because its content was lived before it was reflected upon. These pastoral consequences are viewed positively by some, but they are looked on with suspicion and fear by others. Neither Puebla nor the church hierarchy has condemned liberation christology. But it is evident that the hierarchy seeks or demands a clarification of liberation christology on the crucial point of whether it includes the whole of the "truth about Jesus Christ."

In this work, and in this context, I shall attempt to furnish that clarification—although, as is obvious, I must limit myself to the most important points and not try to handle all of the problems of christology. What I offer here will be what I see as the intent and content of the christology of liberation—although, what I have written here must in the last analysis be my view and responsibility.[8] Furthermore, specifically, I hope to be able to clarify certain difficulties arising from my book *Christology at the Crossroads*.

By way of concluding my explanation of the context of this article, I make two observations.

On the one hand, this book is an attempt to respond to a legitimate demand: that we give an account of the "truth about Jesus Christ." Christians are supposed to be ready to give an account of their hope (1 Pet. 3:15). Theology, then, should be ready to give an account of the truth about Jesus Christ. This is an objective, legitimate demand, and may not be ignored once it is made, regardless of its occasion or intent.

Further, however it may be that this demand is made of theology "from without," theology must respond, must endeavor to explain the truth about Christ "from within." Without this truth, the substance of the Christian faith, and the evangelizing activity of the church, would be eviscerated. Theology itself would be "denatured," and would cease to be of any help to real faith in Christ.

On the other hand, this book will make no attempt to set forth the truth about Christ without taking account of the basic elements of faith in Christ as presently developing in Latin America and being theorized by liberation christology. To be sure, the source and finality of this christology is not the explanation of either New Testament or magisterial formulas concerning the totality of Christ. Unlike other christologies, the christology of liberation is not conceived for the purpose of making these formulas understandable for those who, for contingent cultural reasons, find them doubtful. The intent of liberation christology is more immediately pastoral. Here it will suffice to cite the statement of Juan Luis Segundo:

> Christians of the left, the right, and the center all agree that Jesus Christ is true man and true God, that God is one in three persons, and that Jesus has redeemed the human race by his death and resurrection.[9]

Although this is not its purpose, liberation christology—which, like any other christology, must be enriched by the formulation of the New Testament and the ecclesiastical magisterium regarding Christ—can be of help when it comes to explaining and radicalizing these dogmatic formulations. Neither the limitations inherent in any given christology, nor the unilateral emphasis it may be likely to lay on the historical Jesus, are any impediment to this possibility. To the extent that liberation christology takes account of realized faith in Christ, it will be able to help toward an understanding of the total truth of what is believed. And so I shall first make a brief presentation of the kernel of the christology of liberation, and only then come to treat of the truth of the divinity, the humanity, and the mystery of Christ.

THE FIGURE OF JESUS CHRIST
IN LATIN AMERICAN CHRISTOLOGY

I have set forth elsewhere the importance of the christology of liberation for the evangelizing mission of the church, for the Christian practice of liberation, and for the revival of the faith of so many Christians. Here I present the elements of liberation christology from a point of departure in its positive implications—as well as in its possible dangers—for the theme of this work: the truth about Jesus Christ.

I will say from the outset, however, what it is that appears to me to be the christo-logical and theo-logical kernel of the christology of liberation—the intended object of its service. Any christology must say that Jesus is the Christ. Liberation christology emphasizes that the Christ is no one but Jesus. Any theo-logy must hold that Jesus is God. Liberation christology emphasizes that we only know what God is from a point of departure in Jesus. This, I maintain, is the kernel of our Christian faith, which is at once the Good News and a scandal. As I have written elsewhere—not for the sake of polemics, but simply to maintain the scandal:

> The Chalcedonian formula presupposes certain concepts that in fact cannot be presupposed when it comes to Jesus. [It] assumes we know who and what God is and who and what human beings are. But we cannot explain the figure of Jesus by presupposing such concepts because Jesus himself calls into question people's very understanding of God and human beings. We may use "divinity" and "humanity" as nominal definitions to somehow break the hermeneutic circle, but we cannot use them as real definitions, already known, in order to understand Jesus. Our approach should start from the other end.[10]

This is a scandal for the natural human being who claims to know beforehand what it is to be a human being and what it is to be God and to be able to judge the truth of Jesus on the basis of this previous knowledge. But it is especially a scandal, and remains so even for believers, when, a posteriori, the true human being is revealed as poor, at the service of others, crushed, and crucified, and therefore and thereby exalted, when the true God is revealed as partial to the poor and oppressed, as liberator through love and as the one who hands over a Son (in daring metaphor: as God liberating and crucified).

All of this is doubly scandalous when it comes to light that it is precisely *that* Jesus, living his humanity in the way that he does and definitively rendering God present, who is God and who proclaims the Good News.[11] The unification of scandal and good news is a scandal for natural reason. But it is the substance of Christian faith.

This, in synthesis, is what I have sought to set forth in my christological reflections.

It should not present any obstacle to the appearance of the totality of the "truth about Jesus Christ." On the contrary, it provides the locus in which his true *totality* (God and human being, the mystery of Jesus) and his total *truth* (the mystery of God and the human being *starting from* Jesus) may be asserted.

Of course, making this basic assertion does not clear up potential or real misunderstandings of the christology of liberation—which, for that matter, may be the fruit of limitation, precipitancy, or imprecision in some of its formulations. But it may clear up the underlying misunderstandings. The christology of liberation does not intend to "reduce" Christ, but to show how, from a point of departure in Jesus, the mystery of God and the human being, whose supreme expression is Christ himself, gradually—and scandalously and salvifically—unfolds.

This said, let us analyze liberation christology, its implications for the development of the truth about Jesus Christ, and its possible dangers in detail.

In its origins, the christology of liberation was joined to a historical and ecclesial praxis of liberation, and its more reflexive intention has consisted precisely in Christian assistance to this praxis. True, the need for historical liberation is obvious, and the historical praxis of liberation, in a general sense, requires no justification.[12] But Christians who had inserted themselves into a liberative practice were searching both for a way to see their historical praxis as consistent with their actual Christian faith and for the support and radicalization that faith lends that praxis. Therefore they went back to the figure of Jesus, and this was the origin of an incipient reflection on Christ. Further, in view of certain difficulties that were not only historical but also intraecclesial, they appealed to the new figure of Christ, for which the praxis of liberation had discovered an ecclesial authenticity, and which—who knows?—might even yield a criterion of truth that would be helpful for the resolution of interchurch conflicts aroused by this new practice. Briefly stated, this new reflection on Christ originated in the service of historical liberation and for the purpose of inviting the church, precisely in virtue of its faith in Christ, to insert itself into a task of liberation that would now be seen to be specifically Christian in form.

This reason for reflecting on Christ might be objected to on the grounds that, although both the liberation process itself and assistance to the process to be provided by the faith are correct and desirable, still they sow dangerous seeds for christology. Christology may now become the functionalization of Christ. Now the legitimate "use" of Christ to motivate liberation may be converted into "abuse." To put it systematically: the danger would be that the Liberator would disappear behind the liberation—that the Liberator would be used only when he was relevant for "historical" liberation, ignoring "transcendent" liberation—that the ultimate criteria of liberation, even in its historical aspect, would not be sought in the Liberator, but elsewhere.

The objection can be stated more radically: Although the "use" of Christ may be substantially correct, from a Christian viewpoint christology would lose its proper basicity and ultimacy in favor of a simple theology of history asserting the liberative will of God and the proclamation of the kingdom of

God to the poor. Christ would then appear merely as one of the important mediators of liberation, in the line of Moses or the prophets, and although his major, decisive importance would be acknowledged, his ultimacy with respect to revelation would be obfuscated.

The fear of these dangers as necessarily entailed in the very origins of a christology of liberation cannot be refuted a priori. One must examine the fear historically and try to determine the extent to which it is valid. It is always difficult in the practice of the faith to maintain Christ's totality—first, and independently of liberation christology, by reason of the very scandal inherent in that faith, as explained above. But besides this, it is always historically difficult to maintain the tensions between the historicization of the element of transcendency in faith in Christ and the transcendency of the historical element in that faith. In practice, therefore, it cannot be denied that the danger of so-called horizontalism exists and that this danger has become reality, on occasion, owing to the very nature of the processes of historical liberation. This does not mean, however, that the avoidance of horizontalism will of itself be the guarantee of an authentically Christian verticalism, or that horizontalism in and of itself is a greater danger for faith in Christ than verticalism.

Whatever the horizontalist reductionisms *de facto* occurring in faith in Christ may be, then, what concerns us is to emphasize that they subsist in practice rather than in christological theory, that liberation christology, from its inception, has successfully avoided such reductionism. Below, I shall develop the elements of liberation christology in their totality. For the present, suffice it to cite three antireductionist elements in the origins of that christology.

First, it is important to recall the strictly evangelical tenor of the christology of liberation in its inception. This reflection was undertaken with the conviction that the gospel of Jesus is good news for the poor, and that the poor are the key to our approach to the gospel today. The importance of this statement, so obvious today, resides in the fact that, as Gustavo Gutiérrez has recalled, underlying the theology of liberation from the start were the themes of poverty and Matthew 25. Gutiérrez rightly rejects an interpretation "to the effect that, in its beginnings, the theology of liberation was centered exclusively on the Old Testament theme of the exodus."[13] Obviously, I am not concerned to depreciate the importance of the Old Testament or of the passages dealing with the liberation from Egypt. But it is important to make it clear that the figure of Jesus has been the key to liberation theology from the outset. Matthew 25 is basic, both for doing theology from a point of departure in the poor and for understanding Jesus as he is to be found in the poor. The simple conclusion is that, in the task of liberation theology, Jesus has always held the ultimate primacy and that he cannot be compared to, still less surpassed by, other liberating biblical figures.

Second, Christ is presented not only as the one who moves humanity toward liberation, but also as the norm of liberative practice and the prototype of the new human being for whom liberation strives. Jesus is *norma normans* of liberation, not its *norm normata*. Simply but profoundly this is what is indicated by the Latin American christological title "Jesus Christ the Liberator." The epithet "Liberator" calls for a reference to historical practice on the part of christological reflection. But the article "the" requires that reflection to refer liberation to its herald, norm, and judge.[14]

Third, we must recall the kind of ethical indignation—in addition to an epistemological suspicion—that lies at the basis of an incipient liberation christology.[15] It does not originate as an attempt to quell doubts about Christ, but as an expression of indignation over the use to which Christ has so often been put in the history of Latin America in order to justify the oppression of the poor.[16]

This indignation has two streams. The first, and most visible, is that of the tragic repercussions for the poor of Christ's manipulation. But there is another stream, running toward the very person of Christ. One is indignant that the reality of Christ, his person, has been manipulated, distorted, commandeered, "kidnapped." Behind this second indignation is sorrow not just on account of the oppression of the poor, but also on account of the falsification of the identity of someone of supreme personal significance and meaning for Christians and theologians: the person of Christ. The indignation is like that so often expressed in Scripture: "On your account the name of God is held in contempt among the Gentiles" (Rom. 2:24; see also Isa. 52:5; Ezek. 36:20–22; James 2:7; 2 Pet. 2:2). In parallel fashion, we might say that, on account of a false presentation of Christ, some have abandoned faith in him, although not blaspheming his name.

This indignation and sorrow over the manipulation of Christ is but the other side of the coin of love for Christ. It may seem out of place, like over-psychologizing, to mention the love of Christ here. But if the love of Christ is present in the beginnings of a christology of liberation, then the christological reflection that ensues will have at least one necessary element, however insufficient it may be from other points of view.[17] That this love of Christ is indeed present in liberation christology may be gathered from Leonardo Boff's statement, so admirable in its simplicity, made when the christology of liberation was in its infancy: "True theologians can speak only when Jesus Christ is their point of departure, that is, when touched by Jesus' reality lived in faith and love."[18]

These are some of the objective and subjective elements we find as a christology of liberation gets under way, elements accompanying the unquestionable use of Christ for the liberative task. The person of Christ does not disappear in the principles of liberation christology—and this "on principle": the Liberator is not dissolved into liberation. The least that can be said is that, as liberation christology gets under way, there is a real interest in the person of Christ, and therefore the objective possibility exists that from within the dynamic of reflection there may arise a reflection on the truth of Jesus Christ that does not entail any limitation of that truth.

From these beginnings, the christology of liberation has proceeded to develop a *figure of Christ*. There is no denying that, within the totality of this figure, the so-called historical Jesus has been set in relief.[19] Elsewhere I have developed the "Latin American reasons" for, and precise meaning of, taking the historical Jesus methodologically as the point of departure for reflection on the totality of Christ.[20] Here, suffice it to recall that I have done so (1) to clarify the Christian necessity and specificity of the liberation process; (2) the better to develop the task of fundamental theology and render the acceptance of the mystery of Christ more efficacious; and (3) to deepen and radicalize dogmatic statements.

Let us now examine certain basic details in this figure of Christ, taking special account of their implications for the totality of the truth of Christ.

The christology of liberation presents Jesus first of all in his relationship with the kingdom of God and develops this relationship into the key datum for a comprehension of the truth of Jesus.[21] Inasmuch as this kingdom is the kingdom *of God*, Jesus enjoys a relationship, from the outset, with what is ultimate in God's will: "Your kingdom come" (Matt. 6:10). Jesus himself appears as related, with ultimacy, to what is ultimate in God's will. The christology of liberation understands the kingdom of God from a point of departure in Jesus, in what Jesus says about the kingdom and in what he does in behalf of that kingdom. What the kingdom is, how it is brought to realization, what its values are, how one "corresponds" to it—all of this we know, in principle, starting from Jesus, and, ultimately, only starting from Jesus.

Thus liberation christology runs no risk of reduction to a mere jesuology. True, from a historical point of view liberation christology sees Jesus in relation to the kingdom of God. But from a systematic point of view it sees the kingdom of God in relation to Jesus.[22] It is the ultimacy of this relation that permits a christological and not merely a jesu-ological analysis, an analysis of the relationship between the kingdom of God and Jesus.

The christology of liberation describes the *practice of Jesus* as service to that kingdom of God. Jesus is presented as incarnate, partisan, in the world of the poor.[23] It is to the poor that he addresses his mission in a special, privileged manner, it is with them that he lives; it is for them that he posits the signs of the coming of the kingdom—miracles, the expulsion of demons, wondrous food and drink. It is from a starting point among the poor that he denounces the basic sin and tears away the mask from rationalizations of that sin. Because of all this, he comes into conflict with the mighty, and is persecuted to death.

Liberation christology describes this practice not only as a historical, observable fact, but as *Jesus' response to the will of the God of the kingdom*. Jesus' practice is nourished by a personal conviction that is not open to further analysis, since it is rooted in his relationship with God. Jesus comes in contact with that God by prayer, he trusts in that God, he is obedient and loyal to that God to the end. Jesus appears not only as the person of the practice of the kingdom, but as the witness of faith, and both of these with ultimacy.[24]

Liberation christology emphasizes *Jesus' demands on his hearers*, both in the sense of a radical conversion from sin and in that of the building of the kingdom. Through both, Jesus demands the shaping of the new human being according to the spirit of the Beatitudes.[25]

Liberation christology does not see in Jesus' demand for discipleship the adequate resolution of the thorny problem of his self-consciousness, although it values it highly.[26] However, in plumbing the radical depths of the discipleship he demands and its ultimate basis in his own *person*, it does present Jesus, at least implicitly, in a christological manner.[27]

Liberation christology presents the Paschal mystery as the crowning point of Jesus' history, and as the basic datum for the development of a christology. It emphasizes the historical reasons for Jesus' death: the conflict he aroused, the persecution to which he was subjected, the accusation of blasphemy lodged against him, and his being sentenced to death as a political agitator. But it presents these historical facts as the outcome of his obedience to the Father.[28]

The Jesus who lived and died in this fashion has been raised and exalted by God. The resurrection confirms the truth of Jesus' life and the ultimate truth of his person. The starting point for the christology of liberation is the resurrection. From there it understands the New Testament faith in Christ and the various titles in which that faith comes to be expressed.

Following the New Testament, liberation christology maintains the decisive statement that the one who was crucified has been raised. But it also maintains the converse: the one who has been raised is none other than the one who was crucified. Thereby it can understand what the New Testament properly asserts: the Lord, the Messiah, the Son of God, is Jesus, so that, although these titles are a way of proclaiming Jesus' ultimacy, at the same time it is Jesus who is the content of the ultimacy of these titles. This is properly Christian truth, as well as the scandalous salvific truth that the christology of liberation makes bold to maintain.[29]

Within this truth, following the actual development of the New Testament and the early centuries of church history, liberation christology sets no limits to the logic of faith, which leads to ever clearer and more radical statements about Christ, culminating in his divinity and divine sonship. Liberation christology has not explicitly set itself the task of this development, but it recognizes and acknowledges the radicalness with which the formulas of the New Testament and the councils of the first centuries profess Christ "true God and true man."

From its starting point in Jesus, in his life, death, and resurrection, the christology of liberation has also developed its *image of God*.[30] From Jesus' life, God appears as the God of life, whose will is the life and salvation of all men and women. History is shot through with sin and condemnation. Jesus proclaims a God who comes, who approaches in the kingdom, and thereby sunders the symmetry of a God who may be near and who may be far, who may be savior and who may condemn. God draws near, and this means that God is really love and grace.

This God, who seeks the salvation of each and all, is for Jesus a God of the poor. God feels a special preference and tenderness for the poor. These are the ones who are approached directly in the kingdom, without excluding from it those who, without being poor, wish to become poor and thus enter into the kingdom. Being a God of the poor, God is also the God of the strong prophetic word, who desires mercy and not sacrifice, who blesses the poor and curses those who live in abundance and who vitiate creation by oppressing human beings.

This God is personal. One ought to speak with God in all simplicity in prayer, with the trust and tenderness of a child speaking with a father or mother—but also with the seriousness of one who stands before a God who has a determinate will and who can demand everything of human beings—and with openness to God's word, which is ever new, and can always outstrip human traditions about God.

This God of Jesus is revealed in plenitude, once more through Jesus, in the deed of Easter. Here God is revealed as holy mystery, as love incomprehensible—but comprehensible in its credibility. On the cross, God lets the divine Son die. The almighty does not act in the presence of the power of false divinities, those death-dealing idols: economic power, political power, and religious power. On the cross, the problem of God is raised to the status of mystery. The cross does away with conventional ideas of God, opening the way to a new, revolutionary conception of God.

In the resurrection, God is shown to be the one who raises Jesus, is seen as the one who can call non-life to life, and thereby is seen as love for whoever is small, whoever is crushed and under sentence of death, as hope for whoever is small, crushed, and under sentence of death. If God raised Jesus, then God was also on Jesus' cross, in the horrors of human history.

Out of that action of God in Jesus' life, death, and resurrection, liberation christology is able to formulate the ultimate reality of God as holy mystery. God is mystery because God really transcends, is greater than human beings, and greater than anything human beings could conceive about the deity. But this greater being appears not only in virtue of a qualitative difference between creator and creature in the beginning, and not only in virtue of the difference between history as such and God's absolute future, but specifically in virtue of the divine presence on the cross of Jesus. Here the molds of natural reason are broken, for the one beyond, the transcendent one, has become, incredibly, the one right here, the immanent one. Out of the most absolute nearness appears the mystery of God's otherness. And so, in order to formulate the mystery of God, liberation christology has made use of the traditional formulation of the "greater God" ("Dios mayor") in dialectical relationship with the "lesser God" ("Dios menor").

This mystery of God is holy ultimately because God is love. This is what is variously expressed in formulations like "God of life," "God of liberation," or "God of hope." Lest these formulations be trivialized, the christology of liberation has emphasized the credibility of this love, and the nature of the response to be made to a God who is love.

In Jesus, God's love has been historicized in credible fashion. In Jesus is manifested love as the ultimate element of reality, and in Jesus is manifested just how love is that ultimate element of reality. The revelation of the mystery of God as love might be summed up in three sentences of John: "God's love was revealed in our midst in this way: he sent his only Son to the world that we might have life through him" (1 John 4:9); "God is love" (1 John 4:8); and "If God has loved us so, we must have the same love for one another" (1 John 4:11).

This brief summary of the basic elements of the christology of liberation will suffice to show that the insistence of this christology on the historical Jesus is not reductionistic and does not degenerate into a mere description of Jesus, such as would permit a jesuology and nothing more. Rather it shows the emphasis of liberation christology on the notion that in Jesus there has appeared both God's descent to human beings and the manner of the human being's access to God. From a starting point in Jesus—out of his life, death, and resurrection—the christology of liberation claims to show how the understanding of the human being, the understanding of God, and the understanding of their mutual relationship, can be "christianized."

The christology of liberation not only proposes content about Christ, to be known and believingly accepted, but also—and this emphasis is part of its historical novelty—the manner of knowing Christ, knowing him with a knowledge that, in virtue of the very nature of its object, can only be faith in Christ. It shows access to Christ *in actu*, and it does this as christology, refusing to relegate the task to other theological disciplines, such as fundamental or spiritual theology. Still less does it exonerate theology in the strict sense from this task by relegating it to pastoral pedagogy and practice.

Accordingly, liberation christology has reflected on the locus of the real encounter with Christ.[31] To be sure, many "places" point to the transcendency of God and indirectly to Christ, as is shown by the so-called searching christology.[32] But the christology of liberation emphasizes specifically Christian loci, such as liturgy and the preaching of the word. It places special emphasis on those "places" that, according to the gospel, Christ himself singled out: the community of believers and the poor and oppressed. This latter "place," according to Matthew 25, is the unequivocal place of encounter with Christ. In the poor and oppressed is the hidden face of Christ, and in service to these poor and oppressed there is found, there occurs—independently of any reflex cognition—the encounter with Christ.[33]

Liberation christology has likewise reflected on the manner of thematization and objectivization of the cognition obtained from the real encounter with Christ. Clearly, liberation christology embraces whatever can be known *about* Christ, extracting this content from the gospel accounts and the New Testament and conciliar christo-logies. Typical of the christology of liberation is its proposition of discipleship, the following of Christ, as indispensable for a knowledge of Christ. Apart from this discipleship, one may have correct bits of knowledge and orthodox formulations of it, surely. But this is no unconditional guarantee that a human being may begin in truth to pierce the mystery of Christ.

There are two reasons for this. The first, if Christ is a human being and the Son of God, then we are in the presence of limit concepts not in themselves open to direct intuition. Concepts can and should present the truth of Christ generically. But in order for this generic truth to become real truth, the mediation of something other than pure cognition is required. The total reality of life is required and this includes the practice of love and hope, in which the generic is concretized from within. We call this totality—which includes but is not reduced to pure cognition—"discipleship."

The second reason—more specifically Christian, and attested to by history from the New Testament onward—is that the reality of Christ not only must be formulated in limit concepts, inasmuch as it is a mystery, but that this mystery is historically at diametrical odds with the "natural man." The natural human being tends, in his and her concupiscence, to "think a mystery" according to his and her own logic, and then, in the name of this mystery so thought, to reject the genuine mystery of Christ. This is what appears in the theological composition of Mark 8:27-38. Peter's seemingly correct cognition concerning Christ eventuates as false knowledge: Peter's thoughts are not God's thoughts. The alteration of the falsity of these thoughts is not actually a matter of the cognitive level alone, according to Jesus. According to Jesus, it is a matter of following him on the way of the cross.[34]

The interest of liberation christology in seeking access to Christ grows out of a fidelity to the very content of christology: this access is not only an ethical requirement for those who hear Jesus, but a necessary condition for knowing Jesus. Thereby liberation christology also demonstrates, *in actu*, however implicitly, its strictly christo-logical and not merely jesuo-logical interest: for, from a point of departure in the analysis of Jesus in the past, it presents the manner of access to Christ *today*. This *today* guarantees the transcendence of any mere jesuology.

What I have said about the origin and finality of the christology of liberation, about its basic content and its interest in showing the manner of access to Christ, demonstrates that, at least in intention, there is no reductionism here. Neither are the results reductionistic, even though certain of its emphases focus—not reduce—the content of christology in a particular manner.

And yet there persists a suspicion with regard to liberation christology that might be charitably expressed in the following way. Liberation christology is silent about themes that bear on the divinity of Christ. Imprecision and ambiguities emerge in its presentation of Christ. There is the constant danger that the preeminence accorded the historical Jesus, on the methodological level at any rate, may sooner or later cloud his divine dimension and the fullness of his human dimension.

These "dangers and ambiguities" cause so much concern, at least in the minds of those who do not call in question the healthy, ecclesial intent of a particular Latin American christology, because insufficient account is taken of what the church has authoritatively stated concerning Christ, especially in the councils, which in turn rely on the fullness of the New Testament christologies.

I will conclude with a few words on the ecclesiality of the christology of liberation.

Elsewhere I have described what I call first ecclesiality, the real substance of the church—faith, hope, and love in action, which make the church the people of God, the body of Christ, and the temple of the Spirit.[35] Second ecclesiality, then, would be the historical expression of this substance on the various levels of liturgy, hierarchical organization, the magisterium, theological reflection, and so on. The distinction is in no way intended to depreciate the historical and Christian necessity and validity of ecclesiality understood in the second sense. It simply seeks to call attention to the basic fact that the church presupposes a Christian reality and that this reality does not develop at random—not individualistically, for example—but as *ekklēsia*.

From this it should be clear that liberation christology is ecclesial at least in the first sense of the term. Its theologians know and maintain the formulations of the truth about Christ, but, obviously, they have developed their christological reflection in the context of real faith in Christ. Christians receive and maintain their faith in Christ within an ecclesial community; what this community believes and practices effectuates the renewal of faith in Christ; and the renewal of this faith constantly molds and shapes the being and acting of the ecclesial community. Puebla testifies to this fact by citing the "search for the ever new face of Christ" (no. 173) in the base-level church communities and other groups of religious, priests, and laity.

It remains to be explained, however, in what sense the christology of liberation is ecclesial in the second acceptation of the term. In the few strictly dogmatic writings of this christology, liberation christology accepts the conciliar christological formulations with loyalty and fidelity. Unlike some other theologies, it calls in question neither the content that the church has developed concerning Christ nor its authority to develop such content.

The content is accepted by accepting what the dogmas really say. The dogmas are viewed neither as spurious extrapolation from nor as illegitimate hellenization of what the New Testament states. Liberation christology, then, does not have the problems with which christologies developed in other parts of the world are beset. From the outset it accepts dogma, although it admits the *pastoral* problematicity of its use and the need for its *theological* reinterpretation and enrichment.

The authority of the church to develop content concerning Christ comes to evidence from the ecclesial, and not merely individualistic, acceptance of the faith. The admission of the possibility of novel statements about Christ is admission of the activity of the Spirit, whose historical reality liberation christology thereby actually introduces. That there are sources that, at a given moment, authoritatively proclaim the truth of new statements, is accepted as historical and reasonable and as part and parcel of the ecclesiality of faith.

This does not, however, deprive liberation christology of its reasons for being unwilling to build certain ecclesial statements about Christ—which it accepts—into the methodological starting point for its reflection, or to present them as particularly appropriate formulations from a pastoral viewpoint. I have set forth these reasons elsewhere. The pastoral difficulty of introducing the mystery of Christ from the dogmatic formulas should be evident.[36] There is, however, a special, basic reason that deserves mention here, and it is this: Because dogmatic statements are limit statements they cannot be understood, even at the noetic level, without retracing the steps leading to their formulation. Accordingly, although liberation christology knows and admits from the outset the truth of the dogmatic formulations, it insists on re-creating the process that led to them, beginning with Jesus of Nazareth, and, further, holds that the re-creation of this process is the best way to come to an understanding of the formulas.

All of this being said, however, the irreplaceable role of the christological dogmas of the church for liberation christology, as for any christology, stands firm. This role consists in this: (1) the dogmas set the limits of any christology, in such wise that the transgression of these limits will entail not only disobedience to the magisterium, but sooner or later the impoverishment of the figure of Christ; (2) the dogmas, in their own langauge and conceptuality, radically expound the mystery of Christ, and demand its maintenance as mystery, in spite of certain uses of dogma that tend to the domestication of this mystery; and (3) that christological dogmas expound, at bottom, the truth of the Christian faith concerning the absolute, salvific nearness of God to a sinful, enslaved humanity—a nearness become unrepeatable, unsurpassable, in Jesus Christ.

A radical dogmatic presentation of the mystery of Christ is no threat whatever to the intent of the christology of liberation. On the contrary, it can only enrich and radicalize that christology. Conversely, it is crucial that this presentation indeed be radical, that it go to the root of faith in Christ. As Karl Rahner has said, "It seems to me, we Christians ought to be much more aware of the enormous demands on the courage and strength of our faith that are made by the church's teaching about Jesus Christ."[37]

This "courage and strength of our faith" is demanded, it is true, by the dogmatic formulas, but it is realized only in the heroic and energetic *act* of faith. I hold that this act of faith is furthered by liberation christology as I have outlined it. In order for there to be an integrally ecclesial christology, ecclesiality must be understood in both acceptations of the term. This is what I propose to do in the pages to follow: to recall the doctrine of the church about Jesus Christ, to the end that the christology of liberation continue to maintain the totality of the truth about Jesus Christ; and to illuminate the doctrine of the church from the christology of liberation, to the end that the church continue to maintain its radicalness at the present moment in history.

JESUS CHRIST, TRUE GOD: DIVINE TRANSCENDENCE

After the resurrection, Christians plumbed the reality of the person of Christ, wondering who it was indeed who had lived and died in this fashion and had been raised by God. Through a long process, their faith in Christ, real but only gradually "thematized," was rendered explicit in two ways: by the interpretation, in faith, of certain events of Jesus' life, and by the bestowal upon him of various titles of dignity, frequently related to these events.[38]

In this believing process, Jesus was professed to be the Son of God. "From then onwards the confession of Jesus' divine sonship has been regarded as the distinguishing mark of Christianity."[39] In asserting the reality of Christ as divine filiation, the early Christians sought to set in relief the absolute, unrepeatable relationship of Jesus to God, and conversely, the absolute, unrepeatable manifestation of God in Jesus. This relationship came to be conceived as something so profound that centuries later in the language of the Greek world it was expressed as Christ's "consubstantiality" with the Father. It was asserted that Christ was of the same nature as the Father, that is, that he is a divine reality.

Let us examine briefly from a systematic point of view, without dwelling on exegetical analyses, the development of this faith in Christ's divine filiation, what it means, what mediations have permitted and required its formulation, and finally, how it may be understood in terms of the most typical principles of liberation christology.[40]

It is unlikely that the historical Jesus applied the title "Son of God" to himself, especially since in his time this Old Testament title was frequently used to connote the divine election of and good pleasure in the king, some other person, or the whole people, without, however, necessarily denominating any essential reality in the chosen person, but only a functional one.

Nevertheless, Jesus did demonstrate an awareness of his special relationship with God. He linked the coming of the kingdom to himself. "If it is by the finger of God that I cast out devils, then the reign of God is upon you" (Luke 11:20). He personally felt a special union with the Father, as we know from the celebrated terminological difference between Jesus' reference to "my" Father and "your" Father. Matthew, at least, does not hesitate to attribute to Jesus a matchless intimacy with the Father: "Everything has been given over to me by my Father. No one knows the Son but the Father, and no one knows the Father but the Son—and anyone to whom the Son wishes to reveal him" (Matt. 11:27).

After the resurrection, the actual believing reflection on the unrepeatable relationship of Christ to the Father got under way. This reflection was made gradually and had certain characteristics that it will be well to underline so that we may see their place in today's orthodox profession of the divinity of Christ.

Reflection on the divine filiation of Christ did not arise from an abstract, essentialistic consideration of divinity, nor from a direct attribution of divinity to Christ, but from Jesus' life, death, and resurrection. In virtue of this historical interest, believing reflection related Jesus' filiation, as a believed reality, to an event of his life and lot. At first the special event was the resurrection.[41] As the oldest formulary has it, Jesus "was made Son of God in power . . . by his resurrection from the dead" (Rom. 1:4). Later this filiation was retrospectively referred to other events of Jesus' life, such as his baptism (Mark 1:11; Matt. 3:17), his transfiguration (Mark 9:7), and his conception by the Spirit (Luke 1:35). It would be anachronistic to attempt to see in these believing reflections the "adoptionist" heresy of the eleventh century. They should be considered rather as pioneering believing reflections on the peculiar relation of Jesus to the Father, and we should note their twofold concern: (1) a *historical* concern to relate Jesus' filiation with his life and lot, and (2) a *salvific* concern to relate his filiation with the salvation of human beings.

This reflection gradually laid more and more stress on the filiation as personal union and scandalous revelation, exemplified in the theology of John and Paul.

In the gospel of John, the unity between Father and Son is stated quite clearly (John 10:30). This unity or oneness is expressed as mutual knowledge (10:15) and common operation (5:17, 19–20). But these more "essential" statements are also at the service of the salvific concern that I have cited. Jesus shares in God's life in order to transmit this life to human beings. "Just as the Father possesses life in himself, so has he granted it to the Son to have life in himself" (John 5:26). But once the divine filiation is expressed salvifically, the relation between Jesus and the Father appears in a personal form as well. The Son is related to the Father by obedience, by the submission of his will (John 4:34, 8:29, 14:31). Jesus' obedience to the Father in his salvific mission is the historical form and manifestation of what constitutes his "essential" divine filiation. "The Son is the person who submits himself unreservedly in obedience to God. Thus he is wholly and entirely transparent for God; his obedience is the form in which God is substantially present."[42]

Pauline theology brings out the initerable or unique relationship of Christ to the Father from a starting point in the revelation of the Father on Jesus' cross. Inasmuch as the cross is the vessel of scandal, contradicting Greek and Jewish reason, to assert the revelation of God on the cross of Christ means *eo ipso* to assert that God is revealed in definitive fashion in this Christ. The unification of cross and God can be rejected; but if it is believingly accepted, then the cross becomes the source of a new and definitive notion of God, and the new reality of this God is accessible only from the crucified one. If this crucified one is really the Son, then the divine filiation too has a scandalous revelatory character, and Jesus' oneness with God suddenly becomes a criticism of the current notion of God.

Starting with these mediations of Christ's concrete filiation, the New Testament gradually plumbs the reality of the Son, to the point of asserting his divinity. Actually only lately and rarely is Christ called God in the New Testament; it is especially against the background of his proclamation as Lord that this denomination is made. "In Christ the fullness of deity resides in bodily form" (Col. 2:9). The Letter to the Hebrews calls Christ "the reflection of the Father's glory, the exact representation of the Father's being" (Heb. 1:3), and addresses to Christ the words that the Psalms address to God (cf. Psalms 1:8-9, 45:7-8, 102:26–27). In the Johannine writings the divinity of Christ is asserted more clearly. The beginning of the Gospel of John asserts that "the Word was God" (John 1:1); in a dispute that takes place at the climax of the gospel, Jesus says, "The Father and I are one" (10:30)—one thing, *hen*—and the gospel ends with the profession of Thomas: "My Lord and my God!" (20:28). The First Letter of John ends similarly: "He is the true God and eternal life" (1 John 5:20).

The New Testament, then, asserts the godhead of Christ. Two things should be emphasized: (1) this believing assertion does not consist in the direct, unmediated attribution of divinity to Christ; rather, this divinity is professed according to the logic of faith and through certain mediations—Jesus' history, the salvific nature of his nature and person, his historical relation to God, his resurrection; and (2) the profession of Christ's divinity is made concomitantly with that of the new, scandalous understanding of divinity, the new, scandalous manifestation of God's being-God.

This faith in the divine filiation of Christ was expressed later, in the first three centuries of Christian faith, in various creeds or professions of faith, culminating in the Council of Nicaea's solemn confirmation of these creeds in its condemnation of Arius, in language composed of terminology from the Bible and Christian tradition and the new Greek terminology as well:[43]

> We believe in the one Lord Jesus Christ, Son of God, only-begotten of the Father, that is, of the essence of the Father, God of God, light of light, true God of true God, engendered not created, consubstantial with the Father, through whom all things were made in heaven and on earth, who for us human beings and for our salvation descended and became flesh and human being [DS 125].

The basic content of this statement is the full godhead of Jesus Christ. Faced with the Arian thesis that the Logos is only a demiurge, or the first and most exalted of creatures, the Council states that Christ's being is not creaturely. Against the metaphysical schema of the Greeks, especially of the Platonists and Neoplatonists, the Council insists that there are only two ways of being: uncreated being and created being. But Christ is not a created being. Therefore he belongs to the order of divinity. This is what the Council wishes to say, in contemporary, though nonphilosphical, terminology, when it states that Christ is "consubstantial" with the Father, "engendered," not created.

This conciliar formulation, which takes leave, in part, of the language of the New Testament, though still far from our language and conceptuality, must not be understood as a direct preaching of Christ's divinity understood in itself without the need of mediations—any more than the New Testament assertions of his divinity may be so taken.[44] The assertion of the divinity is clear. But in order to understand what is meant by it, its context must be at least minimally clarified.

The conciliar formula takes the form of a liturgical profession of faith, and thus begins with the expression, "We believe." This means that the formula will clarify and hone the meaning of the content of what is believed, but that it will not proclaim a new reality concerning Christ that has not as yet been believed. The formula refers, then, to an already existing real faith in Christ. The new terminological and conceptual elements are at the service of clarification and precision in a new situation, but the content continues to be the basic content of faith, already present in the New Testament. The new concepts, then, are intended simply to explain that "the Son is by nature divine and is on the same plane of being as the Father, so that anyone who encounters him, encounters the Father himself."[45]

The conciliar formula is to be understood soteriologically, even when it states the reality of Christ in himself. It is not primarily an attempt to explain the reality of Christ speculatively. Athanasius, Arius's great nemesis, had insisted that if Christ is not truly God, then there is no salvation or divinization for our flesh. "For us it would be as useless for the Word not to be true Son of God by nature as for the flesh that he took or not to be real flesh."[46] The divinity of Christ, proclaimed at Nicaea, must be understood, then, from the theology of the early church, which conceives redemption as divinization. The divinity of Christ, even in itself, has an essentially salvific dimension.

In order to appreciate Nicaea's statement in all of its depth, we must recall what Arius found so difficult about accepting the divinity of Christ. Arius could not accept Christ's divinity because the gospels constantly reveal his limitations—his changes, and especially his suffering on the cross. In accepting Christ's divinity in spite of this difficulty—such an obvious one for natural reason—Nicaea is not only saying that Christ is truly divine, but is accepting the scandal residing in God, and thereby accepting a revolution in the notion of God.[47]

The christology of liberation, for its part, accepts these statements of the New Testament and the early councils on the divinity of Christ, even though it has not considered it its specific task to undertake an in-depth analysis of these statements. The statements rather subsist in a symbiosis with the specific elements of liberation christology, whose very radicalness in its presentation of Jesus proceeds, in part and not always in thematized form, but nonetheless really, from its acceptance of the divinity of Christ.

Let us now attempt to thematize the divinity of Christ from the more specific standpoint of liberation christology in a presentation of the figure of Jesus. Were this presentation to degenerate into a pure "Jesuism," ignoring Christ's divinity, what would be the point of a presentation of Jesus in the first place? What would be the point of developing the implications of this radical presentation? For an orientation in our task, I cite a splendid passage from Karl Rahner.

We orthodox Christians ought not to dismiss too quickly this sort of [Jesuism] in its diverse variants. It is a perfectly serious question whether a human being with an absolute and pure love without any egoism must not be more than a human being. If the moral personality of Jesus in word and life really makes such a compelling impression on a person that they find the courage to commit themselves unconditionally to this Jesus in life and death and therefore to believe in the God of Jesus, that person has gone far beyond a merely horizontal humanistic [Jesuism] and is living (perhaps not completely spontaneously, but really) an orthodox Christology.

However, orthodox Christology must give its own implications a thorough examination.[48]

Clearly Rahner is defending the possibility of a real faith in Christ, a full faith, objectively equivalent to the fullness and radicalness demanded by the church, that would not necessarily be subjectively expressed in dogmatic church formulas. But on a deeper level, for purposes of the christological task, Rahner is proposing two ways of discovering an equivalency between the dogmatic formulations that explicitly declare Christ's divinity and a christology based on the historical Jesus.

The first way he proposes is by a *speculative* development of the virtualities, the implications, of the historical Jesus, issuing in a reformulation of his divine transcendency based on his personal history. The second and more novel way is by a *praxic* development of the impact of Jesus. This second way explains the divine transcendency of Christ from a point of departure in the act of faith unleashed by the person of Jesus in his historical reality. Both ways seem to be correct in themselves as approaches to Christ's divinity and historically akin to actual positions of the christology of liberation.

If we seek a speculative equivalency between the christology of liberation and the statements of the church on the divinity of Christ, we need only systematically radicalize the essential element in the christology of liberation.

The core of Jesus' message is the proclamation of the approach of the kingdom of God. The chronology of this approach, and Jesus' knowledge of this chronology, are irrelevant for our considerations. What is important is that Jesus dared to broadcast the unfailing victory of the salvific will of God: Jesus "knows"—from within history and in the midst of its ambiguity—what the denouement of history's drama is to be; he acts in conformity with this conviction to the end; and no historical event prevents him from proclaiming, in words and deed alike, this victorious salvific will.

This definitive knowledge, with Jesus' proclamation of the same, is not the product of a pollyannaish optimism that turns its back on the tragic reality of history and the ambiguity of everything in history that can be pointed to as the approach of God's kingdom. Jesus' conviction goes beyond, and in large measure against, human calculations.

Jesus further proclaims that the approach of this kingdom is love and grace, not judgment. Thus he sunders for good and all the symmetry of a possible salvation and a possible condemnation by God: He unequivocally proclaims that the ultimate will of God is salvation, and that this is because the grace of God will emerge victorious over the freedom of human beings, from within that very freedom. In a word, Jesus appears as the one who utters his pronouncement upon the ultimate mediation of God's will, God's kingdom, and the absolute, irrevocable approach of this kingdom.

Jesus speaks his message, and puts it into action, with ultimacy and without equivocation, in such wise that his person becomes part of his message. Indeed, since Jesus' message about the approach of the kingdom of God is not just one more among many possible messages that human beings might hope for and receive, the truth of this message must be accompanied by its intrinsic credibility—otherwise it will not be grasped as truth, but as just one more of the many things human beings may hope for and wonder about. It is not a message in the gnostic style, which will unveil a truth about God, but a message about the reality of God, who draws near in the kingdom.

For this reason, the conviction with which Jesus proclaims his message and the deeds that he places in the service of the content of his message are essential to the message itself. Jesus' confidence in the coming of the kingdom at the beginning of his activity could be interpreted as merely a good and pious desire, one shared by so many other persons. But once this confidence has been kept up in the face of the apparent failure of the kingdom to come and the rejection of the one who had announced its coming, it becomes the historical way to proclaim this truth with credibility.[49]

And so Jesus' fate becomes part and parcel of the proclamation of God's kingdom. The temptation in the wilderness, the crisis in Galilee, and especially Jesus' passion and death demonstrate his unfailing confidence in the coming of the kingdom. Let the human signs of its possibility disappear as they will, Jesus maintains faithfully, to the end, that not even death can prevent the coming of the kingdom. The resurrection will confirm that this proclamation of Jesus is the truth—that the kingdom of God is drawing near despite all, and even though its approach is something to be reflected upon from a point of departure in Jesus' cross, hence in a new and scandalous way, and that Jesus is the first fruit, the first realization, of this kingdom of God in its fullness.

Jesus himself, then—what he does and says, what he suffers and what happens to him—becomes essential to an understanding of the approach of the kingdom and of the manner of realization of this approach. In his very proclamation of and service to God's kingdom as the mediation of the ultimate will of God, Jesus appears as the mediator of the God of the kingdom.[50]

What we have seen up to this point has of course been something more than a simple historical reading of Jesus. It is a believing reading, based on a historical reality. But it is necessary and sufficient for the purpose of showing Jesus' ultimacy, because Jesus proclaims what is irrevocably ultimate in the will of God and because he pertains, with irrevocable ultimacy, to the manifestation of this will of God.

Jesus' essential relation to the kingdom of God and to the God of the kingdom can be expressed, then, systematically, from a point of departure in

God. God is expressed in the history of Jesus and is engaged in the history of human beings as irrevocable, victorious salvation. In Jesus, the triumph of God's love over the freedom of human beings appears—not through the elimination of this freedom, but by the conquest of its sinfulness from within. In this sense Jesus is God's definitive answer to the human being's eternal question about salvation.

Since God has expressed the divinity in Jesus' history and not in some other history, the reality of God is manifest in a new and scandalous manner. God's salvation is the approach of something that involves solidarity with the very depths of the horror of human history. God's power does not consist in a mastery of human freedom, but in the domination of its sinfulness— ultimately, only by love. God's love is imposed not through majesty, but through credibility, as God's self-bestowal on human beings.

This is the core truth that will be developed in the New Testament. Systematically speaking, Jesus appears as God's definitive saving word to history: the sacrament, the visible expression of God among us, of God's love.

These formulas will suffice for an assertion of the divinity of Christ if they comprise the content of the argumentation that has led to their formulation. A christology that would seek to develop the logic of these statements in the presence of the radical formula of Nicaea need only translate the implications of the argumentation into "divinity" and "creatureliness" respectively.

> This saving event which reveals and makes victoriously present in the world God's definitive saving will, the event in which God "commits" himself, cannot be simply a creaturely reality different from God, existing in infinite separation from God. If it were no more than this, it would always be ambivalent, and could not firmly commit the infinite freedom of God. It would always remain (even if understood as an "expression" of God) subject to an ultimate qualification.
>
> If a finite, creaturely reality is really to be the irreversible self-expression of God, which commits God himself, it must have a different relation to God from that of being merely his creation.[51]

Thus we arrive at an equivalency with Nicaea's formulation. The process consists of three steps: (1) realized faith in the "ultimacy" of Christ (2) the negative formulation of this ultimacy: Christ can neither be, nor be submitted to, the purely creaturely and historical; (3) if Christ is not purely creaturely and historical, his ultimate reality is "on the God side" of reality: he is divine.

Liberation christology need only make radical and consistent use of its own presuppositions in order to arrive at formulations analogous to those of Nicaea. It has instead developed the bipolarity of divine being and creature in the language of liberation or condemnation, an approach of God's kingdom or absolute distance. But it has maintained the radicality that lends force to all christological argumentation: it poses the Christ question in the form of radical alternatives. And so it can simply accept Nicaea's option, respond that Christ is God, and then explicitly extract what is only implicit in Nicaea: that in Christ has been revealed, definitively, but also in novel and scandalous fashion, the Christian reality of God.

Besides this speculative equivalency, one can also find a praxic equivalency between the christology of liberation and the official doctrine of the church. If Jesus indeed causes such an impact that there are men and women who, in life and in death, give themselves to him without reserve and accept in him their God, then the truth about Christ is being asserted indeed, and the content developed concerning Jesus actually becomes understood not only in its factual, but also in its transcendent dimension. This is a praxic focus of Christ's divinity, but it is not thereby less pertinent and fruitful for christology and it is actually more adequate for the realization of the Christian life.

Put systematically: Where there is an act of real faith in Jesus, there, implicitly but really, the transcendency of the *content of this faith* is asserted.[52] At bottom, it is a matter as simple as asserting that nothing strictly created can be the object of faith; and conversely, that where there is faith, this faith is placed in something that is not merely created. This does not mean that the act of faith constitutes its object, but it does mean that the quality of the object of belief can be inferred from the quality of the act of belief. This transcendental correlation between act and object of faith, between *fides qua* and *fides quae*, can be left as a pure conceptual tautology, and is thus fruitless for our purposes. But it can be fruitful if we cite the basic content of the act of faith: surrender to Jesus in life and death.[53]

The christology of liberation, with its presentation of the historical Jesus, has indeed furthered the positing of this act of faith. Of course, this furtherance must be correctly understood as an explanation, an enlightenment of the free decision to follow Jesus. The ultimate roots of this decision derive from God's grace present in the face of the poor. There can be no doubt about this: Liberation christology has posited the *de jure* demand for this act of faith. In stressing the following of Jesus and the need to maintain this discipleship to the end, liberation christology is stating the decisive need for surrender to Jesus in life and death. It is seeking a praxic equivalency with the doctrine of the divinity of Christ.

Within this discipleship, furthermore, transcendence appears in historical form.[54] This Jesus who is to be followed appears to the follower, the disciple, as a "utopic principle." Jesus' discipleship is "utopic" because it is difficult to consummate its full realization. But it is "principle" because it initiates historical realities that make history give more of itself.

This discipleship demands the practice of justice and that justice become more and more human. It demands that this practice be effective, and that, further, it be in the spirit of the Beatitudes, with bowels of mercy, in the quest for reconciliation. It demands struggle with dehumanizing poverty and with the process of impoverishment. It demands indestructible hope in the coming of the kingdom and the maintenance of this hope, often enough as "hope against hope." It demands the initiation of a practice calculated to hasten the coming of the kingdom of God, as structural social reality and as creation of the new human being.

Historically, it is no easy task to bring any of these concepts to realization—justice, reconciliation, hope, the new human being, or a new society. It is still more difficult to maintain their simultaneity: justice and reconciliation, hope against hope, new structures and new human beings, and the struggle against both poverty and impoverishment.

The discipleship of Jesus accepts Christ. In the following of this Jesus, and no other political or religious leader or messiah, in the maintenance of all of the values cited here, in their historical tension, history gradually gives more of itself, transcendence gradually opens up historically and demonstrates its strength historically. The profession of the divine transcendence of Christ is made praxically in the act of maintaining fidelity to his discipleship—and finds an actual historical verification in that this discipleship unleashes an ever "greater" and "better" history, so that, in virtue of this discipleship of Jesus, no limits can ever be set to this history. *Following* Jesus is the praxic form of accepting the transcendence of God; and following *Jesus* is the praxic form of accepting the transcendence of Jesus.

Surrender to Jesus in discipleship during life attains its greatest depth in surrender in death, and in that death that is properly Christian: martyrdom. The christology of liberation has made martyrdom the climax of the act of faith in Christ—but not only because this is evident conceptually, but because it is accompanied by such abundant "martyrial," testimonial reality of faith pushed to its ultimate consequences.[55] This martyrdom testifies to faith in Jesus and to the God of Jesus, to faith in the kingdom of God and in the God of the kingdom, who wills salvation and life and integral liberation from all forms of slavery, who ever furthers the task of liberation, however utopian and "against hope" this task may appear, and in whom one may trust to the death.

Martyrdom, then, is the praxic, but definitive and unsurpassable, response to the question of Christ, "Who do you say that I am?" Christians answer with a profession of his divinity. But the answer can take a different form if we reformulate the question as the familiar spiritual has it:

Were you there when they crucified my Lord? . . .
Were you there when they nailed him to the tree?

The first question—"Who do you say that I am?"—has its ultimate Christian equivalency in the second: "Were you there . . . ?" The first answer has its ultimate Christian equivalency in the second. As Bonhoeffer's poem has it, Christians are the ones who stay close to God in his passion.[56]

The person for whom Christ is such that he moves him or her to posit a like act of faith is asserting the transcendence of Christ, is asserting his divinity. He or she is asserting *that* Christ is God and *that* God is revealed in Christ. If every act of faith is a surrender, a *sacrificium intellectus*, the act of faith will be a greater one when this surrender is a *sacrificium vitae*, and when it explicitly, however unsophisticatedly, calls on Jesus' name.

The christology of liberation is neither speculatively nor praxically ignorant of the divine transcendence of Christ, although it has concentrated on propounding his historical figure. This divine transcendence is implicitly but really present in liberation theology in the content of this figure and in the very focus of this figure. In order to assert the divinity of Jesus after the fashion of the New Testament and the early councils, one need only "explicitate their virtualities," render explicit what is in their content and focus. Liberation christology adds, of course, that the profession of Christ's divinity will only be "Christianly real" and will transcend a mere knowledge *about* Christ—although this knowledge about his divinity is important and indispensable—will only become genuinely "comprehensible"—while ever remaining mystery—will only show itself to be efficacious for salvation—in the humble, unconditional discipleship of Jesus, where one learns "from within" *that* God has come unconditionally near in Jesus and *that* God has promised the divine self to us unconditionally in Jesus: that Jesus is true God and that the true God has been made manifest in Jesus.

JESUS CHRIST, TRUE HUMAN BEING: HUMAN TRANSCENDENCE

In stating that Christ is "on the God side" of reality, we have already formulated his transcendence, to be sure. But we have not yet told the whole truth. This comes only with the addition that Christ is really a human being, indeed, is *the* human being.[57] Thereby we assert his true humanity and the eschatological character (this is the sense in which I use the term "transcendence" here) of this humanity of his.

No detailed analysis of Christ's true divinity is necessary here. This is not where the danger of abridging the totality of Christ resides. We do need a theological analysis of his humanity.[58]

"The New Testament takes for granted the fact that Jesus Christ was a real human being. It is stated as something quite obvious."[59] Only when the church was introduced into the world of Hellenism did the problem of Christ's being human arise, and it was "perhaps the most serious crisis [the church] had ever had to sustain."[60] Gnosticism and docetism preached that Christ could not have had a true body, thus spiritualizing both the figure of Christ and redemption. The theology of Paul as well as that of John combated this radical threat to Christian faith, and the first creeds explicitly rejected it by citing the principal events of Jesus' life, thus presenting him as a true human being.

The Council of Nicaea contented itself with stating that Christ "became flesh and man," without explicitly combating the Arian position that the soul as the spiritual principle of a human being was supplanted in the case of Christ by the Logos.[61] The Council of Ephesus rejected this error, stating that Christ was "true man" endowed with a body and a rational soul (DS 250).

The Council of Chalcedon synthesized the paradox to which the affirmation of Christ's true divinity and true humanity had led. It maintained God's transcendence and therefore the distinction of natures in Christ; it maintained God's immanence and therefore the inseparability of the natures in Christ. This is what Chalcedon asserted in using the adverbs *asunchutōs* (unconfusedly) and *adiairetōs* (undividedly). The "unconfusedly" means that the two natures are not mixed; thereby the perfect humanity of Christ and the transcendence of God is preserved. The "undividedly" denotes the utterly profound, irreversible, unique oneness of God and the human being in the person of Christ; thereby the full immanence of God in the world is safeguarded. It is on this immanence that Christian salvation and the divinization of the human being is based, in conformity with the soteriological intent of the conciliar thinking.

The Third Council of Constantinople, understood in the light of the statements of the Lateran Synod, made an attempt to plumb further the mystery of Christ's humanity by attributing two wills to Christ, one divine and one human. Through its language of human "will," a term more suggestive than human "nature," the full humanity of Christ was reaffirmed, along with "the essential participation of the human liberty of Christ in the deed of salvation."[62]

The logic of these brief reflections on the conciliar declarations is as follows. That Christ is God is a fundamental datum of his reality. But this provides no approach to his mystery unless his total and true humanity is simultaneously professed. Despite the theoretical difficulties with maintaining this humanity to the hilt, once Christ's divinity was admitted the councils made clearer and clearer pronouncements upon the true humanity of Christ and refused to sunder the mystery by denying either the transcendence or the immanence of God in Christ. As with the defense of his divinity, so with the defense of his humanity a soteriological interest is paramount: "What has not been assumed has not been redeemed," as Athanasius wrote.[63]

Clearly, the christology of liberation professes Christ's true humanity, and, together with other christologies, has sought to restore to that humanity the theological importance that it deserves, thereby responding to what the International Theological Commission has called "the christological exigencies of our times."[64] These exigencies, we read further, consist in "the most appropriate clarification possible of the importance of participation in Christ's humanity and the mysteries of his life (his baptism, temptations, agony in Gethsemane, and so on) for the salvation of the human being."[65]

Liberation christology professes the true humanity of Christ in the same way the gospel does—*by telling Jesus' story.* It makes no attempt to write a biography of Jesus of Nazareth and is quite aware that the gospel narratives are narratives issuing from belief. But neither does it ignore the fact that, unlike other New Testament genres, the gospels present Jesus by telling his story, giving his history, by historicizing (even though this historicization remains at the service of faith) his actual life.

This means understanding the human nature of Christ, as the dogmatic formula phrases it, as Jesus' history. It means translating his humanity (genuine and true because it contains the elements that make up humanity—human nature, body, soul, and will) into the truth of his concrete history.[66]

In systematically presenting Jesus' history, the christology of liberation adopts one of several possible viewpoints.[67] One would be to concentrate on certain important events of Jesus' life. Another would be to concentrate on certain attitudes of his, thereupon to attempt to systematize the whole history of Jesus, beginning with some particular event or basic attitude. Liberation christology seeks to present the history of Jesus formally as history, which implies Jesus' practice and Jesus' "becoming" through this practice the transformation of the world and human beings in conformity with the kingdom of God, and the actual transformation of Jesus with reference to the God of the kingdom. This doing and this becoming is seen by liberation christology as the correct way to present Jesus historically, including as it does the analysis of the concrete facts, the mysteries of his life, and his attitudes, to the extent that these are knowable from the gospels. True humanity in Jesus, then, means Jesus' history, both from the point of view of Jesus as agent of that history and from that of Jesus as its human product.

This historical, but not merely "natural," presentation of Jesus reproduces another characteristic of the gospel narratives and New Testament theology. It is a polemical presentation, directed against those who would be unwilling to accept the true flesh of Christ, or against those who would concentrate one-sidedly and "enthusiastically" on the risen Christ, refusing any decisive revelatory value to his flesh. Liberation christology, like Pauline theology, is concerned to safeguard the identity of the one who was raised as the one who had been crucified. It seeks to recover the element of astonishment in the gospel narratives, of which it has been said that the most remarkable thing about them is that they were written in the first place.[68] The presentation of Jesus' history in liberation christology is polemical, then, and directed against those who would seek to undermine, theoretically or practically, the truth of Jesus' humanity. Only thus can we have any ultimate guarantee that Christ will not end up in myth without history. The only feasible pedagogical approach to the mystery of Christ in its totality will be a presentation, in all its radicality, of something that may be a temptation where the mystery of Christ is concerned, but which, once that temptation is overcome, opens the way to belief in the true Christ.

The most specific characteristic of liberation christology's presentation of the humanity of Jesus Christ is its insistence on the *partisan* quality of this humanity. Genuine humanity, of course, involves concretion in the first place. The partisan note adds something to concretion: now this concretion is no longer pure factuality, but a determinate concretion in differentiation, to the exclusion of certain other possible concretions. Where its content is concerned, this partisan note places Jesus in the world of poverty and the poor, where he defends the cause of the poor and assumes their lot. Jesus is true human being in being poor. He becomes the universal human being from a point of departure in the lowly human being.

A partisan approach to the humanity of Christ need not be understood by way of horizontalism and reduction, although it is evident that this partisan quality gives Jesus a certain sociological "location" or "placement," and involves certain social and political consequences for him. But the basic consideration is theological. God's eternal design has been historically manifested from a concrete starting point in poverty and impoverishment. Reductionism is precluded precisely by the fact that the poor and poverty have been selected by God as the privileged loci of divine manifestation. Besides this basically evangelical consideration, there is the fact that a partisan approach to the humanity of Christ responds to the demands of the International Theological Commission: the mystery of Christ "should be presented to each individual is such wise that all may assimilate and celebrate it in their own life and culture."[69] The evangelical viewpoint and the Latin American historical viewpoint actually coincide, then. None of this implies a spurious rereading of Jesus, at least not necessarily.[70] What is at stake is the discovery of the focus that will allow a genuine reading of his humanity as actually manifested.

Further, this partisan approach to the humanity of Jesus Christ is not opposed to, but is precisely open to, the Christian *universalization* of Christ. The profession of the humanity of Christ is not only an assertion of his genuine humanity, but also the assertion that he is *the* human being, that in him the human being has definitively appeared. The New Testament bears witness to the eschatologization of Jesus-the-human-being. In its historical descriptions, it is simply Jesus-the-human-being that the New Testament sets forth. In its theologized formulations, Jesus is presented as the full revelation of the human being. Any christology must make the former series of formulations mediations for a Christian understanding of the latter series. There will always be a certain scandal here, and a certain leap of faith, in that the second series does not proceed mechanically from the first. Liberation christology asserts that, even for the eschatologization of the figure of Christ demanded by faith, the partisan quality of poverty and impoverishment is more adequate historically and leads to a better comprehension of the content of Jesus as the eschatological human being—although here too we have the leap of faith, inasmuch as this transition from the historically partisan Jesus to Jesus the eschatological human being maintains the radical novelty and scandal of what it means genuinely and truly to be a human being.

By thus maintaining the dialectical tension between the historical formulations concerning Jesus, from a point of departure in poverty and the eschatological formulations, we obviate, from the outset, the danger of reductionism, and maintain his partisan quality as well as his universality. Jesus appears as the absolute at its most concrete.

In the following pages I shall attempt briefly, and systematically to relate Jesus' partisan quality and his universality, with a view to an analysis of the theological meaning of his humanity and of the manifestation in him of true humanity.

Jesus the Human Being. The gospel narratives present Jesus as a human being, and a poor human being, in his birth, in the unfolding of the events of his life, and in his death. They present him as a human being in solidarity with the poor and with sinners, whose cause he defends, to whom he proclaims the coming of the kingdom, and whose lot he assumes. This is the partisan presentation of Jesus' humanity.

The New Testament universalizes the humanity of Christ, and presents Jesus as sharing the condition of *every* human being. Accordingly, it emphasizes the suffering (Heb. 2:17, 5:8, 12:2), in obedience and apprenticeship (Heb. 5:8; Rom. 5:19), in which "he had to become like his brothers in every way" (Heb. 2:17) except sin. Pauline theology universalizes him from a point of departure in the historical situation of the generalized human condition. It states that he was "born of a woman, born under the law" (Gal. 4:4) and makes the most audacious assertion that God sent him "in the likeness of sinful flesh" (Rom. 8:3).

In the climactic moments of its universalization of Christ, the New Testament consciously introduces the element of poverty. Christ is the human being, the true human being, in a process of impoverishment—eschatological impoverishment. Accordingly the incarnation is seen as impoverishment, as Christ "took the form of a slave" (Phil. 2:7), making himself "poor though he was rich" (2 Cor. 8:9). The next step is the radicality of the two Johannine assertions: "The Word became flesh and made his dwelling among us" (John 1:14), and, "Look at the man!" (John 19:5).

Seen from God's standpoint, the human being appears when "God wills to be non-God."[71] This is the radical descending proposition. But it is a reduplicative incarnation, including both the movement toward human flesh and the movement toward the element of poverty in this flesh. The true human being appears as the poor and impoverished human being. The historically partisan nature of Jesus' flesh is no obstacle whatever, then, to his eschatologization. On the contrary, the former actually opens the way to the latter. And the former preserves the eternal novelty and scandal of the latter. Henceforth we know that Jesus is the human being, and we know what it means for us genuinely to be human beings.

Jesus the Savior. In Jesus is revealed the new human being, the second Adam, not only in virtue of his poverty and impoverishment, but (and the New Testament states this most forthrightly) because it is Jesus as the *pro*-existent human being who is salvation. As the International Theological Commission has emphasized, "the true autonomy of the human being does not consist in *supra-existence* (proper to one coming forward as superior, and lording it over the rest), or in *contra-existence* (that of the one unjustly subjecting others to slavery for personal profit)."[72] The true autonomy of the human being consists in *pro-existence.*

This pro-existence is salvation inasmuch as it includes gift to others through gift of self, saving others by delivering oneself to (apparent) destruction, loving others efficaciously out of the gratuitous love given to oneself. The pro-existent human being is simply the human being who loves the brothers and sisters in truth and is therefore the true actualization of what it is to be a human being.

Jesus' historical pro-existence is actualized primarily in favor of the poor. To them he proclaims the kingdom of God (Matt. 5:3; Luke 6:20), and it is in this that his mission consists (Luke 4:18–19). The signs of salvation consist in the salvation of the poor (Matt. 11:46; Luke 7:22). This salvation can be described in biblical terms as liberation.[73] And this proffered liberation is the first step in Jesus' approach to all other human beings, including the oppressors. Upon the oppressors he pronounces the word of malediction (Luke 6:24–26), but in the hope of their conversion (see Luke 19:1–10). Stated systematically, Jesus' pro-existence consists, in a first moment, in a proclamation and toil calculated to further the passage of the poor from their infra-existence to the existence of daughters and sons of God.

This partisan pro-existence, this existence in favor of certain others, is the existence that explains historically the pro-existence of Jesus as self-surrender. Jesus is threatened and persecuted (the lot of the poor) even to the passion and the cross. Jesus' death is the maximal expression of his personal surrender.

And yet the gospel narratives themselves register a change of perspective to explain the salvific reality of Jesus, as his surrender gradually comes to be seen as surrender for "all" and for all "sinners." Jesus' very surrender is radicalized as the *gift* of his life is transformed into the *giving up* of his life. The mediator of the kingdom of God gradually appears as the one on whom the demand is made that he be baptized with a new baptism and drink the cup of the passion (see Mark 10:38, 14:36). The question of Jesus' consciousness of the salvific value of his death is hotly debated at the exegetical level. But the least that can and must be said is that Jesus was steadfastly loyal to the will of God, which for him, however mysterious it might be, could not but be salvific—and that to the end, and in the end, he maintained his hope in the kingdom of God (see Luke 22:14–17).

After the resurrection Jesus' pro-existence is universalized. He is presented as the eschatological savior. The salvific value of Christ's death is eschatologized, for it is the historical product not only of the will of human beings, but also of the will of God, who delivers up the Son for our salvation (Rom. 8:31; John 3:16). The sinful human condition of all human beings is eschatologized: "We have already brought the charge against Jews and Greeks alike that they are under the domination of sin" (Rom. 3:10). Jesus the savior, "handed over to death for our sins and raised up for our justification" (Rom. 4:25), is eschatologized in various ways. He is the salvation of Israel (John 11:50), of the "nations" (John 11:51–52), of "all" (2 Cor. 5:14–15; 1 Tim. 2:6), of "the world" (John 6:51).

The figure of this eschatological savior transcends the presentation of Jesus' original pro-existence in behalf of the poor. But it does not eliminate it; indeed it is important for an understanding of the eschatological savior. After all, eschatology, while transcending all historical expression, does not relativize all of it to an equal degree: It hierarchizes it. Universality in sin does not preclude different degrees of participation in that sin. Precisely from the viewpoint of Jesus' cross, sin appears ultimately and essentially as that which genuinely puts the human being to death. The universality of sin, therefore, is composed of historical sins that are more or less grave in the degree in which they put human beings to death or move them toward death. All human beings are sinners, then, but not necessarily in the same manner or with the same gravity. Structurally, those human beings who oppress are "more sinners" than the oppressed, although these latter, too, have their own sinfulness, and may transform themselves into oppressors or may be oppressors in other areas than those of the basic death-dealing oppression.

To be sure, salvation is forgiveness of sin and fullness of life. Life in its fullness transcends any particular type of life—on the level of transcendent life, obviously, but even on the level of historical life. This, however, does not cause differences in life to disappear. Salvation must be offered to all, but the offer must begin with those who are most deprived of life—the poor, who, in the terminology of Jesus' time, are "those who have no life."[74]

Least of all must the eschatologization of the savior distract us from the basic datum of his being-savior. Later explanatory models of Jesus' salvific efficacy may say what they will. The central fact is stated from a point of departure in Jesus' history. And this central fact is that *real sin is conquered inasmuch as it is laid upon Jesus.* Eschatologically it must be said that on the cross Christ took on the sin of the world; but historically it must be added that Christ went to his cross laden with concrete historical sin. In this taking-on of sin, if it is an expression of love for human beings and fidelity to God, sin is vanquished from within, and only thereby is there salvation. Sin is vanquished only by love.

In John's language, Jesus has come to bring life in abundance (John 10:10). To this purpose he voluntarily lays down his life (John 10:18). Laying down one's life is the greatest sign of love (John 15:13), and the One who does so is loved by God (John 10:17). Jesus is the authentic pro-existing human being.

"Partiality"—this partisanship, this taking of sides, this favoritism shown by Jesus toward the poor—is the key to an understanding of the five elements to be found at the nucleus and origin of all soteriology as understood by the first Christians and developed in the various soteriological models of the New Testament and tradition.[75]

Christ gives himself. Historically, he does so in behalf of the poor. Eschatologically, he does so in his death, as total surrender. Love appears here as the basic salvific element, and Christ appears as the one who loves in totality.

Christ takes the place of human beings. Historically, he does so by his subjection to the objective consequence of the historical sin of others. Eschatologically, he does so by taking on the sin of the world, with which the whole world ought to be laden. Here we have the element of solidarity and substitution as found in classic soteriology.

Christ delivers himself up in accordance with the salvific will of God. Historically, he does so by obeying the plural prescriptions of God's will during his life, which move him toward his life's tragic close. Eschatologically, he does so by accepting this tragic close, by being willing to be delivered up by God, and thereby being willing that the cross be his ultimate salvific service. Here appears God's inscrutable design, a design not susceptible of further analysis.

This surrender on the part of Christ is salvation, and protects human beings from the wrath to come. It is the mystery of salvation properly so-called. Historically, God definitively approaches human beings and definitively withdraws the divine wrath. No sin, not even the killing of God's Son, renders God's nearness reversible. Indeed, it is in that very death that God has spoken, in human fashion, the ultimate word, as word of grace: In spite of, and in, the death of the Son, God loves the world and irrevocably makes the commitment to it in love. Christ's surrender and death cause salvation because they express God's ultimate salvific will. In expressing it, they render it real. And in expressing it in Christ's death, they render it humanly credible.[76]

This salvation is not only forgiveness of sin, but renewal of life, the insertion of the human being into the very life of God and the current historical lordship of Christ.

Partiality and universalization are not opposed. It is Jesus' historical pro-existence that makes it possible to profess him as the eschatological savior. The element of scandal in this Christian conception of eschatological salvation, an element not capable of further elucidation, will only be able to be maintained from within Jesus' total historical love for the poor and his total historical surrender to the will of God.

Jesus is Son. This refers not to the divine character of Jesus as Son of God, but to the filiation with respect to God that characterizes the human being. The reality of this filiation appeared in Jesus historically, and appeared in the measure that the mystery of the relationship of the human being to God may be gathered from a point of departure in that human being's conduct—a conduct characterized in Jesus' case by a partiality toward the poor. In other words, Jesus' filiation appears historically as faith in God the Parent in the form of asides-taking faith, in its content as well as in its realization.

Conceptually, there can be no doubt that Jesus thought of God as a God of the poor. This notion is partly drawn by him from the Old Testament and partly radicalized by him. This lies at the basis of his inaugural discourse, according to which the kingdom of God is addressed to the poor—or even, as some think, more radically, only to the poor.[77] They find support for this claim in Jesus' prayer, "Father, Lord of heaven and earth, to you I offer praise; for what you have hidden from the learned and the clever you have revealed to the merest children" (Matt. 11:25).

Affectively, Jesus deals with God in absolute trust and confidence, calling God Abba, which, of course, presupposes his conviction that God is love, but which also carries a nuance that in human language might be termed tenderness.[78] Jesus' parables on the love of God for sinners, especially the parable of the prodigal, demonstrate the tenderness inherent in Jesus' concept of God. Drawing out the implications of this human language, we may say that tenderness signifies kindness and good will precisely toward the insignficant, the despised, love for those whom no one loves because no one loves them. It is a love of special predilection for the "little ones."

Praxically, Jesus deals with God in obedience and loyalty, which, as we have seen, leads him to his solidarity with the poor and to his own impoverishment, even to the supreme spoliation of the cross, an element of which is abandonment by God.

The partiality characterizing Jesus' historical filiation is what permits the New Testment eschatologization of his filiation. Jesus is the Son. New Testament christology actually recognizes this, although it quickly moves to a second position, asserting that Jesus is the *pais Theou*—variously translated as "child of God" or "servant of God," but in any case equivalent to *'ebed Yahweh*, the Isaiahan servant of Yahweh (cf. Matt. 21:37; Acts 3:13, 26; 4:27, 30). This *pais Theou*—described by Isaiah as the one sent to do justice, the chosen one, albeit despised and abhorred by the mighty, the one who trusts in God, who defends God's rights, the one crushed by the sins of human beings, with which he is laden—this *pais Theou* is the eschatological Son (cf. Isa. 42:1–9, 49:1–6, 50:4–11, 52:13–53:12). The Son brings the servant to plenitude, but the Son has no plenitude without being servant.

Precisely because the eschatological Son is also the servant, he can be the first-born, the elder brother, and human beings can become daughters and sons in the Son (cf. Rom. 8:29), can be inserted into divinization—but, to be sure, after the historical manner of servants. Now Jesus can be the witness of faith (Heb. 12:2) who has lived filiation in its historical plenitude in his nearness to human beings. "He who consecrates and those who are consecrated have one and the same Father" (Heb. 2:11). From a theological viewpoint, and surely from a historical viewpoint, human beings, Christ's brothers and sisters, are the poor and the insignificant. Today as yesterday, Paul's expression is valid:

Brothers, you are among those called. Consider your situation. Not many of you are wise, as men account wisdom; not many are influential; and surely not many are well born [1 Cor. 1:26].

These can embrace and contain Jesus' filiation because they embrace and contain, at least spontaneously and at times consciously as well, their own condition as servants. Because they know Jesus as their brother who is near, they can also call God their Father.

Once more the partiality of poverty and impoverishment constitute no impediment to the eschatologization of Jesus as Son, but only christianize it. In this fashion, furthermore, the acceptance of Jesus' filiation is facilitated. In any case, his partisan historical filiation is the believers' path to their reproduction of the image of the Son and the path of their historical and transcendent approach to God.

Jesus the Lord. The New Testament proclaims Jesus as the eschatological Lord. This poses a double question: what is meant by lordship, and how does one come to be Lord? The New Testament asserts that it is in virtue of his glorified humanity, and not only his divinity,[79] that Christ is now the one to whom God has subjected all things (1 Cor. 15:27; Heb. 2:9; Eph. 1:22) and that he has been constituted Lord because of his abasement even to the cross (Phil. 2:6–11).

This eschatological lordship, however, can only be understood from Jesus' actual history. For the historical Jesus, the problem of power was acute. It constituted the environmental temptation of his whole life, coming to a head on certain special occasions. Jesus had to choose between worldly power and the power of truth and love, which lead to human helplessness and death. Jesus chose the latter. True power is in service, not imposition. "The Son of Man has not come to be served but to serve" (Mark 10:44; cf. Mark 10:41–44; Matt. 20:24–28; Luke 22:25–27). Here, to be sure, we are confronted with a revolution in the concept of lordship:

> Earthly kings lord it over their people. Those who exercise authority over them are called their benefactors. Yet it cannot be that way with you. Let the greater among you be as the junior, the leader as the servant [Luke 22:25–26].

The nature of the eschatological lordship of Christ can be understood only from the service of Jesus.

Christ's being-Lord in the present is not only a title qualifying him. It also expresses the exercise *in actu* of his lordship. This lordship will come to its fullness at the end of the ages, when we shall behold regeneration of this world (Matt. 19:28), the revelation of who the daughters and sons of God are, liberation from slavery and decadence (cf. Rom. 8:19–20), the new heaven and new earth (Rev. 21:1; cf. Isa. 65:17; 62:22).

Even in the present Christ exercises lordship as a force for the transformation of reality. The New Testament describes this transformative force as freedom. The believers can live in this world without being subject to its evil (Rom. 8:39–40; 14:8–9); neither life, nor death, nor the present, nor what is to come can any longer separate them from the love of God. As Paul says, "All things are yours" (1 Cor. 3:21), but the eschatological freedom produced by the Lord is nothing more than the realization of the demands of the historical Jesus: victory over selfishness as it appears in the Beatitudes and the Sermon on the Mount and the freedom to give of one's own life, indeed to give one's own life, for love. The Lord's real ability to render persons free is nothing more than the realization of Jesus' words "Come to me, all you who are weary and find life burdensome, and I will refresh you. . . . For my yoke is easy and my burden light" (Matt. 11:28, 30). The freedom produced by Jesus' lordship is nothing more than the encounter with Jesus in his discipleship. This is what renders the human being free and joyful.

The New Testament also speaks of the current lordship of Christ as a cosmic lordship. Audaciously it states that Christ is head and mediator of creation and that all things have their "continuation in being" in him (cf. Col. 1:15–17). This absolute eschatological statement has its mediation in the lordship that Jesus exercised over his world and his history. Lordship is liberation. Jesus is the point of origin of creation's becoming a history according to God: "the blind recover their sight, cripples walk, lepers are cured, the deaf hear, dead men are raised to life, and the poor have the good news preached to them" (Matt. 11:5; cf. Luke 7:22). The cosmic lordship of Christ receives its concrete direction and content from the renewal imposed by Jesus on earthly realities. Therefore believers render that lordship real in the historical construction of the kingdom of God. As the International Theological Commission says:

> This cosmic princeship of Christ is in perfect consonance with the princeship which he is accustomed to exercise in history and in the experience of the human being, especially by the signs of justice, which appear as necessary for the preaching of the kingdom of God.[80]

The lordship of Christ in the present, then, is nothing more than the renewal of reality, both in the believer's personal freedom and in the progressive becoming of the kingdom of God in social realities. The criterion for both continues to be the historical Jesus and the poor, whom he served and sought to liberate.

Once more, Jesus' concretion-in-partiality is no impediment whatever to his eschatologization as Lord. On the contrary, it supplies the content and exercise of lordship by supplying the correct tack or orientation. His eschatologization adds the indestructible conviction and hope that the lordship of Jesus is realized in the very act of its historical exercise by human beings and that it will be fully realized at the end of the ages, when the principalities, the powers, and the last enemy, death, will have been subjected to him (1 Cor. 15:25).

This is liberation christology's presentation of the true humanity of Christ, and these are the reasons why it ascribes supreme importance to its presentation. Certain exegetical evaluations and certain emphases issuing from the actual Latin American historical situation might be open to discussion. But it would not appear incorrect in principle. Rather, it must surely be most fruitful to return to the gospel narratives and present the humanity of Christ as they do: as the history of Jesus. Nor is it incorrect—but rather altogether necessary—to emphasize that humanity polemically, in view of theoretical and practical attempts to reduce, ignore, or reject it. Finally, neither would it appear to be incorrect—but rather, altogether justified from a Christian viewpoint—to emphasize what we have called the "partiality" of Christ's humanity. This partiality must not be understood as an impoverishing reduction, but as an enriching concretion, for, at bottom, this is the way in which the unsuspected novelty and scandal of the human being Jesus may be maintained.

This manner of presenting Jesus in his humanity is no obstacle whatever to the eschatologization of his figure. But it does provide a safeguard against the everlasting danger of denying his flesh in the process of this eschatologization. Like the New Testament, the christology of liberation asserts that Jesus is the human being, as poor and impoverished; that he is the savior, being the one who delivers himself up for love of his brothers and sisters; that he is Son, being servant; that he is Lord, being the one who serves. This concretion appears in virtue of the primordial relationship of Jesus with the world of the poor.

The eschatologization of the human being Jesus is crucial for faith; further, it sanctions for good and all Jesus' specific partiality. Conversely, the eschatologization of the humanity of Christ maintains its Christian character and historical relevance only from a point of departure in the partiality of the history of Jesus.

THE MYSTERY OF CHRIST: CHRISTOLOGICAL TRANSCENDENCE

In presenting Christ's true divinity and humanity, we have already substantially stated in what his reality consists. But his deepest mystery is not encountered until we come to consider divinity and humanity in their mutual relationship, without division or confusion. Here we have the specifically christological transcendence in which the absolute nature of Christian faith is rooted. This is what the dogma of Chalcedon asserts, without pretending to explain the "how" of that relationship, that is, without pretending to explain the mystery.

The christology of liberation has developed no speculative explanation of the christological mystery, however much it may have analyzed the two poles of that mystery. Here I call attention to certain basic requirements for a profession of that mystery, and for such a profession of it that it may remain mystery. Finally, I shall endeavor to clarify certain statements of mine that have been misinterpreted as attacking, or at least as ambiguous about, the mystery of Christ.

The believing assent to the mystery of Christ does not imply an understanding of that mystery. Not even Chalcedon's formula

> pretends to explain, when all is said and done, "how" God and the human being coexist in Christ, as this is the very *ratio* of the mystery, which is susceptible to no positive definition.[81]

On the one hand, theology has sought to develop the notion that "it is not a contradiction that a 'concrete human nature' would exist in a personal manner on a divine ontological level."[82] On the other hand, theology has endeavored to develop the epistemology peculiar to the specific act of faith in the mystery of Christ.

The mystery of Christ has been formulated in orthodoxy in descending fashion, both in the gospel statement that "the Word became flesh" (John 1:14), and in the dogmatic statement of the hypostatic union, according to which the union of natures in Christ obtains in the person of the Logos. Whatever its difficulties, this descending facet of christology is indispensable, as it posits the mystery of Christ formally as mystery. Strictly speaking, nothing created, as such, can be mystery. Only God can be mystery. In order to understand Christ as mystery then, one must understand him from a point of departure in God—although it is precisely this point of departure that renders him ultimately incomprehensible.

Strictly speaking, theology can do no more than assert that mystery, and assert—and this is what is specific to Christian theo-logy, differentiating it from other theo-logies—that the christological mystery is a possibility for God even though this possibility is discovered only from its actual realization.

Let us say something, briefly, about this possibility that resides with God. Theology can only reflect on God in such wise as to consider the christological mystery an a priori possibility. It must therefore reject any understanding of Christ according to which he would have been the union of two realities, divine and human, that would not only be logically independent, but would actually have existed *prius* as independent. Rather, theological reflection must reckon with the possibility that God could and might create that which, while distinct, would strictly pertain to and belong to the divinity.

> But if what makes the human nature ek-sistent as something diverse from God, and what unites this nature with the Logos, are *strictly* the same, then we have a unity which (a) cannot, as uniting unity (*einende Einheit*), be confused with the united unity (*geeinte Einheit*) (this is not permissible); (b) which unites *precisely by* making existent, and *in this way* is grasped in a fullness of content without any relapse into the empty assertion of the united unity; and finally (c) which does not make the *asunchutōs* look like a sort of external counterbalance to the unity, always threatening to dissolve it again, but shows precisely how it enters into the *constitution* of the united unity as an intrinsic factor, in such a way that unity and distinction become mutually conditioning and intensifying characteristics, not competing ones.[83]

To this positive possibility in God, there corresponds in the human being— and once more, this is discovered only in virtue of the reality of the incarnation—a capacity for assumption by God. The human being is "pure reference to God."[84] In the incarnation, God actualizes this possibility— concretizes the generic mystery of being-God in the christological mystery. Still the generic "mystery" of the human being, as "an indefinability come to consciousness of itself,"[85] is defined in God's assumption of a human nature in the very act of causing it to exist.

This human nature of Christ subsists, according to Chalcedon, in a oneness of person with the Logos. Again, the term "person" in this context cannot be understood in any sense as antecedent to the Christ event, however varied its acceptations descriptively and philosophically. In Chalcedon the concept of person is ontological rather than psychological, moral, or phenomenological (the senses in which the term later came to be used). "In Chalcedon's definition, self-awareness, freedom, moral dignity, proceed from the concept of *nature*."[86] Accordingly, what is normally understood by "being a human being" belongs fully to the humanity of Christ. Chalcedon says that what is ultimate and incommunicable in the concrete reality of Christ is in the Logos, not in his human nature.

> This concrete nature, by the mere fact of not determining any mode of existence of its own, exists in another totality: its mode of being is that of the Son; its manner of being and of "possessing itself" is that of the very Word of God.[87]

I shall attempt no detailed analysis of the various theoretical explanations of the non-contradiction of the mystery of Christ.[88] My only concern is to emphasize the permanent importance of "descending christology" for the formulation of that mystery. This importance does not reside in any comprehension of the content of the mystery "from a point of departure in God," but in an insistence that that mystery comes from God, that the possibility that God might concretize the divine mystery christologically has in fact been realized; and conversely, that that mystery is not a possibility on the human being's side, is not a product of flesh and blood, but is gift. A christology "from below" is of the utmost importance to us for an analysis of the concrete content of Christ; but a christology "from above," from God downward, so to speak, from Jesus' assumption in the person of the Son, holds its indispensable element: Christ comes from outside us and beyond us, and we can only respond to the mystery with faith and thanksgiving, if it is indeed the case—and we have seen that it is—that this happening is salvation.

The content of the mystery of Christ demands a specific epistemology, one distinct even from that of a discourse on the mystery of God generally or the "mystery" of the human being generally. The ultimate reason for this is that the copula "is," in the statement "God is human being"

> cannot identify the notion contained in the subject of the proposition (God) with the notion contained in the predicate (human being, being born, and so on) in the same way as other propositions with which we are familiar.[89]

Even the ordinary analogy of being, which spans God and the human being, is transcended here.

To speak of the mystery of Christ calls for an absolute sobriety of language and a reflexively conscious relativization of that language. This state of affairs makes two further demands. The first is openness to a nonverifiable knowledge where the mystery of Christ is concerned. This openness, this availability, is generally described as a *sacrificium intellectus*, or more biblically, as the self-surrender of the whole human being, intellect and will. It is in this sense that I have likened the dogmatic statements about Christ to doxological statements, in which, on the basis of historical statements that are indeed verifiable and that render the act of faith an *obsequium rationabile*, the ultimate nonverifiable statement is made, and made *only in virtue of the self-surrender.*[90] This surrender of the understanding must go hand in hand with a surrender of the totality of the person, understanding and will alike, and, more inclusively, with the surrender of one's actual life, or at least with the openness to such surrender.[91]

The second demand is that the very mystery of Christ be reality in us (however analogously, to be sure), that the incarnation be analogously reproduced in us.[92] This is what happens with grace. Grace is God's self-communication to human beings. In both cases the possibility appears only after its realization, but once the grace event has occurred, it bestows on human beings their likeness and affinity to Christ, in reality and not only in their knowledge. The element of community between the mystery of Christ and human beings favored with grace is grace as God's self-communication. This affinity and community ultimately make it possible for faith in Christ to be an *obsequium rationabile.*[93]

Put abstractly, this statement can of course remain sterile. But if the incarnation is historicized in the history of Jesus, and if grace is historicized in the discipleship of Jesus, then we have identified the locus of genuine affinity with Christ and his mystery. The "average" disciple of Jesus will have no need to render these reflections explicit. Even without doing so, he or she will be living and experiencing the reality of grace and will be capable of a doxological grasp of God's irreversible self-communication in Christ.

The dogmatic affirmation of the mystery of Christ, presented in a "descending" christology, produces a "metaphysical vertigo" not subject to control by reason.[94] It is a limit affirmation, and an obligatory one, but it is not the primordial source of faith. For the very understanding of the dogmatic formula, then, one must begin with something distinct from it and more original than it. The metaphysical vertigo can only be maintained in the presence of a historical vertigo, one filled with gratitude, love, commitment, and historical self-surrender, and presupposing the believing experience.

> In this believing experience of Jesus, antecedent to all manners of "metaphysical" Christology we discover a concrete source of believing cognition, and a criterion for the discernment of this same *metaphysical* Christology.[95]

This sends us back to the original experience of faith in Christ and calls for a concrete manner of approach to the dogmatic formulas from a point of departure in this realized faith in Christ. It is an essential element in the Christian original experience of faith that it embrace the kernel of the christological mystery: the manifestation of God in the human being Jesus, the pertinency of the human being Jesus to God, and the ultimacy of the relationship between the two. This believing experience can be formulated in various ways. "The grace of God has appeared, offering salvation to all men" (Titus 2:11); "The kindness and love of God our savior appeared" (Titus 3:4). It can be formulated in the present as the absolute hope that God will establish the kingdom as proclaimed and brought to reality by Jesus in spite of all difficulties to the contrary. In the maintenance of the ultimacy of God and the ultimacy of Jesus, and in the vital experience of both ultimacies because of Jesus, one undergoes the believing experience that is equivalent to Chalcedon's statement. Citing Rahner once more, this believing experience might be translated as follows:

> In Jesus God has promised himself to me completely and irrevocably. This promise can no longer be revised or cancelled in spite of the infinite possibilities which God has at his command. He has appointed an end to the world and its history and that end is himself, and this decree is not merely present in God's eternal thoughts, it has already been inserted into the world and history by God himself, in Jesus who was crucified and rose again.[96]

This believing experience expresses the content of the descending formulas, but it can only be had on the basis of Christ's historical manifestation: his life, his activity, his death, and his resurrection. The descending christology contains an essential ascending moment: the real impact caused by Jesus as he actually appeared on this earth. The very understanding of the dogma of Chalcedon is inseparable—chronologically and theologically—from the path that led to its formulation.[97]

The descending formulation of the mystery of Christ as incarnation and hypostatic union, consisting as it does of limit propositions, can only be believed. But in order for faith in that mystery to be possible and to have a concrete content, account must always be taken of the concrete content of Jesus that leads and compels one—although it compels only in full respect for one's freedom—to the limit statements of church dogma and the New Testament.

The christology of liberation rejects neither the christological mystery nor its dogmatic formulations, although it has not considered it its task to analyze these formulations speculatively. With other christologies, however, it has emphasized the limitations of human language for purposes of expressing that mystery. The dogmas really speak about God, but they do not speak in God's language. They speak about God in the language of human beings. Furthermore, in order really to speak about God, this very language must be self-critical. Hence the need to maintain a dialectical relationship between "God" and human "language"—or, as José Ignacio González Faus has put it so well, "God's assumption of our 'language' in order to be uttered, and God's destruction of our language."[98]

A recognition of the truth of dogma, then, need not involve a failure to recognize the ambiguity of its language as human language, or the pastoral and theological limitations of its formulation.[99] Language, including dogmatic language, combines the possibility of expressing truth with the perilousness of everything human. Various theologians have recognized this.

Undeniably, a danger lurks here. We note, in the systematization we have just presented, a strong tendency to abstract formulation. Step by step with the accentuation of the abstract terminology, the concrete content of the human subject, "Jesus of Nazareth"—the theological traits of the "God and Father of Our Lord Jesus Christ," and the dramatic fact of their unity, and so forth, are gradually diluted. The systematic synthesis ends in large part as no more than the subtle development of a single type of christology, that is, of the ancient Christian dogma in its extreme ontological form.[100]

Dogma has a positive, regulative, and irreplaceable value for the mainte- nance of the radicality of the mystery of Christ (see p. 19). But its formulation, however true and binding, ever runs the risk of all that is human and therefore must always be understood from within the original event that has rendered it possible: the reality of Jesus of Nazareth and of the God revealed in him. As Olegario G. de Cardenal has expressed it, it is the New Testament itself, "reread and reexperienced, that will be an ongoing threat to further formulations."[101] "Threat" here means neither rejection nor reductionism nor impoverishment, but rather enrichment: it denotes the need to return to the primordial source for a better and more adequate understanding of the irreplaceable kernel of the compact dogmatic formula, which, however true, begins with a "limited historical perspective."[102]

In light of all that has been said, liberation christology has surely devoted the greater part of its energies to an understanding of the total truth of Jesus Christ from the New Testament in general and the history of Jesus in particular. Its approach to the dogmatic formulations has been "ascending": from the history of Jesus to the fullness of Jesus as presented in the New Testament, and from that presentation to the dogmatic formulations.

This ascending emphasis "from below," from Jesus' history, and the desire to demonstrate more vigorously for the contemporary human being in the contemporary situation the kernel of the dogmatic affirmations has led me to make certain statements about Jesus Christ, which, while they neither ignore nor reject the dogmatic statements, nevertheless, by virtue of the relative novelty of their own formulations and at times through a certain imprecision in language, have lent themselves to misinterpretation as attacks on dogma and on the truth about Jesus Christ. For this reason I will conclude this article by explaining some of the formulations that I have used in other writings and clarifying their theological and pastoral context, from which the positive, nonreductionistic intent of these formulations will appear.

My emphasis on the relationship of the historical Jesus to God has led some to conclude that we hold the divinity of Jesus to consist merely in his pyscho- logical, historically experienced relationship with God in trust and obedi- ence.[103]

I have stated above that Christ's divinity consists in his consubstantiality with God (see pp. 19–29), and that his humanity is assumed in the divine person of the Logos (see p. 40). Elsewhere I have stated that Jesus of Nazareth is the eternal Son of God.[104]

What stands in need of clarification, then, is the relationship between historical propositions and transcendent ones, between what constitutes the plane of our knowledge about Christ and the plane of the actual reality of Christ. This latter can be expressed only in doxological formulations, which, in order to be "comprehensible," must retrace the path that led to their formulation. Put systematically, this path consists of three basic steps: (1) the registration or observation of the historical relationship of Jesus to God, which can be aptly described as "filiation"; (2) a consideration of that filiation as the supreme, unrepeatable, and unique oneness of Jesus with God, described in John as a oneness of knowledge and will; (3) the assertion of the "divine" filiation of Jesus—that is, of his being Son of God, consubstantial with God.

There is no question, then, of any opposition between the divine reality of Christ and the historical filiation of Jesus. What is at stake is the recognition of that filiation as the pathway to the profession of the former. What is first on the level of reality is last on the level of our cognition. This is what I have sought to indicate above in stating that the divinity of Christ, while predicated of him really, is not predicated directly, but only through mediations.

This *modus procedendi* is suggested by the New Testament. Jesus' earthly life is described there in terms that make it convenient and necessary to denominate his relation to God as "filiation." Hence the insistence on his trust, obedience, and fidelity. But even when speaking of the exalted Christ, and thus using other titles denoting his relationship with God ("Lord," "Word"), the New Testament continues to use the title "Son of God"—now in the sense of fullness and plenitude—and relates it to the history of Jesus.

Speculatively, as well, theologians have sought to begin with the systematic concept of filiation to help understand the union of Christ with God, to begin with the analogy of humanity and filiation.

> This analogy between filiation and humanity brings us closer to the heart of an understanding of the unity in question. The traditional schema of interpretation goes no further than to posit the unity of the human "nature" with the divine in a nonspecific oneness of activity or *operatio* on the part of the divine hypostasis. Here, we are permitted to conceive of the creaturely relation of the human being to God (as phenomenon and origin or Jesus' human being) as absorbed in the intradivine relation of the Son to the Father as foundation and origin of the divine being.[105]

I do not, then, use the relational category of filiation in order to weaken the ontological reality of the divine nature in Christ. I use it in order to afford the *intellectus fidei* some access to how Jesus can be God by explaining *what* there is in human nature that would entail the likelihood of its being able to be assumed by God in such wise that what would be assumed could actually *be* God.

The use of filiation as a systematic category for an approach to the divinity of Christ has further theo-logical and pastoral importance. Theoretically, the category of "power" could have been selected in order to render Jesus' divinity comprehensible. This is what is expressed by the miracles and by the title "Lord," understood from a concept of power without any dialectic. The miracles have generally been abandoned by exegetes and theologians for this purpose, and power, as already explained, fails to correspond to the reality of Christ unless the power implied in lordship is subjected to a critique based on the actual history of Jesus. At all events, were one to seek to explain the oneness of Jesus and God from a point of departure in power, this would be an effective way of saying that the ultimate reality of God is power and thereby of aggravating the ambiguity and dangers with which an understanding of God is fraught.

The category of Son, however, lends itself to the dissolution of this ambiguity and danger, if the Son is at the same time *pais Theou* and therefore is constituted Lord. In this fashion, the scandalous novelty of the divinity is preserved and the eternal divinity of Christ can be presented pastorally in situations in which peoples are crucified—as is the case with the Latin American peoples—in all its essentials thus promoting the understanding of Christ in his aspect as servant.[106]

Indeed, the divine reality of Christ will be variously presented in various models of theological understanding. Attempting to grasp this reality radically from Jesus' filiation is faithful to the New Testament; but in order to acquire such a grasp it is necessary to return to the historical apparition of this filiation. An emphasis on Jesus' historical relationship to God, then, is not the annulment of his divinity; on the contrary, it actually opens the way to the dogmatic assertion of his consubstantiality with God and offers a pastoral approach to the divinity of Christ.

I have written on occasion that Jesus *becomes* Son of God.[107] This has led some to think that I defend some type of adoptionism, or that I deny Christ's preexistence. This is certainly not the intent of my formulation (see pp. 20–21); furthermore, it is in the context of the human history of Jesus that I use the language of "becoming" (see pp. 30–31). The formula "to become Son of God" is not intended as an antisymmetrical expression of the formula "God's becoming man."

Prescinding for the moment from whether the actual terminology of "becoming" is felicitous or not, let me point out the two things that this language seeks to emphasize. First, inasmuch as Jesus is a human being he has a history, and through this history he gradually reveals what he has always been. This in turn is possible only by virtue of historical revelation. Precisely because Jesus' being Son of God is a full reality, it stands in need of a history, with all of the good and ill fortune, all of the development, all of the novelties and scandals of a human history, in order to be able, asymptotically, to reproduce the plenitude of his being Son. To put it another way, the *revelation* of the full filiation of Jesus occurs, according to the New Testament, not punctually—

witness the New Testament's attempts to relate his divine filiation with several, and not just one, of the historical events of his life (see pp. 20–21)—but historically. Surely it is not only his nature, and not even only one of the events of his life, or only one of his attitudes, or only his fate, but the totality of all of these, that reveals his filiation.

Second, Jesus' historicity affects him in the very depths of his theological relationship to God. This is not an aprioristic statement, but springs from the recognition of the fact that in the gospel Jesus' trust, obedience, and fidelity to God also have a history. The Letter to the Hebrews takes pains to underscore this history. Such a historical approach obviates any doubt that Jesus has lived his relationship to God in its fullness; and this leads it to the most audacious proposition that Jesus' life is one of the origin and fullness of faith (Heb. 12:2). Hebrews not only demonstrates the historicity of Jesus' being a human being, then, but also introduces this historicity into the historical relationship of Jesus with God.

This is likewise the intent of my statement. It may be that the language of "becoming," so easily accepted today to express Jesus' becoming a *human being*, will cause misunderstandings when used to express his becoming as *Son* of God. In this case another language may be sought, which will lend itself less easily to these pastoral misunderstandings, and we may say simply that for the human being Jesus, too, God appeared as a mystery, and all the more so in proportion to Jesus' greater nearness to God and greater fidelity in his response to the mystery. But it would seem to be counterproductive to abandon *all* historical language in describing Jesus even in his relationship to God. This historical language cannot assert that the divine filiation "becomes," but it can emphasize the historical apparition of that filiation. Kasper aptly distinguishes between what Jesus *is* and the manner in which his being gradually *appears*, with special attention to the language used.

> The scriptural eschatological-historical understanding of reality does not involve any supra-historical concept of essence; being is here understood, not as an essence, but as actuality, that is, as being active. The statement, "being is coming to to be," is of course not the same as asserting that being consists in becoming. It is in history that what a "thing" *is* is proved and realized. In this sense Jesus' Resurrection is the confirmation, revelation, putting into force, realization and completion of what Jesus before Easter claimed to be and *was*. His history and his fate are the history (not the coming to be) of his being, its ripening and self-interpretation.[108]

These conceptual and terminological precisions may be of use for the preclusion of any adoptionist conceptualization. But they do not eliminate— on the contrary, they underscore—the fact that Jesus' filiation is shown to us through his history, and that only from the final plenitude of that history can one come to know him as Son of God.

Thus it also becomes clear that the full meaning of Jesus' pre-Easter claim and manifestation, his dignity as Son of God, dawned on the disciples only at the end and after the completion of his way: that is, after Easter.[109]

What must be stressed, in this correct proposition, is that the punctual revelatory moment of Easter draws its vitality and reality from Jesus' whole journey through life, which is not punctual, but genuinely historical. In the Easter moment, Jesus finally shows himself for what he *is*. But this "is," realized in the conditions of human existence, essentially comprises a history, without which not even Jesus would have actualized his being Son of God once the Son had become flesh by God's design.

With these precisions in mind, let us turn to the pastoral reasons for an insistence on presenting Jesus' filiation historically and his historicity theologically. In Latin America, what Vatican II, Medellín, and Puebla call "signs of the times" are not only taken seriously but are taken *theologically*, and are not reduced to sociological, economic, and political signs. Thus they are interpreted as the novel expression of the will of God. Now, just as it is important to make concrete the filiation of a Jesus who is close and near to his crucified people, it is likewise important to present the history of his relationship to God, in order to inculcate an openness to the historical, novel expression of the present will of God—in order to show the urgency of obedience in putting that will in practice and fidelity in its execution. It is also important to feel Jesus to be near to human beings in the face of the novelty of God's will in our day. It is no little consolation for Christians who must discern the will of God in painful and perilous situations when this will becomes demanding—when it becomes luminous in yearnings for liberation and dark in the horrors of crucifixion—when the dialectic arises between struggle with poverty and impoverishment itself—to find, in Jesus, someone who has already stood before God in such situations. In this availability to the will of God, this readiness for change and conversion, for novelty and scandal, Christians experience their gradual becoming, their becoming daughters and sons of God, even though they have always been this by baptism.

Whatever may be the most correct formulation of the theological historicity of Jesus, what is of pastoral interest, what consoles these Christians, is the observation that even the history of Jesus' relationship with God was filled with demands, with lights and shadows, with antinomies not easily reconciled: that Jesus, too, was made "perfect through suffering" (Heb. 2:10) by God. This Son of God, subjected to trial, apprenticeship, and suffering, who thus attained perfection (cf. Heb. 5:9) is a Son of God to whom these Christians feel a closeness.

I have written that Jesus is *in directo* the manifestation of the Son and not in an unqualified sense the epiphanic revelation of the Father.[110] I have stressed that Jesus manifests the correct manner of "correspondence" to God; he is the way and path to God. This has occasioned the deduction on the part of some that I therefore deny that Jesus is the revealer of God.

These are indeed new propositions, and thus call for some explanation. On the one hand, it is evident that the New Testament makes forthright statements about the revelatory character of Christ with respect to God. He is the image of the invisible God (Col. 1:15), the reflection of God's glory (Heb. 1:3), the manifestation of the glory of God (John 17:4–6). In John's categorical pronouncement, "Whoever has seen me has seen the Father" (John 14:9), there can be no doubt that Jesus reveals God. Jesus is God's way of becoming present among human beings.

On the other hand, Jesus does not reveal God epiphanically, as if what appeared in Jesus were divinity after the manner of "motherhood" or "fatherhood." He reveals God sacramentally, as the expression, as the word of God, without his actually being God the Father. What has historically appeared among us is divinity after the manner of filiation. "Jesus has revealed God in the condition of Son."[111] "Jesus lived God as Son in our condition."[112] This is only a return to the dogma of the incarnation, according to which it is the eternal Son, not the Father, who became a human being.[113] But precisely because Jesus is the incarnation of the Son, and because the Son is the intra-trinitarian word of God, therefore Jesus too is the expression, word, sacrament, of God. Historically, what appears *in directo* is Jesus' sacramentality in God's regard, in virtue of the oneness of knowledge and love in the Trinity; doxologically and indirectly there appears the oneness of Jesus with the eternal Son.[114]

Jesus really reveals the divinity, then. *In directo*, he is the apparition among us of the divinity after the manner of filiation, not of parenthood. But because he reveals the divinity after the manner of filiation, and the essence of the Son is to be the expression and sacrament of the Father, therefore Jesus also reveals—sacramentally, and not epiphanically—the Father.

The theological and pastoral intent of my propositions, whatever be their terminological imprecision, is nothing else but the preservation of an important pair of truths. First, I am concerned to safeguard the mystery of God as mystery, even after the appearance of Jesus, indeed, to safeguard the truth that, precisely in Jesus, God is fully manifested and remains mystery, that is, abides as absolute origin—origin without origin—and as absolute future. Paradoxically, God's nearness in Jesus shows God's condition as holy mystery in all of its radicalness. Thus there is no question of reducing the reality of God to christology, although the Christian sense will indeed insist on *concentrating* itself on a point of departure in christology.[115] God's self has been uttered in Jesus; but God has not thereby ceased to be the ultimate mystery. "In being Son, in no wise can he be the Father—in no wise can he reject (except in the imagination) his not being his own origin of himself."[116] One can and must say, then, that Jesus is the sacrament of God, but on condition that one not erect this sacramentality into a means of denying that God is still the ultimate mystery of history and of human beings.

The second purpose of the proposition under consideration is to emphasize the complementarity of aspects in Jesus with a view to our own relation to God. The terminology of "sacramentality" and "revelation" implies Jesus' function in our knowledge of God; the terminology of "Son," then, surely implies, for its part, the correct manner of his "correspondence," as Son, with the Father. Walter Kasper has expressed this complementarity very well: "Jesus is nothing but the incarnate love of the Father and the incarnate response of obedience."[117] That is the sense in which I have spoken so insistently of Jesus as the "way" to God.[118] This is of the utmost pastoral importance in overcoming the restriction of our understanding of our relationship with God to the sole level of knowledge, to the exclusion of praxis.

This complementarity is expressed in the tension between being the "truth" and being the "way" (cf. John 14:6). Puebla has made the pastoral application: "Christ's proclamation . . . 'reveals' the Father to us . . ."; and at the same time "there is no other road that leads to the Father" (Puebla, Final Document, nos. 211, 214).

It will be clear, then, that the intent of my propositions has not been to deny the relationship of Christ to God or to deny the revelatory nature of this relationship. Rather my concern has been to avoid an attempt to understand that revelation *only* gnoseologically or "descendingly." It must be understood praxically and "ascendingly" as well. Christian faith based on Jesus consists in knowing God from Jesus and in corresponding to God as Jesus has done. The former, far from conjuring away the reality of God as mystery, radicalizes it; the latter is no more than doing justice to the revelation of God in Jesus after the manner of Son.

Finally, exception has been taken to my description of God as trinitarian "process,"[119] as if I were thereby denying the reality of the trinitarian God or suggesting that God is formally constituted by history.

In no wise have I sought to engage in speculation upon the Trinity. My intent has been to assert in human language the specific modality of the revelation of God from a point of departure in Jesus. A great deal of material is available on the identity between the economic Trinity (the Trinity for us) and the immanent Trinity (the Trinity in itself).[120] The church has made its pronouncements upon the latter, but, when all is said and done, it has made them based on the manifestation for us from a point of departure in Jesus.

What I have sought to add through my terminology of "process" with respect to the Trinity is that God not only is revealed to us in trinitarian fashion, but that God also takes on human beings' history. This is certainly clear in the incarnation. Hence the use by the New Testament and the church of the language of God's "becoming" a human being, although this language is used with caution.[121] But one can surely speak analogously of God's assumption of human beings' history. "For by his incarnation the Son of God has united Himself in some fashion with every [human being]" (*Gaudium et Spes*, no. 22).[122]

For this reason, by an excellent analogy, [the church] is compared to the mystery of the incarnate Word. Just as the assumed nature inseparably united to the divine Word serves Him as a living instrument of salvation, so, in a similar way, does the communal structure of the Church serve Christ's Spirit, who vivifies it by way of building up the body (cf. Eph. 4:16) [*Lumen Gentium*, no. 8].[123]

These two assertions by the Second Vatican Council were not made in a trinitarian context, it is true; but they indirectly state God's relationship to the history of human beings and to the church, and, conversely, the relationship of this history to God, and they do so with a depth that points to a relationship of this history with the incarnation—although, to be sure, the latter is not predicated of all men and women, but only of Christ (and this is the import of the expressions "in some fashion" and "analogy").

What must be maintained here is that, on one hand, history and the historical process do not formally constitute God, do not make God to be God, any more than Jesus' humanity brings it about that God comes to be God. But on the other hand, neither does it appear possible to escape the notion that history affects God, just as the incarnation really affected God. The "how" of both realities is mystery. That God should become a human being and that God should take on history are mysteries; but they do not cease for all that to be basic Christian tenets. This is the sense in which I have used the terminology of "process" with respect to the Trinity: as a way of underscoring in human language the assumption of processual history by God and God's assumption of this history precisely as open history and not as mere closed nature.

The "evolutionary" dimension implied in the terminology of process only seeks to assert that God is not only the absolute origin, but also the absolute future as well—which means that only at the end of the ages will the tension between the "already" and the "not yet" be resolved, and that this tension will be definitively resolved in the form of salvation, God's triumph, God's definitive manifestation, or, in Pauline language, God's being all in all (cf. 1 Cor. 15:28).

Whatever be the felicitousness of my expressions or lack thereof, their intent is precisely to make possible a radically theo-logical reading of history, not a reduction of it to a merely sociological, economic, political, or cultural reading. God is the one who draws history to its fulfillment—God, and not a mere human ideal of society, however much that is mightily to be striven for. It is God who unleashes human beings' best liberative impulses, who moves men and women to overcome the limitations of these thrusts, and who condemns enslaving thrusts. The belief in Latin America that these impulses, these thrusts, will have a definitive outcome in transcendence arises out of faith in God's nearness. God is in our history without prejudice to the divine transcendence, and God has freely willed to take on our history. From Jesus, God is shown as Father; absolute origin and future; salvific, scandalous mystery that remains mystery. God is shown as Son, incarnate in Jesus' history. God is shown as Spirit, interiorized in human beings and history, and continuing to produce truth and life. In order to assert of God *in se* what appears in the divine revelation to human beings, one must somehow cite God's "openness," which is gradually concretized down the length and breadth of the history of human beings that God has assumed. It is in this sense that I speak of a trinitarian "process."

FAITH IN JESUS CHRIST

I have expatiated with a certain fear and trembling upon the *truth about Jesus Christ*. In doing so, I have been honest with the church and with what the Spirit is unveiling in the churches of Latin America. It is my hope that this explanation will have been useful for showing that, at least substantively, there is no reduction of the total truth about Jesus Christ in the christology of liberation, either in intent or in fact. Perhaps doubts and suspicions still remain. The very limitations intrinsic to the human condition when it comes to speaking adequately about Jesus Christ impose sobriety on any christological reflection. The actual reality of Jesus Christ, which outstrips any of its formulations, calls for ever new reflection. The christological task abides.

I conclude with some brief remarks on something that all christology, whatever its merits or limitations, all pastoral theory and practice, all evangelization, and even all dogmatic statements should serve: *faith in Jesus Christ*. Reflection upon and explanation of the christology of liberation has its importance. But even more important is whether and to what extent there is real faith in Jesus Christ in Latin America, as it is from this faith that a christology of liberation springs, and it is the service of this faith that lends a christology of liberation its entire raison d'être. No one can give a definitive answer to this question, since it pertains to the ultimate mystery of the human being. But certain observations can be made.

If persons and communities follow Jesus and proclaim the kingdom of God to the poor; if they strive for liberation from every kind of slavery; if they seek, for all human beings, especially for that immense majority of men and women who are crucified persons, a life in conformity with the dignity of daughters and sons of God; if they have the courage and forthrightness to speak the truth, however this may translate into the denunciation and unmasking of sin, and steadfastness in the conflicts and persecution occasioned by this forthrightness; if, in this discipleship of Jesus, they effectuate their own conversion from being oppressors to being men and women of service; if they have the spirit of Jesus, with the bowels of mercy and the pure heart to see the truth of things, and refuse to darken their hearts by imprisoning the truth of things in injustice; if in doing justice they seek peace and in making peace they seek to base it on justice; and if they do all this in the following and discipleship of Jesus because he did all this himself—then they believe in Jesus Christ.

If, in the following of Jesus the ultimate problems of existence and history arise, and they have the courage to respond as Jesus has, citing and invoking the name of God; if they have the courage to stand before this God in prayer, the prayer of jubilee when the kingdom is revealed to the poor and the prayer of the agony in the garden when the mystery of iniquity rears its head; if they have found in this discipleship the pearl of great price and the way to God, to whom they give themselves over whole and entire and the heavy burden of the gospel becomes light; if they abide with God in the cross of Jesus and in the number-less crosses of history; and if in spite of all of this their hope is mightier than death—then they believe in the God of Jesus.

If they discover in this discipleship and this faith more happiness in giving than in receiving; if they are prepared to give of their own lives, and life itself, that others may have life; if they surrender their lives instead of keeping them for themselves—then they are bearing witness to the greatest love. They are responding, in love for their sisters and brothers, to the God who has loved us first; they are living in the Spirit of God, who has been poured forth into our hearts; they are living the gift of God, and God as gift—before whom the last word, despite and through the horrors of history, is a word of thanksgiving.

Those who do this, and are this, enjoy the reality of faith in Jesus Christ. It will be an easy matter for them to profess it in words, in eucharistic professions of faith, in the formulations of popular piety, in the reflections of the base church communities, in the official pronouncements of the church. It may even be that some of them have been assisted by the christology of liberation to formulate, and to formulate to themselves, their faith in Christ. But any such formulation will have taken its life from something antecedent to itself: the faith in Christ and love for Christ of those who utter it.

The ultimate language of faith is love. Those who would verify their own truth concerning the Christ will in the last resort have to question themselves about their love for Christ. Is there love for Christ in Latin America? This simple question may perhaps be the ultimate key for an understanding and interpretation of truth asserted about Christ. Only God knows the measure of this love. But it would be unjust not to recognize that in Latin America there are Christians who can make Paul's exultation their own.

> Who will separate us from the love of Christ? Trial, or distress, or persecution, or hunger, or nakedness, or danger, or the sword? As Scripture says: "For your sake we are being slain all the day long; we are looked upon as sheep to be slaughtered." Yet in all this we are more than conquerors because of him who has loved us. For I am certain that neither death nor life, neither angels nor principalities, neither the present nor the future, nor powers, neither height nor depth nor any other creature, will be able to separate us from the love of God that comes to us in Christ Jesus, our Lord [Rom. 8:35–39].

2

The Importance of the Historical Jesus
in Latin American Christology

The theologians of liberation and the Christian people they represent accept, in the reality of their faith and in theological reflection upon that faith, the totality of Jesus the Christ. However, they do not see this totality as a cumulative one, consisting in the sum of the (historical) Jesus and the Christ (of faith), but as a totality constituted by two moments that complement each other *natura sua*. Doubtless Latin American theology has accorded a *methodological* primacy to the moment of the historical Jesus within the totality of Jesus Christ, the better to approach this totality.[1] Thereby it thinks to have found a better point of departure of the articulation of the totality of christological faith (where the reality and relevancy of its object are concerned), and the best route of access today (hermeneutically) to that object.

The intent of this work is to demonstrate the *factum* and the *jus* of this methodological *modus procedendi* by comparing it to, and differentiating it from, other christologies, which, in one fashion or another, are rehabilitating the figure of the historical Jesus. The points of comparison that I shall establish do not, of course, exhaust the problematic of the historical Jesus in other christologies, but are only meant to furnish an explanation of enough points of affinity and difference to assist in a comprehension of what is typical in the use of the historical Jesus by Latin American christology.

HISTORICIZATION OF JESUS CHRIST
IN CURRENT CHRISTOLOGIES

Unquestionably, recent decades have seen, in Catholic as well as in Protestant systematic theology, a tendency to historicize Jesus the Christ.[2] These

---

The purpose of this article, written in 1979 and not previously published in English, is to make a theoretical contribution to the question of the importance of the "historical" Jesus in Latin American christology in comparison and contrast with current christologies that likewise refer to him as their point of departure or that rehabilitate his importance for systematic christology. The translation is by Robert R. Barr.

christologies are engaged in a rehabilitation of the revelatory import of Jesus' earthly existence. The purpose of this rehabilitation is a total understanding of Jesus the Christ.

Latin American christology is formally inscribed in this process, but with its own characteristics. In the following description of this movement to rehabilitate the importance of Jesus' history, one must keep in account the direction of this historicization, the theological and pastoral considerations to which it is responding, and its consequences for systematic christology.

Latin American christology recognizes, and by and large approves, certain achievements on the part of European christology in the return to the history of Jesus. By way of recapitulating what is most substantial and beneficial in this process, we may recall Karl Rahner's enormous speculative effort to restore to Christ his true humanity and thereby to overcome the painful mythological overtones that, besides running counter to the intent of Scripture and dogma, render acceptance of Christ culturally difficult.[3] It is irrelevant for the moment to cite the Rahnerian methodology for achieving the historicization of Christ; but it is important to underscore the christological content that he has developed and his reason for developing it.

Rahner emphasizes the true humanity of Christ, and, furthermore, conceives it sacramentally. Christ was really a human being; but further, his concrete humanity is the exegesis of the transcendence of Christ in such wise that it is useless to look for the locus of the understanding of Christ and of the realization of faith in him outside that humanity.[4] This is no purely academic reflection, nor is it demanded only by the actual reality of Christ; it is needed in order to survive the profound crisis of meaning faced by so many believers when they are presented with a transcendence without history, a Christ without Jesus. Rahner's contribution is therefore profoundly pastoral, and is a response to a determinate crisis.[5]

The theological return to Christ's humanity has followed Rahner's process. From the Rahnerian emphasis on the "true human being" of the dogmatic formula, many theologians, and Rahner himself, have gone on to "Jesus of Nazareth." It is this second step that has given rise to current christologies emphasizing the historical Jesus. The abundant exegetical and biblical literature concerning Jesus has doubtless been a help in taking this step; but the most important consideration is that the translation of "humanity of Christ" into "Jesus of Nazareth" has rephrased the very significance of the systematic christological task. The concrete content of Jesus of Nazareth, over and above the profession of his "true humanity," has forced christology's self-revision.

In this process of revision, systematic christology no longer begins methodologically with the christological dogmas, although it accepts them, and they furnish its reflections upon Christ with their radicalness and limits. The dogmatic formulas, whether in the strict sense of conciliar formulas or in the broad sense of biblical formulas expressing the reality of the Christ of faith, are not the point of departure of the new systematic christologies, but their point of arrival. The methodological return to the history of Jesus shows that only through recourse to this history can the doxological content of the formulations about Christ be invested with meaning.[6] More concretely, it shows that only from a point of departure in Jesus can one avoid the abstract universalization, with its negative consequences in terms of manipulability, of what is essential in christology: the realities of "God," "the human being," and "Christ."

Likewise in this process of revision, the presentation of Christ has been deabsolutized and made in terms of his constitutive relationality. Christ has always been seen, in trinitarian reflection, in relation to the Father and the Spirit; but traditional christologies have presented Christ in a regional and absolutized manner. The return to the historical Jesus has forced these christologies to the discovery of a double relationality. They discover, on the one hand, Christ's constitutive relationship to God, and more concretely, to God's ultimate will, which is the approach of the kingdom of God.[7] On the other hand, they discover the intrinsic relationship of the content of Christ with the ecclesial practices of the communities that sprang up after the resurrection. Christ cannot be adequately understood without reference to these communities that were in the process of recalling him.[8] This double historical relationality (theo-logical and pneumato-logical) of Jesus is of the utmost importance if we are to escape the presentation of christology today in regional fashion, after the manner of the old tractates, and relate our christology to what Jesus himself related. In order to understand Christ, we shall have to understand the God of the kingdom, as well as the faith in Christ stirred up by the Spirit in the communities. All of this effectuates a change in the very notion of method in christology—prohibiting (paradoxical as it may seem) a christology "in itself" and actually making it possible to refer christology in the last resort to a trinitarian context.

Finally, this process has revised christological hermeneutics, which is now seen to have to be adequate to span the historical and cultural distance between Christ and the present. Hermeneutical interest has shifted from the understanding of the Christ of faith and his import for the present to the understanding of the historical Jesus, including a historical understanding of his resurrection. From a point of departure in the historical Jesus, "praxis" has yielded up the element needed to span the historical distance; hence we hear today of praxic, liberative, and even revolutionary hermeneutics. Whatever be the concrete achievements of these various hermeneutics, they all point to the discipleship of Jesus as the way to the attainment of an understanding of Jesus as the Christ; and at all events they are demanded by Jesus, the content of christology.

Accordingly, the process of a return to Jesus has involved a rather generalized abandonment of unilaterally dogmatic or descending *points of departure;* but it has also involved christology's reflection on new content in Christ and on its access to him as another of its tasks.

Latin American theology accepts the direction of this process in its formality, but it has certain reservations, and is even led to the rejection of certain elements, when it comes to the actual christologies emerging from this direction. Of course, in passing such judgment, there is no intent to fall into the anachronism of expecting pioneers to hold more modern positions and make more modern propositions; nor is there any wish to ignore the wholesome pastoral intent that has motivated the authors of these christologies.[9]

Nevertheless, in this process toward the historical Jesus, Latin American theology notes two presuppositions that it cannot share if they are to be transformed into the ultimate motivation for returning to Jesus. The first has to do with the identity of Christ. It is possible to return to Jesus in order to learn who he really is and to gain a reflexive consciousness of not having placed one's trust in a myth. But this better knowledge about Christ is no unqualified guarantee of any radical change in what it means to know Christ, as distinguished from merely knowing about him. The second presupposition has to do with Christ's relevance. It is possible to return to Jesus because his historical life is a better and more effective guarantee of the experience of a meaning that has been called into question. It is more reasonable in today's world to look for the meaning of real life in a real Jesus rather than in what might be presented in mythical fashion. But neither would this substantially change the intent of christology, which would continue, understandably, to be egocentric, although not necessarily egoistic. To give just a few examples: some current christologies make an attempt to recover the historical Jesus so that today's human being may have the experience of radical hope in a future of grace, or in order to reconcile God to the world and thus survive modern society's crisis of meaning, or in order to have an experience of openness that will lend shape to one's life.

The process of the historicization of Christ, then, is at the service of the solution of a double problem: the problem presented by historical criticism to the question of who Christ really is (the problem of the identity of christology), and the problem presented by a developed world in crisis to the significance and importance of Christ (the problem of the relevance of christology).

Latin American theology knows and understands that certain christologies oriented toward the historical Jesus recognize these basic problems and seek to respond to them. Its only reservation is that it does not admit that these are the most radical problems nor the most urgent for Latin America, nor even that they are capable of being solved through an approach *in directo*. It therefore holds that these presuppositions fail to transcend a certain liberalism and idealism.

There can be no doubt that getting beyond a mythologized presentation of Christ has been instrumental in recovering the identity and relevance of Christ for the believer. But this new presentation is insufficient (and contrary to the reality of Jesus) if it fails to break out of the Christ-and-believer circle, and thereby abandons external reality to its own fate, which, in the concrete, is misery, oppression, and death.

Christ's demythologization is important, then; but more urgent in Latin America is his rescue from manipulation and connivance with idols. Demythologization is important because without it Christ remains dangerously abstract and ideal; but it is insufficient unless it leads to Christ's rescue from manipulation. Demythologizing Christ in Latin America does not primarily mean giving an account of his historical faith in the face of rational criticism, although this too must be done; primarily it means avoiding a situation in which, by reason of Jesus' historical abstraction, reality can be left to its misery. More urgent than Christ's demythologization, therefore, will be his "depacification," if we may be permitted the neologism. Christ must not be forced to leave reality in peace.

On a deeper level, however (and here the language may be strong), what we seek in Latin America in returning to Jesus is that Christ not be able to be presented in connivance with idols. An idol is not exactly a myth. Myth is the producer of significations, and it cannot happen that in its name reality is left to itself. An idol, on the other hand, actually shapes reality, for it has need of victims in order to subsist.

The most profound crisis to which Latin American christology must respond, then, lies not along lines of pure demythologization, but along those of the rescue of Christ from appropriation as the alibi for indifference in the face of the misery of reality and especially as an excuse for the religious justification of this misery. It is precisely in this context that the process of the historicization of Christ along the lines of the historical Jesus has gotten under way in Latin America. One might say that what is in crisis is not purely and simply the "name" of Christ, as having lost its meaning and import, but what is actually occurring "in the name of Christ." A post-Enlightenment culture entertains doubts about Christ; Latin American reality produces indignation at what is done in his name. It is the difference between responding to doubt and responding to indignation[10]—an indignation obviously not purely psychological or unfounded in specific reality—that marks the different routes of Christ's historicization from the very outset. The historical Jesus is being recovered in Latin America lest in Christ's name the coexistence of the misery of reality and the Christian faith be acceptable or even justifiable.[11] Or positively: the purpose of the recovery of the historical Jesus in Latin America is that salvation history be historical salvation.[12] Jesus is also being recovered because a minimum of faith in Christ, a minimal reading of the gospel of Jesus, suffices to show the urgency of a rescue of Jesus the Christ and no better, more effective, and more evident way can be found for the rescue of Jesus the Christ than return to Jesus.

It will be clear from what has been said that Latin American christology rejoices that various christologies have returned to the historical Jesus. But Latin American christology serves notice that not simply any return to Jesus, nor simply any finality attaching to this return, is sufficient for the development of a christology that will do justice to Christ and be genuinely relevant.

ECCLESIAL AND SOCIAL POINT OF DEPARTURE OF LATIN AMERICAN CHRISTOLOGY

The historical Jesus is the methodological point of departure for the approach to Jesus the Christ, that is, to the "object" of christology. In the next section I shall analyze the precise import of the historical Jesus in Latin American christology. In this section, however, I shall analyze the point of departure of the theologian—that is, of the "subject" of christology—or, more concretely, his or her ecclesial and social "ubication" or "placement." I reflect on this point at some length because I believe that a circularity obtains between these two points of departure: a determinate placement leads the subject of christology more obviously to ascribe importance to, and to understand, the historical Jesus, and the historical Jesus refers him or her to a determinate placement.

The theologian's ecclesial ubication or placement means here the church as the locus within which that theologian develops a christological reflection, therefore accepting from the start the totality of the faith of a determinate church. In the case of Latin America, this means that the theologian who reflects on Christ possesses and accepts, at least in general and to a greater or lesser degree in function of his or her own faith and that of the community, the totality of faith in Christ. But this is not a purely doctrinal totality, nor indeed—*qua* realized totality—an undifferentiated one. It is a totality of diverse elements, each of which enjoys greater relevance for the totality in a given moment. Let us examine two of these important elements in Latin America today, which *de facto* constitute "points of departure" for the christologist's reflection.

Realized, actualized faith in Christ in many communities comprises many aspects: personal contact with Christ in liturgy and prayer; study and reflection on the gospels with a view to acquiring courage, judgment, and normativity; acceptance of the doctrine of the church concerning Christ (which is actually unknown to the majority of persons, but serenely accepted implicitly). And now realized faith in Christ includes something more novel as well: the exercise of a salvific practice (a practice of "liberation," in Latin American parlance),[13] and includes it as a moment that is, on the one hand a *conditio sine qua non,* and on the other, a moment concretizing and making possible the other elements of faith in Christ. A "practice according to Jesus," then, is a historically essential element in the totality of faith in Christ.

This being the case, faith in Christ is realized and actualized more as invocation of Christ than as pure profession of Christ. As the locus of profession may be worship, the locus of invocation is practice.[14] Christ, in a determinate liberative practice, is invoked and called upon precisely as the unique, unrepeatable, saving Christ. This confers relevance and truth on the profession of Christ in the liturgy and in other doctrinal formulations.

Another important element of ecclesial faith in Christ is the locus of his current presence. This element is important to the theologian not only as believer, but also as "reflexive theologian." It is clear that the articulation of christology stands in need of antecedent material concerning Christ in order to refer that christology to Jesus, to his past. This material cannot be "invented" or "made up." Hence the importance of keeping account of what has been said about Christ in the gospels, in the rest of the New Testament, and in the traditions and dogmas of the church. However, reflection upon Christ must keep account of his current presence and of the discovery of that presence in virtue of what he himself has said.

The theme of the current presence of Christ is classic but is not much developed in the christologies, which normally reflect upon Christ on the basis of documents of the past. It is of the utmost importance, however, that christology take account of the various types of presence of Christ within and without the church community. Kerygmatic theology, for example, has seen this point clearly, and has drawn consequences for christology. Christ is present in the kerygma: he becomes present when his death and resurrection are proclaimed in the word. This presence is important for the christology of the Christ of faith.

In Latin America, realized faith in Christ accords a primacy to the moment of Christ's presence today in the poor. This is simply the classic theme of Matthew 25 taken seriously. That passage is useful not only for learning something about what Jesus has said, but for learning where he is presently to be found.

Ecclesial placement is a point of departure for christological reflection not only because the church is the proper locus of tradition about Jesus, and not only because the modern theory of institutionalization has advantages for the transcendence of the limitation of individual subjectivity in the cognitive order as well,[15] but because in the church community faith in Christ is realized. Theologians do not start their reflection with a *tabula rasa,* therefore, nor do they methodologically bracket the totality of faith in Christ or any of its aspects.

But this realization of faith has two characteristic traits: the practice of liberation and the presence of Christ in the poor. Both traits refer the theologizing subject more spontaneously to the historical Jesus, the former to the discipleship of Jesus, as demanded by Jesus himself, the latter to Jesus' incarnation in poverty and the world of the poor. Both traits taken together specify the theologian's ecclesial locus, ineluctably, as the church of the poor.[16]

In that church the totality of faith is realized, but this totality is mediated by the liberative approach to the poor, as one recognizes Christ in them and corresponds to Christ in the approach to them.[17] In this approach the poor actually evangelize those making the approach (see Puebla, no. 1147). This wellspring of theological cognition is supremely important for theologians and refers them more obviously to the historical Jesus.

Christology's ecclesial placement, accordingly, means one thing in Latin America and something different elsewhere.[18] Ecclesial faith in Christ *de facto* exists; it exists, furthermore, as a response to good news. That faith has two key elements: a liberative practice in conformity with the discipleship of Jesus and the encounter with Jesus in the poor, which requires an incarnation in the world of poverty. These two elements are integrated in the totality of faith in

Christ, but they lend that faith a determinate "partiality": this partiality constitutes the christology's subjective point of departure.

The "ecclesial placement" considered above is *de facto* accompanied by a determinate "social placement." The theologian reflects not only within the church but also within Latin America. This may appear evident, but it is not, for what is at stake is a placement within the *truth* of Latin America. It is difficult, as Paul warns us, to be in the truth of things, for human beings tend to "hinder the truth in perversity," to imprison it in injustice (cf. Rom. 1:18, *tōn tēn alētheian en adikia katechontōn*), and it is especially difficult to stay loyal to that truth and its exigencies. The truth of Latin America, furthermore, is a totality of multiple elements, which calls for a determination of which element or elements will contain a greater concentration of the total truth and afford a better access to the total truth.

A correct determination of this "partial" element of reality has not been easy for theology over the years and the centuries. It has actually been necessary for reality itself to manifest this element in what theology has termed the "sign of the times." "This sign is always the historically crucified people, who join to their permanency the ever distinct historical form of crucifixion," to which they are subjected in a given place and moment.[19] To live in the crucified reality of Latin America, to accept it as it is and not attempt to disguise it in any way, is the first step in any process of theological cognition.

> If the state of domination and dependence in which two-thirds of humanity live, with an annual toll of thirty million dead from starvation and malnutrition, does not become the starting point for *any* Christian theology today, even in the affluent and powerful countries, then theology cannot begin to relate meaningfully to the real situation.[20]

These words of Hugo Assmann certainly apply to Latin America. If theology withdraws from this reality, it will have to listen to accusations of cynicism. But, even more important (where its epistemological condition is concerned): it will be accused of vacuity. "Its questions will lack *reality* and not relate to *real* men and women."[21]

The option "to go with the real," beginning with the flagrant situation of misery in Latin America, is a prerequisite for real cognition in the theological endeavor.[22] The theologian's social placement, then, means being in that concrete, "partial" reality as the locus of access to the totality of Latin American reality and of the hierarchization of its various elements.

This ecclesial and social placement permits and demands a determinate use of the theological "intelligence of the faith," although in theory it could be discovered from other placements that this is how that "intelligence" must function in order to be faithful to its own essence. Ignacio Ellacuría, in his analysis of the philosophical basis of the Latin American theological method, states that the formal structure of *intellectus* is primarily that of the apprehension of reality and of confrontation with it. It is the bringing of the human being into confrontation with him/herself and all other things. It is to be referred to life, and only afterwards—in the concrete exercise of confrontation with reality—will it have the function of grasping the sense of reality and of the subject.

> This confrontation with real things *in quantum* has a triple dimension. It involves *taking on reality*, which supposes being in the reality of things— and not merely placed before the reality of things or being in the meaning of things—a "real" being in the reality of things, which, in its active character of being, is altogether the contrary of a "comme çi, comme ça," inert being, and implies a being among things through their material, active mediations. It involves *taking charge of reality*, implying the basic ethical character of intelligence, which has been given to human beings not that they may evade the responsibility of real commitment, but that they may take upon themselves what things really are and what they demand. And it involves *being charged with reality*, referring to the praxic nature of intelligence (which deals only with that which is, even in its nature as cognitive of reality and capable of grasping meaning) when taking a real being upon itself.[23]

When ecclesial and social placement force the theological intelligence to this manner of functioning, clearly a reflection upon Christ will refer the theologian first of all to the historical Jesus, not because this intelligence cannot come to know Christ as transcendent object and bestower of meaning, but because it has need of historical, material mediations in order to grasp this object first and foremost as reality and not only as idea or meaning, in order to grasp it in the knower's act of "taking it on" in his or her personal ethical commitment, and to grasp it in its demand for a real activity.

None of this is any obstacle to a meaning, and a meaning for us, of Christ in himself, thus grasped through Jesus. Nor does it prevent intelligence from issuing in faith, in a recognition of Jesus as the transcendent Christ. But it precludes any direct confrontation of the believing intelligence with Christ, a confrontation deprived of any historical mediation in its triple dimension and nevertheless knowing him or making him known. In other words, the theologizing subject is also referred to Jesus in the act of finding in Jesus the correct manner of being in the reality of things, of knowing them historically, and of proclaiming the transcendent from them. Jesus' being, which was a being-in-the-reality-of-things, was a "partial" being, in the sense of being partisan or sides-taking, joined as it was with the most crying element of his reality, the wretchedness of the poor and sinners and the demand that misery be defeated and transcended. From this partiality, Jesus understood the totality of reality as a denial of the kingdom of God and a demand for that kingdom, however much it might already be actually approaching in grace. His being-in-the-reality-of-things was a being that was faithful to the actual ethical demands of that reality, which led him to his active defense of the poor and his denunciation and unmasking of the powerful. His being-in-the-reality-of-things was a practice of reaching, healing, exorcism, and so on—things objectively tending to the transformation of that reality. Finally, suffering the reality of things in his own persecution and death and rejoicing in the reality of things, the kingdom approached and was known by the insignificant ones.

From that historical being, a being that was connected with things, Jesus proclaimed the transcendent. Not that Jesus was a "theologian" in the conventional sense of the term; but obviously his cognition also functioned theologically. Jesus proclaimed God and personally wondered about God; of necessity he "theologized" in his life. But as far as we can see from the gospel narratives, he did not do so in a timeless vacuum or generic universalism. For Jesus, the transcendent—God—was "pre-given," so to speak. But the concretion of this generic knowledge of things was realized through his being-together-with-things, in fidelity to their demands and in a transformative practice. Through that being, Jesus came to grasp the transcendent aspect of God, and so the Letter to the Hebrews mentions Jesus' "learning" (Heb. 5:8) and his "loud cries and tears to God" (Heb. 5:7). His grasp of God as reality and meaning was not produced out beyond the pale and purview of his grasp of the historical. It was produced through his grasp of the historical.

Latin American christology therefore believes that the theologian's prioritarian placement must be the world of the poor and the church of the poor, that from this partisan placement the theological *intellectus* functions more adequately, comes to a better knowledge of totality and the meaning of that totality.[24] This placement refers theologians more obviously to the historical Jesus when they address the theme of christology. They believe that they have fuller access to the totality of Christ from this point of departure. This, in the last resort, is the justification and necessity of their *modus procedendi*.

THE HISTORICAL ELEMENT IN JESUS AS CHRISTOLOGICAL POINT OF DEPARTURE

Latin American christology finds its prioritarian methodological point of departure in Jesus of Nazareth, that is, the actual history of Jesus of Nazareth, which includes his person, his activity, his attitudes, his processuality, and his fate. But we must subject the precise import of the "historical element" in speaking of Jesus to a more detailed analysis if we are to understand in what sense it functions as this point of departure, if we are to understand the finality that this historical point of departure obeys.

I will briefly state the points of differentiation between Latin American christology and other christologies that also make the historical Jesus a point of departure, or at least place great emphasis on him.

First, Latin American christology makes no pretense of a biographical focus on Jesus such as that of the theological movement that produced "lives of Jesus." It does not think such a focus possible. Neither does it share one of the historical reasons for which this movement arose: to find in Jesus a "help for the struggle for liberation from dogma."[25] The Enlightenment questioned all knowledge guaranteed by authority alone. But this is not what has formally launched the movement toward the historical Jesus in Latin American christology.

Second there is no question of seeking out the historical Jesus for the sake of his historical proleptic structure—defining the historical Jesus in relation to his resurrection so that only from that event could one discover who Jesus properly is.[26] Important as this consideration is, Latin American christology does not define the historical primarily as that which is open to the future, as the sole criterion for deciding what is really historical.

Third, Latin American christology is not primarily concerned to find in Jesus that concrete element that will preserve the kerygma of Christ from volatization—the task taken up by the post-Bultmannians.[27] To be sure, Latin American christology shares this intention and is concerned to concretize the kerygma of Jesus of Nazareth. But it does not engage in the return to the historical Jesus for this reason formally; or, to put it more generally, it does not return to the historical Jesus in order to solve the general question of the New Testament: the relation between the Christ who is preached and the Christ who preaches.

Fourth, Latin American christology is not preoccupied with finding in Jesus that unrepeatable and unique element that will withdraw total faith in Christ from anthropological and sociological manipulations and thereby preserve the originality of faith in Christ. Its prime concern is not "to preserve a real and actual unique memory, and to represent it here and now," although it readily concedes that this concern is of considerable importance.[28]

Nor, finally, is Latin American christology mainly interested in responding to historical criticism and to the believer's own personal need of finding in Christ something more than "an 'atemporal' model of true humanity."[29] Schillebeeckx's profession of faith, worthy of all respect, "I believe in Jesus as that definitive saving reality which gives final point and purpose to my life," is valid for Latin American christology too, but on condition that christology's point of departure not be a focus of what Jesus means for "my" life, and on condition of not understanding "my" life primarily as the need for meaning and meaningfulness.[30]

Of course, except for the naively biographical focus, Latin American christology does assimilate, or can assimilate, the other focuses on the historical Jesus and the finalities they serve. But it does not formally begin with these finalities or with the understanding of the "historical" underlying them.

Latin American christology understands the historical Jesus as the totality of Jesus' history, and its finality in beginning with the historical Jesus is to serve the continuation of his history in the present. This total history of Jesus contains diverse, interrelated elements, each one enjoying a certain autonomy. We would do well to engage in a theoretical discussion of the correct hierarchization of those elements here, with a view to a clearer understanding of the complementarity of them all. In the following paragraphs I shall present a logical reconstruction of what seems to me to be the hierarchization of these elements on the part of Latin American christology. I call it a logical reconstruction because in the reality of faith and reflection the various elements appear in unity.

The most historical element in the historical Jesus is his practice, that is, his activity brought to bear upon the reality around him in order to transform it in a determinate, selected direction, the direction of the kingdom of God. This is the practice that in his day unleashed history and that has come down to us as history unleashed. The historical here, as Jürgen Moltmann defines it apropos of Christ's resurrection, is what drives history.[31]

The historical element in Jesus, then, is not primarily simply that which can be situated in space and in time. Nor is it the doctrinal element, in the latter's hypostatization unto itself independently of Jesus' practice. Neither is it the prime finality of a christology that returns to the historical Jesus to be able to learn about his geography and temporality or his pure doctrine. This requires an understanding of the New Testament in general and the gospel narratives in particular, not only, and not basically, as description and doctrine, but as accounts of a practice that are published precisely in order that this practice be continued. For us, then, the historical element in the historical Jesus is first and foremost an invitation (and a demand) to continue his practice—or, in Jesus' language, an invitation to his discipleship for a mission.

The historical element in Jesus requires a new conception of hermeneutics. The classic undertaking of hermeneutics has consisted in a development of the possibility of understanding the meaning and import of a text of the past, and of the reality appearing in it, in the presence of the difficulty of understanding occasioned by the historical and cultural distance between past and present. In view of what has been said, however, the continuity thus sought between a text's past and present cannot be primarily on a common horizon of understanding. It must be a common horizon of practice.

Within this common practice, the text of the past will be "understood" indeed; but this community in practice will not be at the service of the mere comprehension of the past. It will be at the service of the renewal of reality in the present. In this wise the current obsession with "understanding" is de-absolutized in favor of a much more primary urgency: that of action, of doing. What must be safeguarded in speaking of the historical Jesus is, before all else, the continuation of his practice.

By no manner of means does this prevent the theologian, in approaching the historical Jesus, from inquiring into the meaning that Jesus bestows, nor does it prevent the question of the meaning of Jesus' practice from arising in the very act of pursuing it. The question of meaning is inevitable and concomitant to all human realization. It is part and parcel of the human lot. From the state of the question we learn that it is from within practice that the question of meaning and its possible answer appears in greatest radicalness; that, for the Christian, Jesus will appear as bestower of meaning for one's own personal existence when *his practice* is pursued, and not when he is made a symbol—however historical—to answer the Christian's questions without any other mediation.[32]

Beginning with Jesus' practice as the most historical thing about him, then, involves an emphasis on the imperative of Jesus' discipleship as a historical practice, within which there can be—and according to faith, there is—continuity as well in the meaning of Jesus' actual life, and through which will also be had the experience of meaning bestowed by Jesus.

It could be objected that in this state of the issue Jesus' "person" disappears behind his practice and that therefore this state of the question only reproduces on another level what rationalism is taxed with: rendering Jesus a pure idea. This is what a personalist theology has struggled to overcome. This is not the case, however. Very simply, this is not what occurs, at least not in principle. I have already noted that this analysis is a logical one—a logical hierarchization of the various aspects of the historical Jesus precisely in order to better recover them all.

The practice to be pursued in continuation of Jesus' practice is not an undifferentiated one, but is endowed with determinate contentual elements. It is a modality and a direction which *de jure* go back to *Jesus'* practice.[33] A practice whose fundamental content is the liberation of the poor, whose modality consists in effective solidarity with them and follows their spirit (as this spirit appears in the Beatitudes), and whose orientation and direction is the kingdom of God, explicitly harks back to Jesus, surely, even though it takes into account the need for new historical mediations (which theologically point to the Spirit of Jesus).

This is the first way—a minimal, but effective one— of recovering the historical Jesus. It is true that it does not yet make the *person* of Jesus a reflex object of reflection. But it nevertheless necessarily refers to Jesus for the purpose of a reflection on practice. In this sense, Latin American christology does not settle for Jesus' practice and nothing else, as certain current materialist readings of the gospel narratives would suggest, but proceeeds from his practice to his person.[34] To paraphrase Willi Marxsen's celebrated pronouncement *"Die Sache Jesus geht weiter"* (this Jesus business isn't over yet), Latin American christology surely seeks to do its reflection in such wise that this Jesus business not be over yet.[35] But it is interested in the person of Jesus both because (as I have said above) it accepts the totality of faith, and because it believes that the memory of Jesus is essential even for better current practice.

I believe that it is Jesus' practice, as a priority moment in his actual historical totality, that affords access to that totality, that makes it possible to explain, understand better, and hierarchize the other elements of his totality: the isolated facts of his life, his doctrine, his internal attitudes, his fate, and what is most intimate to him, what we call his person. What is presupposed here is that practice is the moment of most metaphysical density, and therefore the moment with the greatest potential for organizing other moments and producing the key of access to the person. Whatever be the theoretical value of this presupposition, it cannot be denied that, in practice, christologies that begin, for example, with Jesus' attitude toward God, have a hard time of it when it comes to recovering or validating things as obvious as Jesus' prophetical practice or historical persecution; where christologies that begin with Jesus' practice are still able to account for his personal relationship with God and even to account for the possibility of this relationship.

A view of Jesus from his practice makes for a more obvious discovery and a better explanation of his determinate social placement, the standpoint from which he observes the totality of his surrounding reality, and the persecution and fate that come upon him. It provides a better vantage point for an understanding of his preaching and its basic content: the kingdom of God, the God of the kingdom, the Sermon on the Mount, love for neighbor, and so on. Indeed, now we can explain his actual internal personhood, the most intimate element of his relationship with God, his prayer, and his hope. We are not thereby saying that Jesus' totality, least of all his personhood in its most profound reality, is a mechanical product of his practice. But we do assert that it is from this practice that the totality of his personal reality is best approached.

Latin American christology, therefore, does seek to present Jesus in his being-person. Beginning with his practice does not mean logically deducing, inventing, or arbitrarily reconstructing his other elements. In order to discover those other elements, just as with his practice, one will have to seek out their basis in the gospel narratives. But all of those elements will be differently explained and organized depending on whether or not one prioritizes Jesus' practice.

Through that presentation of the historical Jesus and of what is historical in Jesus, Latin American christology seeks personal access to Jesus. It does so not primarily by presenting pieces of knowledge about him, so that human beings may decide what to do and how to relate to the Jesus thus known, but by presenting his practice in order to re-create it and thus have access to him.

The presupposition in this state of the issue is that that personal access to Jesus is possible, in the last resort, only from continuity between Jesus and those who know him; and that that continuity will have to be posited from a point of departure in the locus of greatest metaphysical density, which is practice. Accordingly, access to Jesus is not first and foremost a matter of knowing about him, knowing about his ideas, and developing, to this end, a hermeneutics calculated to safeguard the distance between Jesus and us and make it possible to know about Jesus. It is a matter, when all is said and done, of affinity and connaturality, from the point of departure in that which is most real in Jesus.

This manner of access to the historical Jesus, furthermore, is the manner of access to the Christ of faith. In the mere fact of reproducing, with ultimacy, Jesus' practice and personal historicity, since what is reproduced are the practice and personal historicity of Jesus, one is accepting an ultimate normativity in Jesus, and therefore pronouncing him to be something really ultimate. One is *eo ipso* declaring, implicitly but really, that this person is the Christ, although it may well remain to render that profession explicit.

To be sure, in declaring Jesus to be the Christ there is a discontinuity, a leap of faith, that cannot be deduced mechanically, not even by virtue of the continuity represented by his discipleship. But that continuity is necessary if the discontinuity of faith is to be Christian and not arbitrary. Christ is professed in faith to be Son by antonomasia—in discontinuity, then—but also to be the *elder brother* who has lived in the fullness of faith "originally"—in discontinuity—but also as the *firstborn* among brothers and sisters—in continuity.

The structure of belief in Jesus as Son is that of our becoming sons and daughters. The acceptance that Christ is Son by nature is effectuated from out of our own filiation, effectuated by grace. In order to believe in Christ we have to believe as Jesus did. In the realization of faith after the manner of Jesus we shall have the locus for professing him doxologically as the Christ.

Faith in Christ, in the radical sense of the word, always means a discontinuity, a leap of faith. Christ in plenitude is always an "other" for us, and one whose otherness is not assimilable by anything that we ourselves can achieve. Latin American christology seeks to identify as exactly as possible the locus of the leap of faith. To this purpose, it does not present knowledge about Christ, about his deeds, about his possible messianic consciousness—all such things as would render faith in Christ reasonable. Rather, without disdaining the presentation of these realities of Christ, it proposes the leap of faith in his discipleship, in his following, in the locus of affinity, and of greater affinity, with Jesus.[36]

It might be objected that there is no mention of grace in this process, as internal moment of faith and as the element that makes real access to Christ possible. The emphasis on practice could lead one to believe that grace disappears in the whole process. At all events, we hear, it must be insisted that the movement of the leap from one's "I" in order to move to Christ is grace, and no human deed.

I do not think that Latin American christology neglects grace, although it formulates it in terms of its own point of departure. It is certain, withal, that "something has been given us," that Christ is not the product of flesh and blood. We might say, with Pauline simplicity, that the goodness of God has appeared; but we might also say that Jesus' life has appeared, Jesus' practice has appeared, unrepeatable, normative, and salvific. To consider Jesus and his practice as something that has appeared, that has been manifested, is the way to continue to maintain the gratuity that exists in the origin of the Christ event. To see Jesus in this manner is the same as to assert him as gift.

Further, the reproduction of his practice is not the "pure" practice of the human being. The follower of Jesus can, and at times does, interpret his or her practice as the gift of "new hands" for activity, and can recognize in this, grace, and the very climax of grace. There is no evident reason why grace might be able to be expressed only in new ears for hearing or new eyes for seeing. New hands, too, are surely the expression of grace. When, furthermore, it becomes difficult to maintain the actual practice of discipleship, when there arises within this practice the temptation to restrain it, the temptation of hopelessness, of the absurd, then the maintenance of the practice is gift and grace. A faith in Christ that feeds on his discipleship is likewise seen as grace.

In starting with the historical Jesus and the most historical element in Jesus, Latin American christology claims to be a strict christology. On the level of method, although the totality of faith in Christ is given in the real faith of believers and theologians from the beginning, Latin American christology considers that christology's logical route is none other than the chronological. Now, chronologically, there appear: (1) Jesus' mission in the service of the kingdom, his practice; (2) the question of the person of that Jesus; (3) the profession of his unrepeatable, salvific reality—faith in Christ.

In today's situation, twenty centuries after Jesus' time, the totality of the chronological process has been communicated to us whole. We have only the finished process, so to speak. The *real* point of departure of Latin American christology, therefore, is total faith in Christ. But the *methodological* point of departure will be precisely the first chronological step. Latin American theologians hold that this is the best way to insure the last step in the process—the full profession of Christ—and to insure that that profession be really Christian and not just a more or less generic faith in Christ such as has so often let important and essential elements of faith fall by the wayside. No better way appears to safeguard all of this than to begin with the historical Jesus.

Latin American christology's return to the historical Jesus with the finality of continuing his salvific practice is a periodic phenomenon in history, having often appeared in moments of grave crisis or moments of Christian renewal. No better solution for the reinvigoration of a Christian faith that has gone worldly has ever been found than the return to Jesus of Nazareth, the return to his dangerous memory. This is how the great reformers of the church have addressed the problem—Francis of Assisi, Ignatius of Loyola, and the great Christians of recent times, such as Dietrich Bonhoeffer. I shall show that this return to Jesus is a phenomenon of the New Testament, as well, and that it is especially needful in today's situation in Latin America.

In the New Testament, we have the totality of faith in the risen Christ. The theology and the christology of the New Testament require this totality. Still, it is likewise true, and from the outset, that the risen one is none other than "Jesus of Nazareth who was crucified," and this becomes the object of christological reflection in a positive as well as a polemical sense.

Be the occasion the enthusiastic, ahistorical understanding of the Corinthians or the danger of gnosticism or docetism, the fact is that Paul sees himself needing to recall the crucifixion of the risen one, just as the Johannine school sees itself needing to recall the flesh of Christ. Here the return to Jesus is doubtless polemical and is proclaimed in opposition to those who would have preferred Christ without Jesus.

More generally: Even after the formulation of faith in Christ, gospel traditions take shape and the gospels are published. Full faith in Christ is already present in the moment of the final redactions of these gospels. And yet in order to present that faith they return to Jesus. They are unable to give an account of their faith in Christ without a historicization of Jesus.

Once the New Testament has recovered the historical Jesus, even though it be via community historicizations, it is important to see which traits of his history are emphasized. Jesus is not presented, in a first moment, in himself, but in relationship to the kingdom of God and the God of the kingdom—which precludes the possibility of beginning directly, with its immediate object, Christ-in-himself. Rather, christology will be possible only if the point of departure is theology in general, whose ultimate correlate is the kingdom of God and the God of the kingdom.

That kingdom of God is not presented only as a utopia to be achieved in hope. It is also presented as a reality to be served, as something to be actualized, whatever may be the gratuity attaching to it. The gospels therefore recount Jesus' practices in "correspondence" with this kingdom.[37] They also recount the historicity of Jesus, his conflicts, controversies, and persecution; they recount his external attitudes, and, minimally, his internal attitudes. Through all of this they gradually paint a picture of the relatedness of Jesus with the God of the kingdom.

They recount Jesus' demands on his hearers for conversion and discipleship. That discipleship is a process of assimilation to Jesus, a becoming like him to be sure, but through the exercise of a practice. That discipleship is demanded by Jesus for reasons of general theology in order to serve God's kingdom and to correspond to that kingdom; but it is also presented as the basic way to have access to Jesus and to the knowledge of his person.

In the *modus procedendi* of the New Testament, then, Latin American christology sees a criterion for its own *modus procedendi.* However it may already possess the totality of faith in Christ, genuinely but often generically, it comes to the historical Jesus in order to concretize and thereby render real the content of that faith. In presenting the historical Jesus, it underscores his constitutive relatedness, which forestalls a christology *in directo,* but which renders one possible that will have historical content, beginning with Jesus' practice in the service of the kingdom. In the historical Jesus it encounters the call to his following and discipleship—that is, to a practice endowed with a modality geared to the service of the kingdom and the approach to Jesus.

Latin American christology, then, sees in the New Testament a *de facto* parallelism with its own *modus procedendi,* a parallelism it considers normative. Its return to the historical Jesus is not mechanical, calculated to make Jesus a concrete letter, a law. But it is indeed a return to him calculated to render the real faith already existing in the New Testament a Christian, effective faith. "The function of the historical Jesus is to introduce us to his dynamics."[38]

The adoption of the historical Jesus as the point of departure for christology is likewise justified by today's situation in Latin America. I have already cited the enormous dangers of beginning with the Christ of dogma, which is susceptible to all manners of manipulation because it is abstract. The Latin American situation leads more spontaneously to the historical Jesus and to an understanding of Jesus such as that presented here.

The Latin American situation and Jesus' situation show striking parallels, although the importance of that parallelism for christology must not be exaggerated and the universal character of Christ must not be ignored. Neither may one ignore that the incarnation of Christ means concretion and partiality and that this concretion and partiality will have greater or lesser similarities with other historical concretions.

A purely notional cognition of the history of Jesus may often be found in more precise scientific and exegetical terms in other climes than Latin America. But a historical situation with a relative affinity to that of Jesus will be open to a better understanding and pondering of his history and will have a more spontaneous grasp on Jesus' handling of or effect on his history and of the way that his disciples should affect or handle their own history.

The similarity of the two situations with respect to a basic point—their misery, repression, oppression, and death—makes it possible for the current situation and the history of Jesus to enjoy a common theological focus. The parallel may appear minimal, but the nucleus of this focus is the horizon of the life and death of human beings and, in the case of Jesus' history, his service to life and his struggle against death. This common horizon affords an understanding of the historical Jesus, demands that Christ be presented from a point of departure in the Jesus who is in favor of life, and causes the historical Jesus himself to be presented from that basic nucleus: his defense of the poor, his denunciation and unmasking of the mighty, and finally the consequences that he must suffer for taking these positions.

To put it simply, the historical Jesus becomes "evident" (once his history has been presented with a minimum of veracity), becomes "demandable" in order for there to be faith in him in Latin America. At the same time, that historical Jesus renders it "evident" and "demandable" what faith in Christ must be, what its basic kernel must be: the following of Jesus as defense of life and struggle against death. All of this may seem a minimum, but it is a fertile minimum, occasioning an advance in the totality of faith. At all events it is an absolutely necessary minimum, without which there is no real advance in faith, and what is deemed advance is but abstract, and frequently dechristianizing, universalization.

Fidelity to the Latin American situation—and the situation of the Third World generally—and to its demands point more obviously to the historical Jesus; and the grasp of the historical Jesus has led more obviously to a deeper knowlege of the Latin American situation and its demands.[39] This is actually one movement with two distinct, complementary movements leading to the historicization (according to the historical Jesus) and the "Latin-Americanization" of faith in Christ.

It may be impossible to go much further on the level of reflection to show this unification, but the unification is a fact. The deeper we plumb the historical Jesus, the more a "Latin American faith in Christ" is facilitated; and the more faith in Christ is "Latin Americanized," the more a "Latin American faith" refers us to the historical Jesus. It can only be observed, after what has actually occurred in Latin America, that an honest grasp of and response to historical situations that are akin generate a closer affinity with Jesus. He is better known "on the inside" as our common brother, and—given the leap of faith—he can be recognized as our elder brother, the Christ.

THE HISTORICAL JESUS AND THE GOSPEL NARRATIVES

A christology that turns to the historical Jesus must give an account, at a certain step in its process, of the historical truth of that Jesus, and, more concretely, of the historical truth of the gospel narratives, which are practically the only documents in which Jesus has been transmitted. This, as we know, has become *de facto* and *de jure,* an acute problem: *de facto,* in that historical criticism presents various degrees of skepticism about the historical reality lying behind these narratives; *de jure,* in that literary criticism has discovered that these narratives belong to the literary genre called "gospel," which narrates Jesus from faith and for faith, and therefore does not pretend to present historical truth in what would be its pure factuality.

Apart from certain work by Latin Americans in the area of exegetical problems, Latin American christology has not undertaken any reflective treatment of those problems. It has confronted them implicitly, however, in the christological task. By way of conclusion, I will elaborate on this point.

Latin American christology accepts the generally received observation on the literary condition of the gospel narratives with respect to their historicity. It knows that the gospel narratives about Jesus are themselves theologized, since what the gospels are concerned to present is Jesus as the Christ. But it also observes—and ascribes great importance to this for its systematic reflection—that in order to historicize Jesus, his life must be historicized in a determinate manner.

This occasions the appearance in the gospels of a theologized Jesus through a previously historicized Jesus, and not properly what we could call a historical-Jesus-in-himself. The factual data concerning Jesus are not directly and immediately accessible from the gospel narratives. The historical problem, then, is presented as the task of discovering the historical Jesus through the historicized Jesus. Latin American christology's judgment on the finality and feasibility of that task is as follows.

Where the finality of the task is concerned—the motivating interest for the discovery of the historical Jesus behind the historicized Jesus—Latin American christology is not especially interested systematically in determining Jesus' "data" with exactitude, his concrete words and actions. Naturally it accepts these discoveries to the extent that they appear to be correct, but it does not make a christology based on the historical Jesus depend on the *ipsissima verba* or *ipsissima facta* of Jesus. Its interest rather consists in discovering and historically insuring the basic structure of his practice, preaching, an end through which the basic structure of his internal historicity and his person are likewise discernible.

As to the feasibility of gaining access to anything historical in the historical Jesus, systematic Latin American christology has not done a great deal of reflection; in its real task, however, it does not share a radical skepticism, but shares what in one way or another is the common heritage of other current christologies (including the European).[40] Thus it accepts these as historical: on the level of event, Jesus' baptism by John, a certain initial success in his ministry, some early conflicts, the selection and dispatch of a group of followers, the use of parables, a crisis toward the middle or end of his public life, the journey to Jerusalem, some kind of meal with those close to him, his arrest, and his crucifixion, with words written on a placard attached to the cross; on the level of behavior, certain attitudes toward the Jewish Law and the Temple, toward the marginalized, the possessed, those in power, certain practices of healing and approach to sinners, the demand for conversion and discipleship, certain specific attitudes toward the kingdom of God and the God of the kingdom; on the level of word, key words and phrases like *Abba,* "kingdom of God," "follow me," and so on.

Neither has Latin American christology developed determinate criteria for judging the historicity of the gospel narratives. At least implicitly, Latin American christology allows itself to be guided by certain criteria (of which Edward Schillebeeckx has written extensively): (1) the appearance of one and the same theme on various levels of tradition; (2) what is specific to and distinctive of a theme by contrast with and even in oppostition to theologies and practices that came after Jesus; and (3) the consistency of Jesus' death with what is narrated of his life.[41]

The first criterion is self-evident and furnishes the foundation for the construction of any christology. The other two criteria serve rather as indirect, but efficacious, verification of the first. The two latter criteria, furthermore, acquire special evidence in the concrete situation of Latin America, and therefore are not only intrinsic criteria. From the current social and ecclesial reality of Latin America, the third criterion is evident. There the death of hundreds and thousands of persons is analogous to Jesus' death, and the causes of their death are historically similar to the causes of Jesus' death. That Jesus must have lived and acted in the way he is reported to have lived and acted is not only plausible, it goes without saying. The second criterion also possesses a currency of its own in view of Latin American reality. To take a simple example, but one that is easily understood in a Latin American context: After Archbishop Romero's murder, some persons wished to see his memory die with him; in order to try to negate that memory, those persons focused their explanations on the archbishop's words and actions. In other words, in attempting to oppose and negate what Romero had done and said, they effectively worked to revive the memory of the key deeds and themes in Romero's life.

On a purely logical plane, one can never dismiss the possibility that the gospel narratives were the fruit of the imagination of the communities. That they are this in part is more than likely. That they are this in their totality is rather unlikely, even logically. Hence the necessity of meticulous exegetical and historico-critical work. At all events, Latin American christology holds a presupposition in favor of the basic historicity of the gospel narratives in virtue of the actual situation in which they were composed. To anyone living and suffering history on the South American continent it seems altogether probable that "Jesus was like that." The gospel narratives acquire an internal consistency in their "basics" because the internal consistency of the life they narrate continues to be repeated in its "basics" all through history.

Although Latin American christology offers no special originality on the foregoing point, I believe that it is original in its emphasis on the "gospel" element of the narratives: Jesus must be presented as gospel, as good news. Only thus can justice be done to the historical Jesus. From the critical standpoint, this is a problem. From the standpoint of systematic reflection, it is an advantage: the narratives about Jesus are necessarily evangelical.

Latin American christology resumes this evangelical character of the presentation of Jesus. The christological task itself is performed in an evangelical tone, not in order to recover the literary genre of the gospel, but in order to transfer the gospel tone to another more reflexive and conceptual literary genre. What is important is that Latin American christology begins with the real conviction that (1) Jesus is good news; and (2) this good news is for the communities and therefore there is a correlation between Jesus and the communities, in virtue of the quality of Jesus as good news.

As to the first point, Latin American christology shares, *de facto,* the same intention and historical conviction that underlies the writing, publication, and proclamation of the gospels: there is good news to be announced. This basic conviction historically differentiates Latin American christology from other christologies, not by any merits of its own, but because this is the way Christ is still grasped in Latin America. For whatever reasons, Christ is not automatically and spontaneously seen in other places as good news. The laborious effort and best intentions of other christologies aim precisely at the recovery of the formal nature of the gospel narratives as good news (and not only the investigation of their truth). In Latin America, however, such is not the case. The gospel continues to be *eu-aggelion,* "good news," for the Latin American, and, as in Jesus' time, for the poor of Latin America. On this subjective conviction of the theologian, a conviction rooted in objective reality, the evangelical tone of christology and of doing christology as good news rest.

Hence the attempt on the part of Latin American christology to establish that Christ is good news, without exhausting its best efforts in showing Christ's unique and unrepeatable aspect. To be sure, it supposes and develops this formal aspect of Christ as well; but its emphasis is on his content as good news. Elsewhere, the best efforts of theologians are brought to bear in presenting Christ under both aspects , as for example when he is called "absolute bearer of salvation" (Karl Rahner), or "Omega point of evolution" (Teilhard de Chardin). Both of these theologians surely stress the salvific elements of Christ; but given their cultural situation, their christological reflection has to concentrate on showing that Christ can be *the* savior. In Latin America the emphasis is just the opposite. Christ is already *the* savior for christology; its concern is rather to show him to be liberator.

To present Christ "evangelically," therefore, does not mean only according the gospel narratives the primacy over other, more dogmatic presentations; nor does it mean only presenting Christ as good news as if this were merely one more among so many elements of his reality, which could just as well have been absent. Rather it means presenting him *essentially* as good news.

As to the second point, Latin American christology produces, *mutatis mutandis,* the *modus procedendi* of the first communities. Precisely because it makes no attempt to reflect *in directo* on Christ-in-himself, but on Christ in his quality as good news, the reference to the community for which he is good news is essential.

That there are four gospels and countless little gospels that stand behind these, far from making christology difficult, shows it how it ought to develop. Christology develops by placing a determinate community in contact with the historical Jesus or with his memory. The community selects and historicizes, up to a certain point, its memories of Jesus in such wise that he continues to be concrete good news for the community. This is how the community develops its christology. This is also what makes a certain christology Latin American, with the obvious difference that one cannot go back to "recent" memories of Jesus, but can only move through the historicizations already made by the first communities. There can be no doubt, however, that the various emphases on the part of Latin American christology (Jesus' relationship with the poor, his liberative practice, his conflict, his self-surrender in and for love) have developed because the communities "remember" these aspects on the basis of their own needs.

This *modus procedendi* entails no manipulation of Christ, at least no substantial manipulation, or manipulation in principle. The very fact that today's Latin American communities, like the first Christian communities, continue to go back to Jesus to hear and to practice the good news and to submit themselves to its judgment shows that Jesus is still the *norma normans*. Indeed there obtains a circularity between Jesus who is for the communities and the communities that go back to Jesus—a circularity that christologies should reflect. The magisterium will rightly propound on one side the "minimum christology" and on the other—in respect of radicalness—the "maximum." But within that christology there can and should develop christologies (in the plural) because Jesus is good news and in order to continue to present him as good news.

All of this means that the fact that the information reaching us about Jesus is obtained via a literary genre called "gospel" is not a difficulty for the christological undertaking in Latin America. Rather it constitutes a demand there that christology be effectuated in the last resort as gospel. Latin American christology learns two important lessons from the New Testament. The first is that the figure of Jesus cannot be theologized without being historicized—without narrating his life, practice, lot, and so on. That is, one cannot speak theologically of Christ without returning to the historical Jesus.

The second lesson is the converse of the first: Jesus cannot be historicized without being theologized. That is, very precisely, he cannot be historicized without being presented as God's good news. Latin American christology seeks to be neither reflection upon the "idea" of Christ, nor on the other hand a mere "jesuology." This mutual relationship, consisting in theologizing by historicizing and historicizing by theologizing, is what Latin American christology seeks to incorporate, in its particular enterprises, in order to be faithful to its object, Christ, who has been handed down not just in some random way, but through the gospel of Jesus and in Jesus as gospel.

PART II

JESUS, THE KINGDOM OF GOD, AND THE LIFE OF THE POOR

3

Jesus and the Kingdom of God: Significance and Ultimate Objectives of His Life and Mission

Of necessity, the theme of Jesus and the kingdom of God is broad and complex, since it is the point of departure for the explanations undertaken by christology, theology, ecclesiology, eschatology, and the Christian moral discourse. This article will attempt to shed light on the theme "The Church and the Kingdom of God." Accordingly, I shall proceed in systematic fashion, without delving into the exegetical complexities that would point up the Synoptics' different perspectives and thus nuance and fine-time certain statements about the kingdom of God as found on Jesus' lips. The global outlook of the Synoptics will more than suffice to provide us with a view of what the kingdom of God meant in Jesus' life and the consequences of that meaning for his life. The correct approach for the church today is to question itself about its positive relationship to the kingdom of God.

As my intent here is systematic and practical, I shall center my investigation around three basic questions: (1) What is ultimate for Jesus? (2) What is the kingdom of God for Jesus? and (3) How does the kingdom of God come, how does it draw near? The interrogative form of posing the problems will be a help to the seriousness of this reflection and will help us not to suppose that we already know enough about the subject.

WHAT IS THE ULTIMATE FOR JESUS?
A THEOLOGICAL PROBLEM

I open with this question of the "ultimate" for Jesus because the history of Christianity has given different answers to it and the diversity can cloud the

---

This is a translation by Robert R. Barr of an article that appeared in *Sal Terrae* (May 1978). The entire issue was devoted to the theme "The Church and the Kingdom of God." In keeping with that theme, Jesus is presented here in his relationship with the kingdom of God, not only in order to assimilate what Jesus thought about the kingdom of God, but also that the church today may strike a correct relationship with that kingdom.

simplicity of Jesus' answer. The *"ultimate"* can have the name of God, Christ, heaven, the church, grace, love, and so on; or, negatively, sin, hatred, condemnation, and so on. So complex a panorama can cloud the identification of what was really and truly ultimate for Jesus—that from which other ultimacies derive a Christian hierarchy.

As we seek what was really ultimate for Jesus, let us pose the problem theologically, and seek a reality that will be genuinely ultimate, that will impose itself as such, and that will preclude the temptation to replace it with something only seemingly ultimate. Since this search seeks to be critical and to keep account of what has come to pass as the ultimate for Jesus without really being so, I shall proceed dialectically, denying ultimacy to what does not have it in an absolute sense.

Jesus is not the ultimate for himself. Today this should be evident. On the plane of Jesus' consciousness it is clear that he did not preach himself.[1] Any attempt to make Jesus the absolutely ultimate breaks down in the face of the evidence of exegesis, and not only the historical Jesus, but the risen Christ as well.[2] The whole argumentation of modern indirect christology—the argumentation to show Jesus' peculiarity and his divine filiation—demonstrates that even christology can only be *relational,* not absolute. One can only understand Jesus as from something distinct from and greater than himself, and not as from something directly residing in himself.

Jesus expels demons, and this is a sign of the novelty of his person. But this symbolizes not his own ultimacy but the approach of the kingdom of God (Luke 11:20). The antitheses of the Sermon on the Mount—"You have heard . . . What I say to you is . . ." (Matt. 5:21–47)—show forth the ultimacy of a new way of life. The radical following of Jesus is demanding (Mark 8:34–38). It is at the service of the ultimate salvation or condemnation of the human being. When Jesus says that no one should be ashamed either of him or of his words, the reason he gives is that otherwise the "Son of Man" (distinct from Jesus in Mark 8:38 and Luke 12:8) will be ashamed of them.

All of these statements are calculated to show that Jesus did not conceive of himself as the absolutely ultimate but rather in relation to something distinct from himself. Jesus does have a kind of ultimacy, as we shall see in the third part of this article. But in order to understand exactly in what his ultimacy consists, we must first understand his own ultimate pole of reference.

The ultimate for Jesus is not simply "God." Up to this point what has been said is fairly evident and commonly accepted. But this is not so with the next step: Jesus did not simply preach "God." "God" is not simply and absolutely Jesus' ultimate pole of reference. This seemingly shocking statement should, however, be evident, and theologians assert it by implication. Jesus preached the kingdom of God, not himself.[3] "The centre and framework of Jesus' preaching and mission was the approaching Kingdom of God."[4] Now, it is this implication that I wish to underscore. Theologians today agree that in order to name what was ultimate for Jesus one cannot simply cite "God," but must make a dual statement: God *and* kingdom, God *and* nearness,

God *and* his will, God *and* motherhood/fatherhood, and so on.

Systematically, then, the ultimate for Jesus is God in relationship, rendered explicitly as kingdom with the history of human beings—God's nearness, will, parental love; or conversely, a history "according to God." But in order to state this clearly, and especially, keeping in mind the practical repercussions of ignoring the duality of the ultimate, it is appropriate to emphasize what is implicit in that ultimate: that it is not simply "God" that is the ultimate for Jesus. To state that God is would be equivalent to saying that what is ultimate for Jesus is not essentially related to history and that history is not essentially related to it.

The profound reason for which Jesus did not simply preach "God" is that Jesus is heir to a series of traditions according to which God is never God *in se,* but is always in relationship with history. Whether we take the exodus traditions, with their God who hears the cry of the oppressed and strikes a covenant with the people; or the prophetical traditions, with their God who seeks to establish right and justice; or the apocalyptic traditions, whose God seeks to renew reality eschatologically; or the sapiential traditions of a God who provides for creation; or the traditions of God's silence in the face of the world's wretchedness and sin—all of these traditions have one thing in common: God is not a God in and for God. God always stands in some type of relation to history. The concrete element of that relation will depend on the underlying theology of each respective tradition and hence will vary. But the formality of a God in relationship with history is in all Old Testament traditions. As a good Jew, then, Jesus cannot name the ultimate simply as "God." And if this causes a certain surprise, it is because Christianity has not sufficiently gotten beyond the Greek origins of much of its theology and has failed to assimilate—despite so many formal assertions to the contrary—its biblical origin.

Nor do the foregoing statements oppose—rather they confirm—the activity of Jesus that would most appear to have its correlate simply in "God": Jesus' prayer. We need only analyze the content of the two prayers that have been handed down to us to be convinced that in neither of them is the ultimate simply God. The correlates of the prayer of thanksgiving (Matt. 11:25–26) and of the prayer in the garden (Mark 14:32–42) are the realized will of God in history and the intended will of God for history. Jesus' prayer thereby appears, surely, as dialogue with God, but with God precisely as Father, and so against a broader horizon than that of the simple "Thou" of God—rather, in a context of God's parenthood, found or sought.[5]

All of this shows that the ultimate for Jesus is not simply "God," but God in concrete relation to history. Therefore any hermeneutical presupposition, conscious or unconscious, along the lines of a pure personalism is a serious obstacle to understanding what the kingdom of God was for Jesus.

The ultimate for Jesus is not the church or the kingdom of heaven. The reading of the gospels by the church customarily equated the kingdom of God with the "kingdom of heaven" and with the "church." Equivalence with the "kingdom of heaven" would mean that the kingdom of God is "heaven" in its absolutely transcendent version, in distinction from and in opposition to the realization of that ultimate in the history of human beings in any form. This misunderstanding arises from the expression found frequently in the Gospel of Matthew, "kingdom of heaven." But exegesis has clearly shown that Matthew's expression is a reverent circumlocution for the name of God. Reading "kingdom of God" as "church" would mean that the kingdom of God has a historical version, too, and that this is precisely what the church is. The calamitous consequences of this equivalency, and, positively, the correct relationship between church and kingdom of God, are treated in other places. Here suffice it to recall that, according to responsible biblical exegesis, the historical Jesus did not intend to found a church such as arose later in the New Testament, although he did desire the restoration of a remnant of Israel, faithful to the best traditions of his people.

The ultimate for Jesus is the kingdom of God. In this dialectical procedure—denying what is not absolutely ultimate for Jesus—we now come to the simple statement that the genuinely ultimate, that which gives meaning to Jesus' life, activity, and fate, is the kingdom of God. Even though it has not yet been made explicit what that kingdom would consist in for Jesus, certain systematic considerations of importance can help our understanding of what is to follow.

In Jesus, the ultimate is presented in a unity of transcendence and history. This unity, this oneness that necessitates a dual explanation, is due to the conception Jesus has of God as the God of the kingdom. The so-called vertical and horizontal dimensions, then, are equally "originary" in Jesus' relationship with the absolute. There is no longer any history but one, and its duality will not be adequately expressed as history of the "beyond" and history of the "amidst" (supernatural history and natural history), but will have to be expressed as history in the direction of the kingdom of God (history of grace) and history counter to the direction of the kingdom of God (history of sin).

No institution can lay claim to an absolute value that would threaten the absolute value of the kingdom of God. This is true not only factually, in that Jesus *de facto* did not intend the church concretely, nor did he equate the projects of the rabbis, Pharisees, Essenes, or Zealots with the kingdom of God.

This is true in principle as well, in that the values of the kingdom will be criteria of judgment upon any type of human configuration, religious or sociopolitical, that explicitly or implicitly seeks to put itself forth as the actual kingdom of God, although service to this kingdom will call for concrete configurations all through history.[6]

WHAT IS THE KINGDOM OF GOD FOR JESUS? A HISTORICAL PROBLEM

It is a well-established historical datum of the life of Jesus that he preached the kingdom of God. In this sense, the exordium of the Gospel of Mark, although it is only a theological summary, does make Jesus' ultimate horizon and its consequences explicit: "This is the time of fulfillment. The reign of God is at hand! Reform your lives and believe in the gospel!" (Mark 1:15).

In making this proclamation, Jesus continues that of John the Baptist (Matt. 3:1), whose disciple he probably was.[7] In this sense Jesus does not proclaim anything absolutely new, but summarizes the hopes and expectations of the best traditions of his people. Typical of Jesus is his concentration on this theme. "The per se traditional expectation of the kingdom of God to come is transformed in Jesus into the decisive, sole outlook."[8]

Now we are on the correct methodological track. From the Old Testament we learn the formal notion of the kingdom of God, and especially its content, addressees, and negation, in the prophetico-apocalyptic tradition. From the New Testment, from the Synoptics, we learn what Jesus' concentration on the kingdom of God was. We learn what the kingdom basically was for Jesus, not only from what might be extracted from his notion of the kingdom, but also from *Jesus' actual life in the service of the kingdom*. This last statement is important, incidentally, for solving the difficulty proposed by Walter Kasper: "Jesus nowhere tells us in so many words *what* the Kingdom of God is. He only says that it is near."[9] In order adequately to deal with this difficulty we must consider not only what Jesus explicitly *says* about the kingdom, but what he *says and does* in the service of the kingdom.[10]

The reign of God in the traditions before Jesus. There frequently appears in the Old Testament a nomenclature of God as king, especially in the Psalms and in the liturgy. The nomenclature is not original with Israel. It existed throughout the ancient Near East. "In adopting the institution of the monarchy, originally foreign to them, Israel adopted its symbols as well, to expresss their belonging to the God who had saved them and made them his own."[11] But Israel historicized so many of the concepts of its milieu and the symbol of the king came to be applied to God—"eventually was used to set in relief his ability to intervene in history."[12]

Yahweh's historical intervention is seen in various ways in the stages of Israel's history. In the Mosaic times the reign of God is seen as a military and civil chieftancy. In the time of the Judges it is seen as the exclusivity of the kingship of Yahweh—hence, for example, Gideon's refusal of the title of king. In the time of the monarchy, Yahweh's kingship becomes compatible with that of the human king of Israel—not without grave theological conflict—who becomes Yahweh's adopted child.

After the collapse of the monarchy, the national catastrophes, the exile and captivity, a new conception of God's reign springs up. Now it is seen as the future, and more attention is paid to the content of the kingdom as the prophets develop it. The apocalyptic approach universalizes that expectation, even to cosmic proportions, expressing it in a hope for a renewal of all reality, including the resurrection of the dead.

In Judaism, especially in the era in which Jesus appears, the reign of God is intensely awaited, and the nomenclature of the "kingdom of God" is revived. The most crucial question is how to await, how to hasten the coming of that kingdom. Will it be by fulfilling the prescriptions of the Law? By armed insurrection? By attention to signs from heaven?

The notion of the kingdom of God, the kingship of Yahweh, and so on, runs all through the history of the people of Israel in one form or another. But it is important to clarify the *formality* of this notion from the outset. As we know, the term "kingdom" suggests a series of spontaneous interpretations other than those that lie behind the original *malkūtā Yahweh*. The kingdom of God is not geographical, nor does it imply a static situation in which Yahweh is officially acknowledged as king. "Kingdom of God" has two key connotations: (1) God will rule through dynamic act;[13] and (2) God's purpose will be to modify and establish a determinate order of things.[14] Both connotations are expressed in Psalm 96:13: "For he comes to rule the earth. He shall rule the world with justice and the peoples with his constancy."

What is important here, then, is that instead of speaking of "kingdom," one should refer to Yahweh's "reign"—what occurs when the one ruling the world is really Yahweh and no other power. Systematically, it is important to observe that the primary note of the kingdom of God is not the ascending movement of Yahweh's liturgical, orthodox, or official acknowledgment on the part of a particular people as king, and not another divinity; rather it is in the descending movement of a concrete historical reality: that the history of a determinate people be actually in conformity with what Yahweh wills. What is at stake, therefore, is that the kingdom of God comes to be historical reality and not just the profession of Yahweh as king.

The reign of God is the establishment of justice and right with regard to the poor. The prophetical period from which Jesus obtained his categories for understanding what the kingdom of God is, has a clear answer to the question of what happens when God reigns.[15] God is definitively a loving God. God is not condemnation but love. Yahweh therefore appears as a loving father (Hos. 11:1), faithful husband (Hos. 2:20), or consoling mother (Isa. 66:13). Yahweh has not abandoned the people. "Can a mother forget her infant, be without tenderness for the child of her womb? Even should she forget, I will never forget you" (Isa. 49:15). "I will be their God, and they shall be my people" (Jer. 31:33). This love of God's is seen as effective—capable of doing something novel. It is not only the interiorist declaration that the ultimate meaning of reality consists in love. It is also the declaration of a reality in conformity with God's love. The following passage from Isaiah on God's dream for this world will do better than a lengthy disquisition on the topic.

Lo, I am about to create new heavens
    and a new earth;
The things of the past shall not be remembered or come to mind.
Instead, there shall always be rejoicing and happiness
    in what I create;
For I create Jerusalem to be a joy
    and its people to be a delight;

I will rejoice in Jerusalem
    and exult in my people
No longer shall the sound of weeping be heard there,
    or the sound of crying;
No longer shall there be in it
    an infant who lives but a few days,
    or an old man who does not round out his full lifetime;
He dies a mere youth who reaches but a hundred years,
    and he who fails of a hundred shall be thought accursed.

They shall live in the houses they build,
    and eat the fruit of the vineyards they plant;
They shall not build houses for others to live in,
    or plant for others to eat.
As the years of a tree, so the years of my people;
    and my chosen ones shall long enjoy
    the produce of their hands.
They shall not toil in vain,
    nor beget children for sudden destruction;
For a race blessed by the LORD
    are they and their offspring.
Before they call, I will answer;
    while they are yet speaking I will hearken to them [Isa. 65:17–24].

The prophet's dream proclaims the hope of good news, but not merely as conciliation. Rather it is proclaimed as reconciliation. The dream takes into account the current situation in history, a history dominated by sin, which is in formal opposition to hope. In its anathema against sinners, the dream observes *sub specie contrarii* what the hoped-for reconciliation ought to be: a world without oppression. This is why the prophets condemn those who "sell the just man for money, and the poor man for a pair of sandals"; who "trample the heads of the weak . . . and force the lowly out of the way" (Amos 2:6–7), "storing up in their castles what they have extorted and robbed" (Amos 3:10); who "oppress the weak and abuse the needy" (Amos 4:1); who "turn judgment to wormwood and cast justice to the ground" (Amos 5:7), who "hate him who reproves at the gate and abhor him who speaks the truth" (Amos 5:10), who have "trampled upon the weak and exacted of them levies of grain . . . oppressing the just, accepting bribes, repelling the needy at the gate" (Amos 5:11–12); who "hasten the reign of violence . . . lying upon beds of ivory, stretched comfortably on their couches" (Amos 6:3–4); who "trample upon the needy and destroy the poor of the land" (Amos 8:4); who build their houses without justice, who love bribes and look for gifts, who defend not the fatherless, "and the widow's plea does not reach them" as they are murderers (Isa. 1:21–23); who "join house to house and connect field with field, till no room remains, and [they] are left to dwell alone in the midst of the land" (Isa. 5:8); who "enact unjust statutes and who write oppressive decrees, depriving the needy of judgment and robbing [the Lord's] people's poor of their rights, making widows their plunder, and orphans their prey" (Isa. 10:1–2).

This list, taken from just two of the prophets, shows what they understand the kingdom of God *not* to be. The prophets speak not only of a world of limitation and natural misery, but of a world of historical misery originating in the oppression of some human beings by others. That world is the one that must be transformed and reconciled. Therefore the utopia of the kingdom is seen not only as the overcoming of misery (see the extended citation above from Isaiah 65), but as a world of reconciliation among human beings.

> Then the wolf shall be a guest of the lamb
>   and the leopard shall lie down with the kid;
> The calf and the young lion shall browse together,
>   with a little child to guide them.
> The cow and the bear shall be neighbors.
>   together their young shall rest;
>   the lion shall eat hay like the ox.
> The baby shall play by the cobra's den,
>   and the child lay his hand on the adder's lair.
> There shall be no harm or ruin on all my holy mountain;
>   for the earth shall be filled with knowledge of the LORD
>   as water covers the sea [Isa. 11:6–9; cf. 65:25].[16]

In that kingdom, the sorrows of war will give way to the joys of toil, for "they shall beat their swords into plowshares and their spears into pruning hooks" (Isa. 2:4). In that kingdom one may have true knowledge of God, which is nothing but the actualization of justice (Jer. 22:13–16; Hos. 4:1–2), and the true worship of God, not based on sacrifices, but on mercy and justice (Hos. 6:6, 8:13; Amos 5:21; Isa. 1:11–17).

This universal reconciliation, in the prophets as well as in the teaching of Jesus, has one basic and essential characteristic: the kingdom of God is for the poor. In the description of the sin that is the opposite of reconciliation we already have abundant testimony as to who are the ones oppressed by the anti-kingdom. Third Isaiah clearly declares:

> The Lord has anointed me; he has sent me to bring glad tidings to the lowly, to heal the brokenhearted, to proclaim liberty to captives and release to the prisoners, to announce a year of favor from the Lord [Isa. 61:1–2].

What the reign of God means for the prophets can be learned from the utopia they herald in the presence of the concrete historical reality of oppression, which is at once ignorance of the God of the kingdom and injustice to the poor.

The reign of God, then, will be that situation in which human beings have genuine knowledge of God and establish right and justice toward the poor.[17] This is also the kernel of apocalyptic thought, garbed though it may be in other conceptual attire (resurrection of the dead, radical transformation of the ages). What is most profound in apocalyptic thought continues to be the expectation of God's justice in a world in which the innocent suffer and the unjust prosper.[18]

For Jesus, the kingdom of God "is at hand." With apocalyptic intensity, Jesus proclaims that the kingdom of God—what all have been waiting for—is at the very gates. The present world of misery has come to its end. Jesus seems to expect the irruption of this kingdom—God's definitive yes to history—during his own lifetime (Matt. 10:23; Mark 13:30, 9:1).

Unlike the Baptist, therefore, Jesus preaches the kingdom of God as good news. God sunders the divine symmetry: no longer is God equally near and far, equally just and merciful. Now God draws near in grace.

Of course this still gives us no information about what the kingdom of God will be in itself when it comes in plenitude, when the present world really comes to an end. The reason for this is simple: the end has not come, as Jesus acknowledges (Mark 13:32). The only thing that we can know of the kingdom of God in its intrinsic fullness is the *notion* that Jesus must have had and that we must gather from apocalyptic tradition.[19] What we know from Jesus is what the *reality* of a kingdom of God *at hand* consists of; and correlatively, *what Jesus does* in respect of this approach, how Jesus "corresponds" to the kingdom at hand. This observation seems to us to be important for knowing Jesus, as well as for understanding the relationship between church and kingdom of God. It will be of little avail to attempt to construct argumentation as to the correct behavior of the church from the ultimate realization of the kingdom of God. That ultimate realization is empirically unknowable. But it will avail much to observe the behavior of Jesus in the process of this kingdom's approach, for this process is our historical situation.

The kingdom of God is near for the poor. Joachim Jeremias writes:

> To say that Jesus proclaimed the dawn of the consummation of the world is not a complete description of his proclamation of the *basileia;* on the contrary, we have still to mention its most decisive feature. . . . The reign of God belongs *to the poor alone.*[20]

The kingdom of God is at hand because the good news is proclaimed to the poor (Matt. 11:5; Luke 4:18) and the kingdom of God is theirs (Luke 6:20). Thus we have a first important characterization of what it is for the kingdom of God to be "at hand." Since the absolute utopia is for the poor, it is to them that the kingdom is preached and proclaimed.

Jesus had two ways of describing the poor. According to the first way, the poor are sinners, publicans, prostitutes (Mark 2:6; Matt. 11:19, 21:32; Luke 15:1), the simple (Matt. 11:25), the little (Mark 9:2; Matt. 10:42, 18:10, 14), the least (Matt. 25:40-45), those who practice the despised professions (Matt. 21:31; Luke 18:11). The poor are the vilified, persons of low repute and esteem, the uncultured and ignorant, "whose *religious* ignorance and *moral* behavior stood in the way of their access to salvation, according to the convictions of the time."[21] The poor are therefore society's *despised,* those lesser than others, and for them the prevailing piety proclaims not hope, but condemnation.

According to Jesus' second way of describing the poor, the poor are those in need in the spirit of Isaiah 61:1. The poor are those who suffer need, the hungry and thirsty, the naked, the foreigners, the sick and imprisoned, those who weep, those weighed down by a burden. The poor are therefore those who suffer some type of *real oppression.* The poor, to whom the good news of the kingdom is addressed, find themselves in some kind of misery and see themselves weighed down by a double burden: "They have to bear public contempt from men and, in addition, the hopelessness of ever gaining God's salvation."[22]

When Jesus proclaims that the kingdom of God is at hand for the poor and not for the just (a piece of irony directed against the Pharisees, who set themselves forth as the just), he is making a first important statement on what it means for the kingdom of God to be at hand. He is saying that this approach of the kingdom is not generic and universal. It is "partial." It has a prioritarian addressee and at the same time a prioritarian locus for an understanding of how one "corresponds" to a kingdom of God that is at hand.

This way the kingdom has of being at hand produces scandal (Matt. 11:6): scandal that God would give hope to those who are deprived of it in the secular sphere, scandal that God would restore to dignity those from whom religious and sociopolitical society have wrenched it away, scandal that God would really be partisan love, mercy, and re-creator. Jesus' polemics against the Pharisees shows the importance of this scandal. It betrays the partiality of the "kingdom at hand." The Pharisees refuse to accept the approach of the kingdom precisely by reason of their own partiality. It would shatter the seeming equilibrium and justice of the law. Therefore they criticize a Jesus who eats with sinners and publicans (Mark 2:15–17) and heals a withered hand on the Sabbath (Mark 3:1–6). Therefore they criticize his disciples, who do not fast (Mark 2:18–22), who gather a handful of grain on the Sabbath (Mark 2:23–28), and who eat without washing their hands (Mark 7:1–7).

Jesus' polemics with the Pharisees is only superficially casuistic. It is not really legal prescriptions that are at stake, but God's partiality. The simplest conclusion to be drawn from this manner of the kingdom's approach is that persons ought to correspond to it by taking up the defense of the poor and acting in solidarity with them.[23] This is the "place to live" when the kingdom is at hand.

One corresponds with the approaching Kingdom of God in love and justice. But now we must ask whether the approach of the kingdom of God is exhausted for Jesus in the recovery of hope by the poor in knowing that they are loved by God, in knowing that they are actually God's favorite persons. If the answer were to be in the affirmative, the prophetical horizon sketched above would appear vain, since it depicts the poor not only as knowing something special about themselves, but as ceasing to be the oppressed of the secular sphere. We ask, therefore, whether, according to Jesus, the approach of the kingdom entails the surmounting of real misery and the transformation of society to the advantage of the poor. In order to answer this question, it seems most appropriate to observe in the concrete what Jesus says and does with respect to these problems in the time of a kingdom "at hand."

From this perspective, it is evident that Jesus' proclamation is not limited to God's scandalous, partisan love for the poor. It includes his quest to deliver the poor from their real misery. Here the important thing is to observe the *structure* of the liberation striven for by Jesus, without anachronistically looking to Jesus for the concrete mechanisms of liberation sought by so many Christians, and so rightly and so necessarily, today. At bottom, then, the problem is not the concrete mediations of Jesus' liberation. The problem is whether Jesus corresponded to the approach of the kingdom *only* by arousing a hope. Was it also through a determinate *praxis* objectively calculated to change the situation of the poor? Let us make some brief observations about this.

In the first place, Jesus' miracles and exorcism constituted a liberative activity. If we transport ourselves from the traditional christological concern to demonstrate Jesus' authority and power to the deeds themselves, then the miracles are not only prodigies and works of wonder, they are works *in favor* of the one in need. They constitute the transformation of an evil reality into a different reality, a good one.

In the second place, Jesus promoted solidarity among human beings not in generic and merely declaratory fashion, but by bringing his activity to bear on human beings' concrete historical situation. Jesus' concrete "placement" or status with his people, his efficacious acts and attitudes of solidarity show what he himself understood by solidarity. Jesus states that solidarity does not exist in his society, and then he moves toward those whom that society has ostracized. He defends prostitutes, he speaks with lepers and the ritually impure, he praises Samaritans, he permits ostracized women to follow him. These are positive actions of his, calculated to create a new collective awareness of what solidarity is, that it actually exists, and the partisan way in which it ought to develop. Jesus' meals with the poor have special importance for this point. Of course they are only symbolic. But symbols are effective. Correspondence with a kingdom of God "at hand" is had when human beings feel solidarity with one another around a common table. Jesus approaches the ostracized not only individually, but in their community, re-creating them as a social group through the materiality of the dining table.

In the third place, what, according to Jesus, is the impediment to the common table? Surely, sin; but sin not only as a closing up against a God who draws near in grace, but also sin as a rejection of the ideal of the kingdom as expressed in the prophets. The sin unmasked by Jesus in the shadow of the kingdom, as it were, is sin against the ultimate content of the kingdom. Jesus therefore denounces any action, attitude, or structure that keeps human beings divided into wolves and lambs, into oppressors and oppressed.

Jesus' anathemas are condemnations not only of individuals, but of groups and collectivities that through their power keep the poor in a state of oppression. They are anathemas of sin, sin against the kingdom. To the rich he says, "But woe to you rich, for your consolation is now" (Luke 6:24). He is not just threatening the rich with ultimate failure (Luke 12:16), or condemning them for leaving the solution of economic problems to God (Luke 12:31). First and foremost he is denouncing the unjust social situation. "For there can be no doubt: Jesus considers it an injustice that there are poor and rich. . . ."[24] That is an intolerable situation, even in the short time before the imminent arrival of the kingdom.[25] And the reason that Luke gives is that wealth is simply unjust (Luke 16:9), for it is the fruit of oppression. Therefore Jesus proposes another way of using wealth as the kingdom approaches—a way that will render it just: give it to the poor (Matt. 19:21; Mark 10:21; Luke 18:22).

The *priests,* who hold religious power, are accused by Jesus of having adulterated the meaning of the temple, transforming it into a den of thieves (Mark 11:15–17). Religious power has been converted into a means of profit-making and thus of oppressing the weak. The *scribes,* who hold the intellectual power, are accused of laying heavy burdens upon others without lifting a finger themselves (Matt. 23:4), of preventing others from entering into the kingdom (Matt. 23:13), of having removed the key of knowledge and left others in ignorance (Luke 11:52), of devouring the living of widows on the pretext of having long prayers to recite (Mark 12:40). The *Pharisees,* who represent the power of exemplary holiness, are accused by Jesus of being blind guides (Matt. 23:24), and of having abandoned what is most basic in the law (Matt. 23:23). Jesus accuses the *rulers,* who hold political power, of governing with absolute power and of oppressing the masses (Matt. 20:25).

The denunciation of the sin of oppression is an action by Jesus in favor of the content of the kingdom now "at hand"; and the concrete identity of what is denounced enables us to appreciate as well the positive element in the proclamation of this kingdom. One corresponds to the kingdom of God by doing justice, by eliminating crass social discrepancies—by using power in a new manner, to the advantage of the poor.

Finally, Jesus himself lives and proposes the practice of love as the "law of life under the reign of God," as Joachim Jeremias phrases it.[26] I will not elaborate upon this theme at any length, but will make some brief observations on the reality of this love, not in its ultimate plenitude, but in the time in which the kingdom is at hand, as Jesus sees it. The first observation concerns the addressee of that love. Jesus' words about the final judgment leave no room for doubt: the prioritarian addressee of this love is anyone in need, and the need in question is surely made explicitly in Matthew 25:35–38. Further, we see that "my least brothers" (Matt. 25:40) has a universal extension not reducible to Jesus' disciples, but applicable to any human being in need. It is they who are the addressees of the kingdom; they are in the majority in society and are the fruit of society's oppression. So the love in question must be translated into the active word of justice.

The second observation concerns the agent of the practice of this love. The parable of the Good Samaritan admirably illustrates that true love is measured by the objectivity of what is done, not by the intention or a priori quality of the doer. The despised Samaritan lives the love that corresponds to the approach of the kingdom. He understands the locus of the praxis of love. Unlike the priest and the Levite, who make a detour so as not to meet up with the one in need (Luke 10:31-32), the Samaritan draws near (v. 34). Thus he becomes the victim's neighbor, and not the other way around, as Jesus notes (vv. 29, 36). And so my "neighbor . . . is not [the one] I find in my path, but rather [the one] in whose path I place myself."[27] The kingdom of God is at hand when men and women actively seek that efficacious love that will transform this world according to the ideal of the kingdom to come.

The third observation bears on the absolute element of that love as the way to correspond to the approach of the kingdom. Where there is love among human beings, seemingly so "horizontal" a love, we have the great paradox that God is approaching. We are familiar with the two passages concerned with the "great commandment" (Mark 12:28-34; Matt. 22:34-40; Luke 10:25-27) and with the superiority of the human being to the Sabbath (Mark 2:23-28; Luke 6:1-5). Both passages state that it is in love that human beings achieve their fulfillment, for it is in love that they correspond to the kingdom "at hand"—correspond to the love of God for human beings.[28]

We *respond* to the approach of the kingdom in the hope that God is at last "at hand" in grace and partisan love; but we ultimately and absolutely *correspond* to it by becoming like the reality of the God who is "at hand." In God's seeming self-forgetfulness, as God demands our love for other human beings, the kingdom comes near—a new world "according to God" is under way. Correlatively, in love for another human being, human beings are loved by God. In corresponding to God's loving reality they simultaneously correspond to God's love.

This is John's profound intuition. He deduces the demand of love for neighbor from one's awareness of being loved by God: "Beloved, if God has loved us so, we must have the same love for one another" (1 John 4:11). Luke's intuition is the same: "Be compassionate, as your Father is compassionate" (Luke 6:36).

Why is this of crucial importance for what was the real ultimate, the absolute, for Jesus? The biblical passages use generic language—like "love" and "compassion"—and therefore current mediations are always needed. But what is being asserted in these passages is that for Jesus the ultimate is *the realized will of God*. Therefore this absolute is not simply "God," and this in virtue of the very notion Jesus had of God. Jesus proclaims the irruption of the definitive kingdom of God, the work of God. In the meantime, in the time of the kingdom "at hand," he strives for a world according to God. Precisely because that God of his is love and not pure sovereign power, partisan, sides-taking justice for the poor, and not the universal moral law, because that God is not egocentric—for this reason, and not by reason of any secularist intention, God is the absolute only insofar as God's reality of being-love is actualized in this world.[29]

Here is the theological kernel of what is meant by a kingdom of God "at hand." True this kernel is not simply to be deduced from the apocalyptical notion Jesus may have had. But it is to be deduced from seeing Jesus in *action*—preaching to the poor, forthrightly denouncing injustice and oppression, placing everything he has at the service of the approach of the kingdom, creating human solidarity from a point of departure in the poor, and staying faithful to that task even though the kingdom of God in its fullness did not come, and the kingdom "at hand" seemed tragically far-off in his death. What is ultimate for Jesus is not, when all is said and done, discoverable from his notions, but only from his life. The absolute for Jesus is what he *maintained in deed* as ultimate through his life, throughout his history and in spite of history: the service and love of the oppressed, in order to create a world in which right and justice will be established—a world worthy of the undying hope that, despite all, the kingdom of God is still at hand.

HOW DOES THE KINGDOM OF GOD COME TO BE AT HAND? AN ESCHATOLOGICAL PROBLEM

From what has been said thus far, I shall now explain what it means to say that the kingdom of God is eschatological. The eschatological character of the kingdom was rediscovered at the turn of the century by Johannes Weiss and Albert Schweitzer, and an earnest discussion on the part of scholars has continued from that day to this. The discussion bears on two points. First, while the kingdom must definitively have come with Jesus, either it has not yet come *in absoluto,* or—in Oscar Cullmann's formulation—it has "already" come, but "not yet." The question, then, is that of the *temporal nature of the kingdom.* The second point of discussion is whether the kingdom of God for Jesus is the pure work of God or also that of the activity of human beings. The question here, therefore, is that of the gratuity of the kingdom.

These discussions are crucial for explaining what Jesus really thought about the kingdom of God. I conclude this article by re-positing the eschatological problem from a systematic standpoint so that the theme "Jesus and the kingdom of God" may likewise be useful and normative for us.

It seems that Jesus thought of the eschatological coming of the kingdom as about to take place, in the near future, probably during or at the close of his life. The kingdom, then, was not fully present for him, but only "at hand." And yet Jesus preached it as something ultimate-and-present. He conceived of the kingdom as a gift of God. Nevertheless, he sought to foster it in a determinate manner throughout his life. However surely a point of departure in the mere notion that Jesus had of the kingdom of God leads us to the notional aporiae of eschatology—such as those of the reconciliation of present and future, or of gift and human task—if we begin instead from Jesus' real life, we gain a new approach to the eschatological.

From this viewpoint, what Jesus offers as eschatological and ultimate is a life in the shadow of God's kingdom. How the kingdom comes, what its element of gratuity is, what is historical about it and what transcendent—all of these questions are answered in the measure that Jesus' call is accepted: "If a man wishes to come after me, he must deny his very self, take up his cross, and follow in my steps" (Mark 8:34).

The following of Jesus is the primordial locus of all Christian theological epistemology and therefore of the understanding of eschatology as well. The *thought* tension between gift of God and human task dissolves in Jesus' discipleship, where grace is *experienced,* not only in new ears for hearing the good news, but also—and furthermore as fullness of grace—in new hands for fashioning a history itself at hand for the kingdom. The *thought* tension between the present and future of the kingdom is *experienced* as undying hope. In the *praxis* of love and justice one knows that the kingdom is at hand, is becoming present; and in conflictive *praxis* in the midst of the world's sin one maintains hope in God's future.

Jesus' discipleship does not furnish us with a response to the question "What is the fullness of the kingdom, and when will it come in that fullness?" Jesus' discipleship does offer us a place to ask these questions meaningfully. The ultimate reason for this is that this plenitude as reality can only be understood starting from and in historical reality. The continuity between plenitude and history is not to be found in thought. The following of Jesus provides, then, the living of a reality, the fashioning of a reality, of a kingdom "at hand," from which, at least in hope, an ultimate reality acquires meaning. That "God may be all in all" (1 Cor. 15:28) in the end is something that we can formulate only in serious, humble toil calculated to render God a little more present in our world today.

This is important for the church today in identifying its relationship to the kingdom of God. A routine repetition that "the church is not the kingdom of God but its servant" will not suffice—although it will be no small matter to be convinced of this. It will likewise be insufficient merely to recall that the Catholic Church must not walk alone but must collaborate with and learn from the other Christian churches and from all men and women of good will, who likewise objectively serve the approach of the kingdom and who even outstrip us.

The church must positively place itself in the locus from which its concrete task, to be realized in a determinate era, will be illuminated—the following of Jesus—and from there learn to evaluate its mission, not hastily appealing to the apocalyptic, to the unknown plenitude, and ignoring or undervaluing the historical present, but rather following the historical path of Jesus. The apocalyptic should be the ultimate horizon for the church today, too—but not at the price of ignoring the ultimacy of history. The mission of the church must be thought and accomplished not only from a point of departure in the kingdom of God, but from a point of departure in the kingdom of God *at hand.* This mission, then, today as in Jesus' time, takes on concrete, verifiable forms.

Because the eschatological existence available to the church is the following of Jesus and not a mere mechanical imitation of him, the church will have to learn how the kingdom of God "at hand" is served historically. Jesus will direct it along the proper channels: that God is greater than any historical configuration, even of the church; that, paradoxically, God is also smaller, for God's face appears in the least and the oppressed; that sin has concrete names in history, and takes flesh not only in the individual, but in society; that the praxis of love is the ultimate thing that can be accomplished; that this love must be really efficacious, really transformative, and therefore must reach not only the person as individual—one's spouse, one's relatives, one's friends—but society as such, the oppressed majorities—that is, that it must be justice; that the following and discipleship of Jesus is partisan, prioritizing the poor and oppressed; that one must be ready to change, as Jesus was, to be converted, to pass by way of a breach, a rupture, to "let God be God"; that one must be ready for surrender, for sacrifice, for persecution, for giving one's own life and not keeping it for oneself.

As it allows itself to be swept along the channel of discipleship, the church will gradually learn from within, by trial and error, which concrete mediations today bring God's kingdom near; what social, economic, and political systems render the kingdom-at-hand more illuminating; where the Spirit of Jesus is hovering, in the centers of power or the face of the oppressed; how to conceive and organize the church, from institutional steeples or popular foundations; which concrete sins call inexorably for denunciation; and so on.[30]

It is a simple matter, then, to pose the problem of the eschatology of the kingdom . All one need do is learn from Jesus how to live, how to be church, in the faith that the kingdom is at hand; and then, in the shadow of the approaching kingdom, how to go and transform human beings and society. The nearness of the kingdom is understood, without any tinge of false piety, in Jesus' nearness, in his discipleship and following. This is what is genuinely ultimate for the church, for here we grasp what was ultimate for Jesus.

I conclude these reflections with the words of the Salvadoran priest and martyr, Rutilio Grande, s.j., who grasped in Jesus' discipleship what he had to do, how he had to speak, because he *believed* that the kingdom of God was coming and because he *wanted* it to come to his *campesino* town of Aguilares.

The Lord God gave us a material world—like this material Mass, with its material cup that we raise in our toast to Christ the Lord. A material world for all, without borders. That's what Genesis says. I'm not the one saying it. "I'll buy half of El Salvador. Look at all my money. That'll give me the right to it." No! There's no "right" to talk about! "It's called right of purchase. I've got the right to buy half of El Salvador." No! That's denying God! There *is* no "right" against the masses of the people! A material world for all, then, without borders, without frontiers. A common table, with broad linens, a table for everybody, like this Eucharist. A chair for everybody. And a table setting for everybody. Christ had good reason to talk about his kingdom as a meal. He talked about meals a lot. And he celebrated one the night before his supreme sacrifice. Thirty-three years old, he celebrated a farewell meal with his closest friends. And he said that this was the great memorial of the redemption: a table shared in brotherhood, where all have their position and place. Love, the law code of the kingdom, is just one word, but it is the key word that sums up all of the codes of ethics of the human race, exalting them and presenting them in Jesus. This is the love of a communion of sisters and brothers that smashes and casts to the earth every sort of barrier and prejudice and that one day will overcome hatred itself.[31]

4

The Epiphany of the God
of Life in Jesus of Nazareth

Theology in Latin America has rightfully stressed that the Christian should follow a liberator Jesus and should invoke a liberator God. But unlike other geographical areas where liberation bears a direct relationship to "freedom,"[1] in Latin America it bears a relationship to something even more fundamental and original: it bears a relationship to "life," which, in its complexity, includes freedom, but is a more basic datum.

That is what I wish to analyze in this study on Jesus of Nazareth. I wish to recall attention to the most fundamental of theological realities: that God is a living God and that God gives life. However, to do justice to the study of this fundamental truth, this Christian tautology, we must analyze its implications, concretize what is said in it in a general way, and point out the historical options and their consequences for our position. Otherwise, we might be only mouthing a routine avowal of a God of life, but actually ignoring, manipulating, or even denying its truth.

If, as believers, we assert that the true divinity has manifested itself in Jesus, then we must distinguish that divinity from false divinities. But raising this issue—ostensibly such a simple matter—is of extreme importance owing to its theoretical and practical consequences. This is because the true concept of divinity can be arrived at on the basis of the internal coherence of the qualities that are attributed to divinity and from the explanatory capacity of a given conceptualization of God for a better understanding of nature, history, or—in a word—everything.[2]

However, in pursuing this undertaking, we need not search for what might be the most profound coherence within God per se, because, according to the

This article was published in Pablo Richard et al., *The Idols of Death and the God of Life* (Maryknoll, N.Y.: Orbis Books, 1983). It was originally translated by Barbara E. Campbell and Bonnie Shepard and has been edited for inclusion in the present volume.

biblical tradition that was inherited and shared by Jesus, it consists in the coherence between "the true God" and "the living God," between being a living being and engendering life in history. We must not forget that the Jews did not swear by the "true" God, but rather by the "living" God.[3]

If this is so, distinctions among the various divinities who are invoked and, moreover, the distinction between true and false divinities, are not drawn in all their radicality by recourse to the principle that there is one true divinity and the others are false, but by recourse to the principle that there is a living God who gives life and there are other divinities that are not living and do not give life. But the second part of this principle is still rather mild and exploratory; it grants too much and is not definitive. In theory, it might be claimed that false divinities neither have life nor give it; in other words, they do not have any influence on the real lives of human beings, because they themselves lack life. The conviction that false gods are *nothing* is clearly present in biblical tradition (see Ps. 10,81; 1 Chron. 16:26).

The deepest aspect of the distinction between true and false divinities is found in the genesis of the false divinities. According to the Scriptures, if false divinities are nothing, then they do not exist of themselves but have been created by humans. And the creation of divinity by humans—in other words, idolatry—leads historically not just to the absence of life, but to death. This historicization of idolatry appears in two of the classic passages dealing with it (Wis. 13–14; Rom. 1:18–32): human beings become dehumanized and dehumanize others; they themselves go to their death, and give death to others. Thus the final option wherein the problem of true divinity is posed is that between the living God who gives life and the gods who are not such and whose invocation leads to death. Hence, idolatry is not just an intellectual mistake but the choice of death and the fruits of death.

The early Christians stated the reality of the true God very well, from the positive standpoint: *gloria Dei, vivens homo* ("the glory of God—a living human being"). However, there must be added to this the tragic reality of the other side of the coin: *vanitas Dei, moriens homo* ("the denial of God—a dying human being"). The deep correlation between "God" and "life" is what makes it possible to progress in the knowledge of the true God and in the unmasking of false divinities. The God in whose name life is engendered will be the true divinity; and the worship of the true God will progress in the process of engendering life. Conversely, the gods in whose name death is produced will be false divinities; and there will be an increasing lapse into idolatry as death proliferates.

To raise the issue of true divinity in this manner is not an idle or merely academic undertaking in Latin America. What lies behind a theology of "liberation" and a theology of "captivity" is the fundamental perception that no theology can be elaborated realistically apart from this basic point. In Latin America, life and death are not merely fruitful concepts for progress in the speculative understanding of God; they are brute realities. And because ours is a continent that has not yet been exposed on a massive scale to secularizing influences, they are realities that come about through the invocation of various divinities. These divinities have been made explicit in a religious, and particularly in a Christian, framework, and have become implicit in secular substitutes, such as various social, economic, and political ideologies.

Hence it is not academic to question whether or not the true God in Jesus is really addressed in various invocations, even when they are explicitly Christian; to determine whether the *vivens homo* or the *moriens homo* proceeds historically from various invocations. It is a matter of recovering the luminous simplicity of the profound correlation between God and life, and of not understanding what is religious as something added to life, but rather understanding life as the essence of what is religious.

I base this analysis on Jesus of Nazareth. Associating Jesus with God is "automatic" for a Christian, by virtue of the faith and dogma of the church and, more generally, by virtue of an institutionalized Christian culture. But associating Jesus of Nazareth with the God of life deserves special attention. It is a matter of reaffirming the simplicity of something that is obvious but often distorted in the complexity of manipulations.

One need only open the gospels at the beginning and reflect on the very name "Jesus" (Luke 1:31; Matt. 1:21). The scenes in which the angel conveys the name of the child to be born are, of course, the product of theological reflection by believers, but hence all the more important in their significance: they are theological summaries of the entire background reality of Jesus of Nazareth. They are not a prologue, but an epilogue.[4]

The child's name is "Jesus," *Yeshua,* an abbreviation of *Yehoshua,* which means "Yahweh is salvation." To be sure, one would have to read the entire gospel, and even the subsequent history of the gospel—namely, the life of the church—in order to fathom the depths of what is said here. But what is fundamental has been said: since the coming of Jesus, the first and last thing that can be said about God is that God saves—to the full.

The essence of that salvation has also been well expressed in the canticles of Luke's Gospel: mercy, alliance, friendship, peace, salvation of enemies, enlightenment, and justice. If we move from a christological consideration—that is, the consideration of Jesus as a mediator of salvation—to a theo-logical consideration, we discover that the fundamental mediations of the reality of God are nothing other than life and everything that fosters it. We also find ourselves, concretely, in the presence of the threatened poor. Here "Yahweh is salvation" does not have any ethereal, spiritualistic, and univerifiable meaning or a religious meaning that would apply only to this or that part of the world. It has, rather, the significance of giving real life in the presence of threats to life and the oppression of life, in the presence of the machinations of other divinities.

What we are now attempting, in analyzing the reality of God in Jesus, is only to fathom the meaning of "Jesus" and "Yahweh is salvation." It is an attempt to comprehend the mediator, Jesus of Nazareth, so as to comprehend the mediations of God's reality. They are what lend a final meaning to the person of

Jesus, and, for the believer, they are the final criterion for distinguishing the true God and for recovering that God from the idolatry of death.

Hence, analyzing the reality of God in Jesus deals with two meanings, both of which must be stressed: the historical meaning and the faith meaning. In the first meaning, Jesus should be considered a historical figure, parallel, for example, to the figures of Moses or Jeremiah. The attempt is to understand who God is to Jesus, and to make a historical analysis of how that God appears in the mediator and his mediation. This analysis of the historical Jesus must take into account Jesus' notions of God and, more particularly, his praxis and final destiny, which demonstrate the concrete reality of those notions.[5]

In the second meaning, Jesus should be considered a participant in the very reality of God, as Son. This is the analysis carried out by faith. In it one grasps and accepts the basic norms set for the mediator and his mediation. In this way, the Parent of Jesus, through the path of the Son and in the history begun by the Spirit, becomes God *for us.* This is not merely a matter of learning who God was to Jesus, as one might learn who God was to Moses or Jeremiah, but rather of grasping Jesus' fundamental relationship with God, wherein one will learn who God is, in what sense God is a God of life, how life is given, the relationship that exists between giving life and giving one's own life, and so forth.

In this study, I shall emphasize the historical aspect, although in accepting in faith the fundamental normativity of that history we are also asserting its faith meaning. In other words, by associating ourselves today with the fundamental structure of the role of the mediator and of his mediations, the God of Jesus will also be a reality to us as a God of life. We shall consider two points from the historical aspect: Jesus' struggle against the divinities of oppression, on which we shall expand further, and the positive significance of God to Jesus.

Because this topic, by its very nature, is so extensive, we shall attempt to summarize the fundamental points in a series of theses. We shall describe Jesus' path in a systematic manner, illustrating it with major passages from the synoptic gospels. This is a systematic, not an exegetical, study, but based on the fundamentally historical features of the life of Jesus and what is revealed in them concerning the reality of God to him.

JESUS' STRUGGLE AGAINST THE DIVINITIES OF DEATH

That Jesus was a noncomformist with respect to the religious situation of his time and his people is both obvious and generally accepted.[6] What is important is to ascertain the extent and, in particular, the origin of that nonconformity, not only in the realm of Jesus' possible psychological or even ethical attitudes, but also in the theo-logical realm—that is, the realm of his vision of God.

To summarize briefly, Jesus struggled resolutely against any type of social force that in one way or another, mediately or immediately, dehumanized human beings, causing their death. In this respect, the human being, living and living fully, was a clear-cut criterion of Jesus' course of action.

In that struggle, Jesus discovered that the forces of death had come to be justified by explicit religious concepts of life, or those that implicitly assumed some type of divinity as absolute. Hence much of his public ministry was aimed at unmasking false divinities.

In this process, Jesus set his activity more and more within a context of position-taking, as attested to by his many controversies. His controversial involvement brought upon him many attacks and much persecution and, in the end, death. The gods of oppression, against whom he had struggled, dealt him death.

Thesis 1: *To Jesus, God's archetypal plan is for human beings to have life. Life, in all its fullness, including its materiality, is God's prime mediation. This insight explains Jesus' attitude toward the Jewish law (as a manifestation of God's will), his interpretation, criticism, heightening, and deepening of it. There must be "bread," as a symbol of life, for everyone.*

In order to understand Jesus' perception of the reality of God, and the subsequent struggles that it occasioned for him, we must begin with something very fundamental: Jesus proclaimed life as the archetypal plan of God for human beings; therefore the fulfillment of life is the prime mediation of the reality of God. To be sure, we shall have to observe in Jesus *how* life is engendered; but what is important now is to stress *that* God's first mediation is the engendering of life.

Even though this seems simple, it must be stressed. First, because automatically relating God's plan to the spiritual redemption of the soul is still very common. Two other reasons, which have their own validity, should be brought up, at least logically, only after, not before, stating the more fundamental truth. There is every reason to stress in Latin America that a creation-oriented theology is inadequate and "ideologized." The inertia of creation does not lead from historical sin to the engendering of life.[7] It is also important to keep in mind, in the elaboration of the concept of true life, that life must be according to God's plan and in alignment with the historical circumstances that govern it and make it possible.[8] Both of these considerations must be integrated into God's archetypal plan for life.

We shall consider, from two vantage points, how Jesus viewed God's archetypal plan with regard to life. To Jesus, the fundamental thing about the divine law was that it was an expression of God's plan. It contains something very profound concerning God's will—profound, not because it is a law, but because it is an expression of the divine will.

We have already noted that Jesus was a nonconformist with respect to the Old Testament law, but we must probe why and in what way. In order to understand Jesus' attitude toward the law, we must remember that in his time there was both the written Torah—that is, the Pentateuch—and the oral Torah, called Halakah, the scribes' interpretation of the written Torah.

In the gospels Jesus talks about the written Torah as if it were something recent—because it contained the abiding laws of the will of God.[9] The passages in question relate to the observance of the second part of the decalogue (Mark 10:19 and elsewhere)—in other words, respect for human life in its various manifestations, assistance to parents in need (Mark 7:10; Matt. 15:4), and the equating of love for God with love for one's neighbor (Mark 12:28–34 and elsewhere). This archetypal will of God must be respected because it governs the communal life—and hence simply the life—of human beings.

In addition, Jesus probes deeply into at least two specific areas of the law concerned with its preservation. Insofar as marriage is concerned, he calls for a return to the original decree of the true will of God (Mark 10:6; cf. Gen. 1:27), whereby man and woman become one and whereby the man leaves his own family (Mark 10:7; cf. Gen 2:24). Jesus defends married life in his radicalization of adultery (Matt. 5:27ff.), relating it to the ancient law (Exod. 20:14).

Radicalization of the law to the advantage of life can be observed when Jesus talks about life itself. The "thou shalt not kill" (Exod. 20:13) applies to anger and abuse of other human beings (Matt. 5:21ff.). Not only must life be protected, but its origins must be insured as well. The law of retaliation, which even went so far as to exact a life for a life (Exod. 21:23), is abolished (Matt. 5:38–42). In other passages, as they are not directly concerned with the law, but rather with life, the synoptic gospels make major omissions. The whole emphasis is on the God of life. When Jesus responds to the Baptist's emissaries (Matt. 11:2–6; Luke 7:18–28), he points out positive signs of life—the blind see, the lame walk—but he omits the continuation of Isaiah's text on the extermination of the ruthless (Isa. 29:20). The same type of omission occurs in the quotation from Isaiah 61:2 made by Luke when he recounts Jesus' words in the Galilean synagogue. Luke concludes with the mission of "proclaim[ing] the year of the Lord's favor" (Luke 4:19; cf. Isa. 61:2a); but he omits "a day of the vengeance of our God" (Isa. 61:2b).

From the Old Testament quotations, Jesus' reinforcement of them, and the omissions, we see how Jesus interprets the archetypal will of God as life and how he probes deeply in that direction. In these considerations the primary concern is to extract consequences not for a Christian ethic (which must take into account a series of current historical mediations) but rather for theology, for the concept of the God of Jesus as the God of life.

That intention is more clearly evident in the criticism that Jesus makes of the Halakah—that is, of the interpretation of the law. In Mark 7:8–13 (cf. Matt. 15:3–9), it becomes evident that the human traditions presumably created in the name of God run counter to God's original intention. This logion involves casuistic traditions entailing disregard of the obligation to assist one's parents, even when "the support that had to be given to them was fictitiously given to the temple."[10]

And there is the general criticism of the human traditions contrary to God's original will in the passage about the human being and the Sabbath (Mark 2:23–28 and parallels). Jesus tried to argue in various ways to a position contrary to that of the Halakah, citing the case of David (Mark 2:25ff.; cf. 1

Sam. 21:2–7), who, in need, took the bread of the presence, and the action of the priests in the temple on the Sabbath (Matt. 12:5); he also argued *ad hominem,* using the same method as those who criticized him (Matt. 12:11). But the fundamental argument, based on principle, lies in the will of God itself: "The Sabbath was made for the sake of man" (Mark 2:27); the Sabbath is God's creation, not for its own sake, but for the life of the human being, in the form of rest (Deut. 5:14). As Joachim Jeremias comments, the fact that the creation of human kind took place on the sixth day, whereas the ordinance for rest was given on the seventh day, informs us that it was God's creative will that the day of rest be in the service of human beings, and for their benefit.[11]

Jesus' criticism of the Halakah and radicalization of the Torah have ultimately, therefore, a final theo-logical motivation: at their source is God's archetypal will that the human being should live. The fact that the concrete details concerning what "living" means are of course devised in accordance with the various mentalities in different periods does not detract from this fundamental assertion. "The will of God is not a mystery, at least insofar as it relates to brothers and sisters, and deals with love. The creator who can be placed in opposition to the creature is a false God."[12]

This fundamental understanding of God, whose archetypal will is the life of human beings on the most elementary level, and hence on the level of making life possible, can be found throughout the gospels. We shall focus on only one element of life, but it is the symbol of all life: bread, food.

Jesus spoke more than once about bread and food. In the Lord's Prayer the petition for bread occupies an important place. Although Matthew and Luke do not coincide on all the petitions, both include this one. It is the first petition made in the plural, aimed at expressing the best desires of and for human beings. We are already familiar with the discussion about the meaning of *epiousion* ([bread] sufficient for the day—Matt. 6:11; Luke 11:3), which can mean "what is necessary for daily existence," or "for the future, for tomorrow."[13] On the basis of this latter meaning, one could spiritualize the petition for bread in the sense of an expectation of the bread of life. But even Jeremias, who, for linguistic reasons, upholds the latter meaning, warns that "it would be a crass misunderstanding were we to think that this amounted to a spiritualization of the petition for bread."[14] The bread of life and earthly bread are not opposed. It is right for us to ask that the bread of life come now, in the midst of our poverty-stricken existence.

We must recall again the passage concerning the grain plucked on the Sabbath.[15] In the final versions, the incident occurred on the Sabbath, which Jesus' disciples apparently violated by plucking the ears of grain. This was followed by Jesus' dispute with the Pharisees. It is the intention of these later versions to show that Jesus was the master of the Sabbath and (as observed above) that the Sabbath is for the sake of humankind, and that therefore religious laws must be humanized.

Underlying this controversy is something even more fundamental than the proper use of what is religious. In the earliest account, the discussion is not about the Sabbath and its observance. When Jesus argued about what David did—eating the bread of the covenant—he did not mention the matter of the Sabbath at all. The question about David was not that he had taken bread on the Sabbath, but rather merely that he had taken and eaten it. What the Pharisees objected to was the fact that the disciples had picked and eaten grain from someone else's field, not that they had done so on the Sabbath. It is a strictly human, not a religious, problem: the disciples' hunger and their taking another's food to satisfy it. Jesus is asserting, in defending them, that "in the case of need (here, the disciples' hunger), every law must give way to a vital need."[16]

At stake in this controversy is not primarily a religious problem, but rather a human problem: the disciples' hunger. Jesus taught that there cannot be a law that prohibits the satisfaction of basic needs of life, whether it be on the Sabbath or not. Such a law could not be a mediation of the will of a God of life. Hunger could not be assuaged in the name of a god that would decree such laws. The logion of the Sabbath would become generalized later, for the human being may not be dehumanized in the name of religious laws. It is important to stress the primarily material aspect of this controversy because it explains clearly the primary relationship between God and life.

Bread and food are thus primary mediations of the reality of God. This is why Jesus favors and defends them; this is why he eats with publicans (Mark 2:15-17 and parallels). This is why he pays so little heed to ritual ablutions before eating (Mark 7:2-5; Matt 15:2), the former being human institutions and the latter a divine institution. This is why the miracle of the multiplication of loaves (apart from the christological and liturgical intent of the evangelists) emphasizes that those who are hungry must be fed and stresses that they ate and had their fill (Mark 6:30-44 and parallels; Mark 8:1-10; Matt. 15:32-39). This is why the one who feeds the hungry has encountered both the human being and the "Son of Man" (Matt. 25:35-40).

For Jesus the first mediation of the reality of God is life. God is the God of life and is manifested through life. This is why we must ask for bread and why we may pluck grain from another's field in order to satisfy hunger. From the foundational horizon of the archetypal will of God, Jesus observes that God is a God of life and fosters the life of human beings. This is certainly a primary and generic horizon, which was to become historicized and concrete in the life of Jesus himself. Life would appear as a reconquest of life in the presence of oppression and death; giving life would be salvation, redemption, liberation; life would have to be rescued from death, death itself yielding life. But, logically and in principle, one can understand the God of Jesus only from the positive horizon of life. God is an unfathomable mystery, and our attempts to conceptualize God dare not allow this basic truth to be forgotten.

It is paradoxical (paradoxical in principle, though a frequent occurrence in history) that when Jesus announced this God of life and historicized the announcement, controversy, persecution, and death emerged. The divinities of death did not allow the one making this proclamation to go unpunished—a proclamation that was a response to the innermost essence and deepest desire of every human being.

> **Thesis 2:** *The eschatological horizon of Jesus' mission is the kingdom of God, a kingdom of life for everyone. But, in order for it to be a reality it must be shared in by those who for centuries have been deprived of life in its various forms: the poor and the oppressed. Hence Jesus' proclamation is "partial," partisan, and the God of life appears only as taking sides with those deprived of life.*

Jesus began his public ministry by announcing the good news of the kingdom of God. In its ultimate essence, that kingdom is nothing but full life in which everyone can participate. However, the overall content of the preaching of the kingdom of God does not sufficiently explain what is meant by the God of life, or why Jesus, who announced "good" news, came to such a dire end in his mission.

The reason lies in the fact that then as now, "kingdom of God" was a symbol of fullness but was open to different interpretations. If that fullness had referred only to the universal scope of the intended hearers of the message, then dire consequences would not have resulted for Jesus—but the essence of the revelation of the kingdom would have been misunderstood.

It is not that the universality of the hearers is an incorrect notion per se. There are in the gospels enough symbols of that universality: Jesus' contacts with Martha, Mary, Lazarus, Zaccheus, the Roman centurion, Nicodemus, and others. This does not mean that the universality of the hearers should be ignored on the basis of the gospel. It means that such a view is not the primary or the most correct one for understanding the fullness of life of the God of Jesus.

The most correct view is gained rather from a different standpoint. Jesus announced the kingdom of God to the poor; he announced life to those who had it least. The notion that God is God must undergo a historical verification, which is nothing but the giving of life to those deprived of it for centuries: the poor and oppressed majorities.[17] Therefore, as part and parcel of the announcement of the coming of the kingdom of God (Mark 1:15; Matt. 4:17), the poor appear as its privileged recipients (Matt. 5:3; Luke 6:20).

In order to highlight the true locus of the relationship between God and life, Jesus, like the prophets before him, deliberately pointed out a partial, partisan locus, that of the poor deprived of life. I shall illustrate this—it can be found in many places throughout the gospels—with the passage from the first preaching in the Nazareth synagogue (Luke 4:16-44).[18] This passage is of unique importance. It introduces the program of Jesus' public ministry according to Luke. The fact that Luke puts it at the beginning of Jesus' public activity, changing the sequence of Mark (where it follows later, 8:22-9:9), and the fundamental content of the passage attest to its vital significance. In it, Jesus' prophetic anointing (v. 18a), the determination of his mission as an evangelizer (vv. 18

and 43), the content of that mission as the good news of the kingdom (v. 43), the urgent need for carrying it out (v. 43), and its fulfillment in the present (v. 21) all appear.

This scene introduces Jesus the mediator, the mediation that he must perform, and the recipients of that mediation. The central point of the scene is Luke 4:18: "He has sent me to announce good news to the poor." Let us observe two important aspects of it. The content of that good news is, as has already been noted, the kingdom of God (4:18 and 4:43). The special significance of his evangelizing is, through the parallelism with Isaiah 61:1ff., "not only the proclamation, but also the fulfillment of the message that was proclaimed."[19] "That news will be good only insofar as it achieves the liberation of the oppressed."[20]

Who the poor and oppressed are can be inferred from the meaning of poor in Isaiah 61:1–2a and 58:6, quoted in Luke 4:18ff. In Isaiah the poor are all those who are bent under any type of yoke. The mission of the anointed one of Yahweh is that of total liberation, which includes, and very specifically, liberation from material poverty. When Luke quotes Isaiah in those passages, he makes some changes that help us to better understand his text. On the one hand, he omits the expression "to bind up the broken-hearted" and replaces it with "set free those who have been crushed," from Isaiah 58:6. He thereby precludes the legitimation of a spiritualizing interpretation, and underscores the material aspect that is an essential factor in total liberation. On the other hand, he omits the second part of Isaiah 61:2, "a day of the vengeance of our God," and concludes with the proclamation of the year of God's favor, "thus presenting salvation in Jesus as the jubilee year in which the liberation of the enslaved takes place."[21]

In the parallel passages from Luke 7:22–23 and Matthew 11:4–6, where John the Baptist's emissaries are given the same signs, there is also an indication, given in the same manner, of who the poor are and of what happens to them when the God of the kingdom approaches them. They recover life because, among the ancients, even verbally, these persons—the blind, lame, lepers, and others—are compared with the dead. "The status of such persons, according to the thinking of that time, could no longer be called life. They are virtually dead. . . . Now those who resembled the dead are brought to life."[22]

According to Jeremias, therein lies the innovation of Jesus' announcement of the good news, in which the poor return to life. Therefore whatever else the fullness of life may include, "the material liberation from any type of oppression, resulting from injustice, is associated with the biblical message as an essential religious value."[23]

Jesus' vision of God obliged him to preach and to act on behalf of life and its fullness. In these passages the fullness of life is not measured in view of a life already well established, which then notices what is lacking to its fullness, but rather starts with the conviction that there can be life in an absolute form—that is, the awareness of fullness comes first. To make this consideration realistic, Jesus, like the prophets, concentrated on those areas where the life of individuals is most precarious, most threatened, or even nonexistent. For that reason the program for his mission is one of partiality, and announces a God of partisan life to those who lack it on the most elementary levels.[24] Apart from that locus, any announcement of a God of life cannot but be idealistic.

That partiality caused scandal (Matt. 11:6; Luke 7:23).[25] The fact that life is offered to the poor, that God's salvation is addressed to them, and furthermore "only to the poor,"[26] caused scandal among powerful minorities and brought about the persecution of Jesus. Only in God's partiality toward those without life is there a guarantee that God is a God of life for everyone.

> **Thesis 3:** *Lack of life is not caused only by the limitations of what has been created, but also by the free will of minority groups who use their power for their own interests and against others. That is why Jesus anathematizes the rich, the Pharisees, the scribes, the priests, and the rulers: because they deprive the majorities of life, in its various forms.*

Jesus points out that the absence and annihilation of life, in addition to its obvious natural limitations, are the result of human sin. Hence his reproaches and anathemas. These are abundant in the synoptic gospels and may be regarded from different standpoints, either as an unmasking of false values and hypocritical attitudes among those who are anathematized or as an unmasking of deprivations in others' lives. The second viewpoint is of direct concern to us, although we do not question the reality of the first. It is not merely a matter of observing how Jesus anathematizes individuals because of their direct relationship to wealth, power, knowledge, and the like. We also observe the type of oppressive relationship that is established with other persons. Let us note a few clear-cut examples of anathemas and reproaches from this twofold standpoint.

"Alas for you who are rich" is the comment in the first denunciation (Luke 6:24). Here is an absolute condemnation of wealth, primarily because of its results for the rich person. "You have had your time of happiness" (Luke 6:24) and it will do you no good on the day of judgment (Luke 12:13–21). But, in particular, there is condemnation of the intrinsic root of the evil of wealth, which is relative; wealth is unjust. The moderate Jerusalem Bible comments: "It is called 'unjust,' not only because those who possess it have acquired it by evil means, but also, in a more general way, because there is some injustice in the origin of nearly all fortunes."[27] Hence wealth is not merely the possession of goods, which makes it extremely difficult to open one's heart to God (Matt. 19:13–26; Mark 10:23–27); it is an accumulation of goods that deprives others of the goods to which they are entitled. For that reason, the rich are the oppressors of the poor, according to Luke. Thus Zaccheus is praised not only because he gave away his riches, but also because he distributed them to others (Luke 19:8). The rich are "oppressors of the poor,"[28] and states of poverty are "caused by the oppressor."[29] The rich deprive others of what is necessary for life, and that is why Jesus anathematized them.

Chapters 23 of Matthew and 11 of Luke contain the famous anathemas against the scribes and Pharisees. In the existing literary format, these anathemas are preceded by some comments that are also made by Mark (10:43b and 16:37b–40) on religious hypocrisy and the vanity of the scribes and Pharisees. The latter flaunt the external signs of compliance with God's will, keep their phylacteries wide and their cloak fringes long, seek the first seats at banquets and in the synagogues (Matt. 23:5–7; Luke 20:46, 11:43; Mark 12:38–39). They seek thereby to remind others of God's will and to appear as the ones best complying with it.

In view of this, Jesus cautions his disciples against the casuistry of the law and against the hypocrisy of the scribes and Pharisees. In doing so, he condemns not only their false subjective attitude, but also the objective oppressive consequences for others. "Beware of . . . [those] who eat up the property of widows, while they say long prayers for appearance's sake" (Mark 12:38–40). More generally, Jesus condemns them because they "load men with intolerable burdens, and will not put a single finger to the load" (Luke 11:46).

The conceit and hypocrisy of the scribes and Pharisees is particularly emphasized in these passages. That hypocrisy evokes Jesus' severe judgment: "They will receive the severest sentence" (Mark 12:40; Luke 20:47). The fundamental flaw, however, was not the overweening malice of their hypocritical subjective attitude, but rather the fact of oppressing others, imposing heavy burdens on them and taking the property of widows. That is the fundamental sin, the fundamental negation of the will of God, subjecting it to hypocritical pride.

The anathemas pronounced against the scribes and Pharisees (Matt. 23:13–36; Luke 11:37–54) concur fittingly with these rebukes. Both lists have much in common. We shall therefore arrange them as Boismard has done,[30] starting with a list of the anathemas in Luke. The first three anathemas are directed against the Pharisees, whose hypocrisy is thrown directly in their faces:

> You clean the outside of cup and plate: but inside you there is nothing but greed and wickedness [Luke 11:39].
>
> You pay tithes of mint and rue and every garden-herb, but have no care for justice [11:42].
>
> You are like unmarked graves [11:44, explaining the contrast with Matt. 23:27: "covered with whitewash; . . . but inside they are full of dead men's bones and all kinds of filth"].

The internal/external contradiction—that is, the hypocrisy—of Pharisees is clearly present in these implications. But, once again, what at bottom makes these attitudes hypocritical are the objective consequences to others stemming from the Pharisees' internal wickedness. Their hearts are filled with greed and wickedness (Luke 11:39; Matt. 23:35); they have no care for justice and the love of God, and that is precisely what must be "practiced" (Luke 11:42; Matt. 23:23). The solution to the hypocritical inconsistency between the external and the internal lies not only in internal change, but in external objectivity: "Let what is in the cup be given to charity, and all is clean" (Luke 11:41).

The anathemas against the scribes do not explain their false internal attitude so much as they demonstrate directly their objective and oppressive wickedness, based on the consequences of their actions:

> You load men with intolerable burdens, and will not put a single finger to the load [Luke 11:46].
>
> You build the tombs of the prophets whom your fathers murdered, and so testify that you approve of the deeds your fathers did [11:47–48].
>
> You have taken away the key of knowledge. You did not go in yourselves, and those who were on their way in, you stopped [11:52].

Here there appears not only the hypocrisy, but also the direct oppression of the people by the scribes. Their malice is disclosed clearly, whether or not hypocrisy is present. Others suffer and are deprived of their rights by what the scribes do.

In the final additions to Matthew's text there is also repeated a phrase addressed to the scribes and Pharisees: "Blind fools" (Matt. 23:17; cf. 23:29, 26).[31] They travel over sea and land to win one convert; and when they have gained one, they make that person fit for hell (Matt. 23:15). This is the stress placed on the intrinsic wickedness of the scribes and Pharisees: not only are they headed in the wrong direction, but they also misguide others and lead them into danger.

Hence, whatever the pride and hypocrisy of the scribes and Pharisees may be, the anathemas focus on the objective reality of the deprivation of others of something important, and of oppression. They commit injustice against others, they rob them, they impose intolerable burdens on them, they deprive them of knowledge and of entry into the kingdom, they lead them along a dangerous path, and they kill the prophets. Jesus condemns conceit and hypocrisy because of the evil that they entail; but he also condemns the objective basis that makes such hypocrisy possible: depriving human beings of life in the various spheres of their existence.

Jesus' castigation of the priests climaxes in the expulsion from the temple (Mark 11:15–59 and parallels). These narratives, plus those that follow, on Jesus' authority (Mark 11:27–33 and parallels) have been highly theologized in christology and in Jewish eschatology as bearing on the future of the Jewish people as the chosen people. But the original core of the narrative appears to be in Mark 11:15–16.[32] The priests have committed the horrendous crime of defiling the essence of the temple. But, once again, their crime does not entail a religious wickedness alone, but a human one as well. "The priests have converted the temple into a den of thieves, a den from which evildoers continually emerge to commit their evil deeds. The priests misuse their vocation, which is to conduct worship for the glory of God. Instead, they engage in business, and accrue profits."[33] Although not in the form of anathemas, these harsh rebukes by Jesus have the same logical structure: fellow human beings are being oppressed in areas of their human existence, and with the overbearing wickedness that makes this possible in the name of an institution willed by God.

Finally, Jesus rebukes "those with political power," saying that "the recognized rulers lord it over their subjects, and their great men make them feel the weight of authority" (Mark 10:42 and elsewhere). This is certainly a general rebuke, unlike the other, detailed ones, although it is confirmed by Jesus' harsh words about the ruler Herod (Luke 13:32). Once again, the point is the relational aspect of political power. Regardless of the fact that, in a given era, power may have grandeur and honor, and even God's blesssing, Jesus condemns a power whose historical consequences are oppression and the deprivation of life—here, in the realm of political rights.

When we scan Jesus' anathemas and rebukes, we see that they sharply attack the individuals at whom they are directed, either because they have upset the scale of values, with their possessions and power, or because, overturning the values of religion and knowledge, they hypocritically boast. Something more profound underlies these anathemas. Jesus made it clear that the anathematized were dehumanized themselves—something that cannot take place without dehumanizing others. So, in his anathemas, he does not use merely formal logic, analyzing how certain attitudes dehumanize the human being, but material logic as well, observing how human beings become dehumanized by dehumanizing others.

The understanding that Jesus had of the God of life lies at the root of this logic. What makes the attitude and actions of the anathematized intolerable is the fact that they deprive others of life, whether of life itself, or of the possessions, freedoms, knowledge, and the like, necessary for life. It is important to stress this, so as not to confuse two areas. As we shall see later, Jesus will anathematize the dehumanization of others in the name of God, under the invocation of God. That is the sin against religion. But at the root of this sin is the fact that a human being is dehumanized; it is a sin against humanity. To deprive the human being of life in the name of God is a double evil because God is the God of life. This observation is important, as we must not resolve the issue of religious hypocrisy on the basis of its internal aspect alone. It would be of little use not to be hypocritical internally if one were to continue oppressing others externally. The greatest disharmony with the God of life lies precisely here.

Thesis 4: *Jesus' understanding of a God of life comes into conflict with the private interests of those who do not want to give life to others. This explains the controversies that Jesus entered into. Underlying the more explicit issue of the law and its casuistry are problems relating to the lives of human beings.*

Jesus' controversies also touch on the issue of the God of life, which, by that very reason (ironically but tragically), is seen to be controversial. Because of their value as exemplars, I shall concentrate on the five famous controversies that Mark puts almost at the beginning of Jesus' public activity (Mark 2:1-3; cf. Luke 5:17 and 6:11), and Matthew divides into two sections (Matt. 9:1-17 and 12:1-4). The five controversies have to do with : (1) the cure and pardon of the paralytic; (2) Jesus' dining with public sinners; (3) the question of fasting; (4) the grain picked on the Sabbath; and (5) the cure of the man with the withered hand.[34]

In their final version, these five accounts all have the literary structure of a controversy. It is fitting to divide them into two groups so as to observe just what the controversy and its theo-logical dimension are. Controversies 2, 3, and 4 have several features in common. Incidents are recorded in which, by their nature and in the society of that time, controversy was inherent: eating with sinners, not fasting when others did, taking what belonged to another. This is the core of the controversy. What is involved here is the breaking of accepted social norms: fasting, respecting private property, and avoiding the company of sinners. To break with such norms was unacceptable, and this is why Jesus and his disciples were accused of wrongdoing.

The other two accounts (1 and 5), at their core, relate a miracle—something that, of itself, should not have triggered a controversy. In their final written form, however, they are made controversial by additional circumstances. In the first account, Jesus declares that he has the power not only to heal, but also to forgive sins. In the fifth account, Jesus works a cure on the Sabbath. In these accounts the controversy is not inherent in the social event described—unlike the other three—but rather a social event is given a religious dimension. The account of the grain-plucking takes on a controversial significance when the shift is made from the original incident of simply taking another's property in a case of need to a consideration that the incident took place on a Sabbath.

The importance of this analysis, as regards Jesus' understanding of God, is twofold. In the first place, Jesus defends the human and historical mediations of whatever is according to the will of the God of life. To the society of his time, these mediations could be of two types: the socially accepted type, such as cures, or the socially unaccepted type, such as friendly relations with publicans, not fasting, and taking what is necessary for life even though it belongs to someone else. The latter type caused controversy, even before it was formulated in religious terms. And, in defending his "anti-social" attitude, Jesus not only provoked controversy, but also declared that God is, before all else, the God of life.

In the second place, when a controversy is interpreted from a religious standpoint, it becomes clear in the synoptic gospels that Jesus is giving a religious explanation of his understanding of the God of life, defending it against those who attack him and condemning their understanding of God. This appears in various ways in the five accounts, depending on the nature of the attacks and on the theological perspectives of the authors.

Confining ourselves to a few key points, we can say that Jesus makes use of a controversy in order to present a new image of the proper relationship between the human being and the religious realm. Religion is not worship alone, but a worship that is at least compatible with, and positively contributive to, giving life to human beings. Therefore religion that prevents the furtherance of life is false. This is proved by the reference in Matthew to Hosea 6:6 in connection with a meal shared with publicans (Matt. 9:13) and the plucked grain (Matt. 12:7). It is consistent with Matthew's view of Christian worship (Matt. 5:23).

This appears more clearly in Jesus' famous statement about the Sabbath. Jesus does good works on the Sabbath; he cures the crippled (Luke 13:10–17). In defending himself, he sometimes argues *ad hominem* (Luke 14:1–6); but he argues mainly on principle: the Sabbath is for the human being, not the human being for the Sabbath (Mark 2:27). The same formula can be framed in terms of what we might call the rights of God and the rights of human beings. In the Jewish mentality of the time, the Sabbath served as the day of God's celebration with the angels in heaven, and the Jewish people, by reason of its divine election, was allowed to participate in that celebration. Hence it appeared to them that nothing could be allowed to impede or threaten the divine celebration.[35] However, Jesus claims that the rights of God cannot be in contradiction to the rights of humans when these rights foster human life.

In the narratives of the synoptic gospels, the immediate justification for Jesus' stand is *christo*logical: "The Son of Man is sovereign over the Sabbath" (Matt. 12:8 and elsewhere). But the ultimate justification is *theo*logical, as stated in the quotation from Hosea and in what has been noted previously. Any alleged manifestation of God's will that runs counter to the real life of human beings is an outright denial of the most profound reality of God.

This is how the two levels of the controversy—the human and the religious—are combined; and hence it is possible to make a human controversy the substratum of a religious controversy. The controversies do not essentially involve different religious explanations of the reality of God, which would also entail different legal requirements. They involve different understandings of the reality of God, which will naturally come out in religious explanations. Because the understanding of the reality of God can differ from person to person, discussion emerges. Because the realities compared are not only different but conflicting, controversy emerges.

Thesis 5: *Jesus knows that human beings have not only different, but conflicting, notions of God, and that their invocation causes life and death; human beings invoke divinities even when death is the result. Thus, Jesus not only explains the true concept of divinity, but also exposes the use made of false concepts of divinity to oppress human beings and to deprive them of life.*

Jesus realizes that there are different, and even opposing, concepts of God; but he also realizes that actions contrary to the reality of the will of God are justified in the name of God. Therefore, his controversies not only affirm and clarify the true reality of God, but also expose the religious justification of human oppression.

The passage in Mark 7:1–23 (cf. Matt. 15:1–20) is the classic example in the synoptic gospels. The occasion is an undramatic incident: his disciples have eaten without washing their hands—in other words, they have eaten with impure hands (Mark 7:2)—thereby breaking the ancient tradition on which the Pharisees insist. Such traditions abound, particularly in regulations for legal purity. And according to the synoptic gospels, Jesus and his disciples break these unabashedly (Mark 1:41, 5:41; Luke 7:14, 11:38).

When attacked by the Pharisees, Jesus gives two types of response. The first relates to the value of human traditions (Mark 7:6–13), the second to true purity (Mark 7:14-23). In both responses, not only is the true doctrine pointed out, but also opposed traditions are exposed as being a means of ignoring the true will of God and thus of oppressing one's neighbor in their name.

In the first case, Jesus exposes how humans make their own traditions and shows that their legislation "is in contradiction with God's commandment."[36] The contradiction can be seen clearly in its content: parents do not receive the assistance they need from their children—in the name of religious legislation exacted by humans (Mark 7:12). The word of God is thereby abrogated (Mark 7:13) and the "rights of one's neighbor are violated." [37] What Jesus repudiates in these remarks is not that human beings explain and interpret the word of God or the methods that they use for this purpose. What he repudiates is the "explanation itself,"[38] for the word of God is abrogated by it.

As regards legal purity, Jesus explicitly responds to the issue of what is pure and impure. The fundamental assertion is that what comes from outside does not make persons impure (Mark 7:15). Therefore, religious traditions that arbitrarily assign a criterion of the will of God to what is external (eating without washing one's hands, touching a corpse or a leper) are false. This is a thundering assertion because it meant "putting in doubt the suppositions of the entire ancient liturgical ritual, including everything involved in its practice of sacrifice and expiation."[39] "There is invalidated here the entire Old Testament legislation, with its distinctions between animals and meals that are pure or impure."[40]

The positive aspect of Jesus' teaching is clear. The criterion of wickedness is not found in regulations external to the human being, but in what originates from within the human being. Evil deeds are evil because they run counter to the will of God: "acts of fornication, of theft, murder, adultery, ruthless greed, and malice; fraud, indecency, envy, slander, arrogance, and folly"(Mark 7:22).

The entire passage from Mark shows that the Pharisees dealt wrongly with the issue of the true will of God, locating it in laws and traditions merely because they used—misused—that issue in order to conceal evil acts against a neighbor (Mark 7:22) and to positively oppress a neighbor (Mark 7:12). Hence Jesus' exposé of the spurious use made of legislation as a presumed mediation of God's will, in order to act counter to the true will of God.

The law, as a human mechanism, cannot survive in independence of the originative will of God. "In the exposition that Jesus makes of this for us,

God's will is crystal clear: there is nothing incomprehensible about it."[41] Human beings had made it artificially complex and artificially difficult. In this way the law seemed to mirror the incomprehensibility of God. But human beings, out of self-interest, used the law's contrived difficulty and complexity in order not to do what God truly wanted. That is what Jesus exposed. In the name of that spurious use of the law, it is possible, and may even be thought "obligatory" in practice, to fail to take care of one's parents in need, and it is possible to conceal internal impurity with external purity.

In the matter of identifying the chief commandment, Jesus made another illuminating clarification (Matt. 22:34–40 and elsewhere), although not in such an explicit manner. In his time this was not an idle question; it was discussed assiduously.[42] Moreover, at that time "there was no lack of declarations explicitly forbidding the making of a distinction between what is primary [in the law] and what is secondary."[43] Inasmuch as the entire law came from God, no human discriminations were allowable.

The danger of manipulation contained in this idea is obvious. Hence, Jesus' response is all the more important. In the first place, Jesus prioritizes the commandments, and hence the will of God. Not everything is equal: some things are more urgent than others. But, secondly and more importantly, Jesus sets forth the first commandment (love of God) in such a way that human beings cannot have recourse to it in order to disregard clear-cut obligations to fellow human beings, an innate tendency amply documented in history.

The synoptic gospels present this aspect of Jesus' teaching in various ways.[44] In Mark, Jesus answers the scribe's question about the first commandment by adding to it the second commandment regarding love for one's neighbor and concluding: "There is no other commandment greater than these" (Mark 12:31). By using the plural, "these," he therefore includes love for one's neighbor in "the great commandment." In Matthew, Jesus responds in the same way, adding that the second commandment is "like" the first (Matt. 22:39). In Luke, the correct response is given by the lawyer himself who questioned Jesus in order to test him, and he puts the two commandments together (Luke 10:27). Immediately thereafter, Luke puts in Jesus' mouth the parable of the good Samaritan so that there would be no doubt about who one's neighbor is and in order to expose those who passed for experts with respect to the first commandment—the priests and Levites (Luke 10:31 ff.)—but who did not keep the second commandment.

In his teaching on the love for God, Jesus touches on the human tendency to manipulate not only certain provisions of the law, but even the greatest and most sacred of commandments—love for God—precisely to disregard the express will of the God whom one must love: love for one's neighbor. Hence, Jesus exposes the use of religious law because in its name disregard is shown for what God, in fact, wills for human life.

Thesis 6: *The defense that Jesus makes of human life as a fundamental mediation of the reality of God causes others—generally the leaders of* *the Jewish people, who, objectively, invoke other divinities—to reproach and persecute him, the mediator. Alternative divinities, reflected in the plurality of mediations, are also clearly reflected in the wish for alternative mediators.*

As we have observed, Jesus' anathemas, controversies, and exposés have an objective purpose: to elucidate the true reality of God and God's defense of human life. However, it is both natural and understandable that the objective controversy also becomes a subjective controversy—in other words, that personal attacks and, in this instance, the persecution of Jesus ensue. The attack on him increasingly assumes the features of an exclusionary alternative. The persecution of Jesus aims at eliminating him.

The Synoptic Gospels

The dimension of basic alternatives runs through the synoptic gospels in various forms. I cannot analyze it in full here, but can only enumerate some of its formulations as prototypes. On the anthropological level, it is affirmed in the Beatitudes and the denunciations (Luke 6:20–26) and in the words on saving and losing life (Mark 8:35 and parallels). On the christological level, it is asserted that one must be with Jesus or against him (Matt. 12:30). On the level of divinity—the most important one for our purposes—the alternative is expressed clearly: "No servant can be slave to two masters; for either he will hate the first and love the second, or he will be devoted to the first and think nothing of the second. You cannot serve God and Money" (Matt. 6:24; Luke 16:13).

Jesus probably did not present that alternative in all its radical essence at the outset, although in the programmed announcement of the kingdom, belief in the good news is linked with repentance (Mark 1:15; Matt. 4:17). But the depth and radical essence of the alternative at stake—the fact that human beings simply do not accept God and that they manipulate God in order to serve another god—is disclosed gradually.

Jesus' determination to present God as an alternative, and an exclusive alternative, becomes intensified concurrently with the fate that he himself experiences upon announcing the true God who cherishes human life. It has been rightly claimed that *temptation* was the atmosphere in which all of Jesus' life took place and that it related to true messianism—that is, to the true will of God concerning him.[45] But it is also a fact that *persecution* was the atmosphere in which his mission took place, at least as of a certain date. Although it is difficult to determine the various periods of Jesus' life exactly,[46] "the gospels are faithful to history when they state that successes and failure, sympathy and hostility, were the fabric of Jesus' life from the beginning."[47]

From his preaching and healing ministry, Jesus embarked on controversies, something that he did not seek out in the first stage of his mission.[48] His interpretation of the will of God, his closeness to those officially rejected by society, and his forgiveness of sins made him suspect. His extraordinary healing powers evoked a clear expression of that suspicion, explicitly on the theological level: "If his critics were not willing to admit that the 'finger of God' was evident here, then there was only one alternative remaining for them. . . . Hence the conclusion: 'He casts out devils by Beelzebub, prince of devils'; in other words, he was a sorcerer."[49] This is the fundamental issue: whether or not the finger of God is present in the divinity mediation represented by Jesus. Because the leaders of the people did not believe in the mediation, they therefore persecuted the mediator.

A brief summary of the provocation and persecution of Jesus, to the time of Judas's betrayal, will be helpful to our purposes. Luke puts the first serious attack against Jesus nearly at the beginning of his mission in Nazareth, when he refused to repeat the wonders that he had worked in Capernaum. The conclusion of the passage tells us that his infuriated fellow townspeople threw him out of the town and tried to hurl him over a cliff (Luke 4:28ff.).

This local controversy was compounded from nearly the beginning of the gospel by persecution, not because of village issues, but because of Jesus' interpretation of the will of God. After the fifth controversy in Mark, when Jesus cured the man with the withered hand on the Sabbath, the Pharisees conspired with the Herodians to find a way to eliminate him (Mark 3:6 and parallels). They were already lying in wait to see whether he would work cures on the Sabbath so that they could bring charges against him (Mark 3:2 and parallels).

During the period preceding his entry into Jerusalem, it is evident that many of the questions directed at him by the scribes and Pharisees were designed to tempt him, to put him to the test. They hoped to seize upon some remark out of which they could make an accusation against him (Matt. 19:3; Luke 10:25, 11:16, 53–54, 14:1). In Luke 13:31, the Pharisees themselves warn Jesus that Herod wants to kill him—although their intention was perhaps just to have Jesus leave the place.

Once he was in Jerusalem, and even before Judas's betrayal, it is obvious that the malicious plots against Jesus were mounting, and that the leaders wanted to put an end to him. All three synoptic gospels present five scenes in which Jesus is in danger. In the passage concerning the tribute to Caesar (Mark 12:13–17, and parallels), the Pharisees and Herodians are sent to "trap him with a question." In the passage on the discussion about the resurrection of the dead (Mark 12:19–23 and elsewhere), the Sadducees try to discredit him. The passage on the expulsion of the money lenders from the temple (Mark 11:15–19 and parallels) concludes with the deliberations of the high priests and scribes to kill him, although they feared the people. The passage from the parable on the murderous vintners (Mark 12:1–12 and parallels) also concludes with the intention to arrest him because the chief priests and others realized that the parable was aimed against them; but they were afraid of the people. Finally Matthew and Mark, who introduce into this scene (Mark 12:28–34; Matt. 22:34–35) the discussion of the first commandment, also present the incident as an insidious temptation of Jesus by the Pharisees. All these passages conclude with a summary, preceding Judas's betrayal: "The chief priests and the doctors of the law were trying to devise some cunning plan to seize him and put him to death" (Mark 14:1 and parallels).

St. John's Gospel

I shall now summarize what St. John's Gospel contributes to the understanding of the persecution of Jesus throughout his public life, noting that, for theological reasons, John makes the Jewish people as a whole responsible for it, and not merely their leaders, as the synoptics gospels do.

From the beginning of his first stay in Jerusalem, Jesus distrusted "the Jews" (2:24). During his second stay in Jerusalem, "it was works of this kind done on the Sabbath that stirred the Jews to persecute Jesus. . . . This made the Jews still more determined to kill him, because he was not only breaking the Sabbath, but, by calling God his own Father, he claimed equality with God" (5:16, 18). When the Feast of Tabernacles was approaching, "Jesus went about in Galilee. He wished to avoid Judea because the Jews were looking for a chance to kill him" (7:1). They were asking, "Where is he?" (7:11). And, in the temple, Jesus asked them, "Why are you trying to kill me?" (7:19). Some Jerusalemites remarked, "Is not this the man they want to put to death?" (7:25). "At this they tried to seize him, but no one laid a hand on him because his appointed hour had not yet come" (7:30). "The Pharisees overheard these mutterings of the people about him, so [they] sent temple police to arrest him" (7:44).

In another discussion with the Pharisees, Jesus was teaching in the temple, "Yet no one arrested him, because his hour had not yet come" (8:20). At the end of this discourse, "They picked up stones to throw at him, but Jesus was not to be seen; and he left the temple" (8:59). The parents of the blind man cured by Jesus were afraid to speak, "because they were afraid of the Jews; for the Jewish authorities had already agreed that anyone who acknowledged Jesus as Messiah should be banned from the synagogue" (9:22). At the end of his discourse at the Festival of the Dedication, "Once again the Jews picked up stones to stone him" (10:31), and his reasoning "provoked them to make one more attempt to seize him. But he escaped from their clutches" (10:39). On the way to Bethany, to visit Lazarus' family, his disciples said, "Rabbi, it is not long since the Jews there were wanting to stone you. Are you going there again?" (11:8). After the resurrection of Lazarus, many Jews believed in him; the Pharisees met with the Council and Caiaphas and "from that day on they plotted his death" (11:53). At the last Passover feast, "the chief priests and the Pharisees had given orders that anyone who knew where he was should give information, so that they might arrest him" (11:57).

This brief review of the synoptic gospels and of St. John's Gospel demonstrates, although not in every detail, that, historically, persecution followed

Jesus throughout his life and mission. It certainly serves to prove that his final persecution and death were not fortuitous.

But, more important still, it highlights the objective theological background of the persecution, although the reasoning has been theologized by the evangelists in the light of subsequent reflection. Jesus was persecuted for reasons that have been made theologically explicit in the strict sense: for his position regarding the Sabbath and for the relationship he claimed with God (particularly in John). The persecution itself contains a deep theological symbolism. In Luke, the first attack occurs in the synagogue. In John, the heaviest attacks occur in the temple. The fact that Jesus is driven out of the synagogue and out of the temple is a symbolic expression of excommunication and of Jesus' nonacceptance by the prevailing religion. Persecution leads to exclusion from the places most closely associated with God's presence.

The essential datum is that divinities are battling; their different mediations are battling; and hence their mediators, too, are battling. Whereas Jesus' controversies point out the fact of alternative divinities, the persecution of Jesus seeks the exclusionary alternative. The false divinities and their mediators want to exclude, and eliminate, the mediator of the true divinity.

Thesis 7: *The politico-religious trial of Jesus clearly demarcates alternative divinities: either the kingdom of God, on the one hand, or the Jewish theocracy, or Pax Romana, on the other. The divinities that are not the Father of Jesus are not only false, but lethal. The mediator of the true God is killed in the name of the false divinities.*

Jesus was violently deprived of life, as is seen in the formulations of the original kerygma, both in their historical versions (see Thesis 9) and in their theologized versions (Acts 2:23, 3:13-15, 4:10, 5:30, 10:39, in Peter's discourses, and Acts 13:28, in a discourse of Paul). The fact that in these texts the Jews are held responsible for Jesus' death and their blame is emphasized—because the initial Christian polemic took place in Jerusalem—does not detract from the underlying truth. Jesus was a victim of the oppression he had preached against, and a victim of the most acute form of oppression—death.

Granted the historical fact of his death, an analysis must be made of the theological context of that death. We are not dealing here with soteriological significance that believers subsequently ascribed to that death after the resurrection, but rather with what is discovered about God from the fact that Jesus was executed. The first thing that is discovered is that he was killed "in the name of God," he was killed by those who invoked God in what they were doing. This appears indirectly in the trial before Pilate, and explicitly in the trial before the Sanhedrin.

The tendency in the synoptic gospels, especially Luke, is to ascribe the ultimate blame for Jesus' death to the Jews and their leaders, not to Pilate.[50] Nevertheless, Jesus died on the cross as a political criminal, and by the type of death that only the Romans, the political authority, could enjoin. Passing over details that are not pertinent here, the important thing is to consider the type of charge that made conviction by Pilate likely. What is historically most probable is the account in Luke 23:2 and John 19:12–15.[51] Jesus was accused of inciting to rebellion and of not paying tribute to Caesar. The historical aspect of these charges may be related to the uprising mentioned in Mark 15:7, in which the Jews may have wanted to implicate Jesus.[52] Or, more generally, the Jews "might have stressed how politically dangerous the apocalyptic impulses in Jesus' preaching were."[53]

Although the first charge—that of subversion—lacks historical grounds, the insinuation that Jesus' action ran counter to the political interests of Rome is coherent, even though Jesus himself may not have sought it directly. In fact, as is noted in the gospel accounts, Pilate did not decide to convict him on the basis of participation in the uprising, as a concrete, isolated event, because he found no evidence for that. What prompted him to convict Jesus was the alternative presented in John 19:12: either Jesus or Caesar. Not isolated matters, but symbolic totalities, are involved here. "It may be said that Jesus was crucified by the Romans not only for tactical reasons and reasons based on the standard policy of calm and order in Jerusalem, but essentially in the name of the gods of the Roman state, that guaranteed the Pax Romana."[54]

In the trial before Pilate, the alternative of two persons, two mediators— Jesus and Pilate—appears directly. In the realm of "persons" there is very little logic in the trial, and Pilate wants to release Jesus. But if one moves from mediators to mediations, then one understands the conclusion of the trial: Jesus' condemnation to death. For the alternative was between the kingdom of God and the Roman empire, and these two sociopolitical totalities invoked different gods: the Father of Jesus, and the Roman gods. So Jesus died, not because of a mistake by Pilate, but because of the logic of the divinities of death, of oppression. The ultimate reason for which he could be sent to his death, without denying his personal innocence, is the invocation of the divinity of Caesar. Death could be imposed in the name of that divinity.

That Jesus died in the name of a divinity appears more explicitly in the religious trial, owing to the very nature of the matter at issue. It lends itself to a more theological formulation of Jesus' conflict. There has been a great deal of discussion about historical aspects of the trial.[55] For our purposes, it will suffice to note that at the Festival of the Dedication, as described in John 10:22–39, a clear-cut religious conflict appears between Jesus and the Jews. The interrogation before the chief priest (John 18:19–24) may have been a private interrogation. And the meeting of the Sanhedrin may have taken place the morning after the arrest of Jesus for the purpose of preparing the charges before Pilate, who could have him executed. Hence, the synoptic traditions may have wanted to historicize the cause of Jesus' death: "the increasing hostility of the Jewish leaders (especially the chief priests), which, in John, reaches its high point at the Festival of the Dedication."[56]

This historicizing is done in such a way that the death alternative was posed between the chief priests and Jesus. It is stressed that they wanted an "allegation . . . on which a death-sentence could be based" (Matt. 26:59; Mark

14:55), and the conclusion was that "he should die" (Matt. 26:66; Mark 14:64). Important for our purposes are the accusations that created a logic calling for his death. According to John, the interrogation before Annas related to the teachings of Jesus and his disciples (John 18:19). But in the accusation before the Sanhedrin it related to two key points concerning Jesus as a mediator and the mediation of the God of Jesus. The cause of the conviction appears in the charge that Jesus has blasphemed by declaring himself the Christ (Matt. 26:64; Mark 14:62; Luke 22:67; John 10:24). But, in addition to this cause, which probably comes from redactional sources, we must consider the other cause, which relates not so much to Jesus' claims about himself, as to the claims of a new mediation of God, and not only new, but different and contrary: the temple (Matt. 26:61; Mark 14:58; John 2:19). Only by understanding what the temple meant in the religious, political, and economic spheres[57] can one understand the totality that Jesus offers as an alternative to the temple. Jesus offers not a change in, but an alternative to, the temple. The destruction of the temple implies the surpassing of the law, as the leaders of the people interpreted it, and even as it appeared in some of the prophetic and apocalyptic traditions; and it implies no longer making the temple the center of a political, social, and economic theocracy.[58]

Therefore, Jesus—and here we are not treating more strictly christological considerations of his own person—is the mediator of a mediation of God that is in opposition to the concrete mediations included in the practical understanding of the religion of his time. And the divinity on whose name the temple is based is what brings Jesus to death. The editorial adjunct in Matthew 26:63 demonstrates this symbolically. The chief priest "charges him by the living God," in order to be able to send Jesus to his death—even though that decision had already been made. Jesus dies at the hands of false divinities, and they are explicitly invoked for his death, even though, ironically, it is the living God who is named.

Hence, the deepest significance of both trials will not be discovered by considering them as a confrontation between persons, between Pilate and Jesus, between the chief priest and Jesus—in other words, between what we have termed *mediators*. The deeper significance lies in the *mediations* of the true divinity—mediations that are in conflict. And these mediations are associated with the life and death of human beings. What appears in the trials is the *total* character of the alternative mediations. It involves the Pax Romana and a theocracy based on the temple, on the one hand, and the kingdom of God on the other. Hence it involves totalities of life and history, ultimately based on and justified by a certain understanding of God. As a result of the invocation of the divinities, Jesus was killed. This is the underlying fact that reveals Jesus' historical destiny: the divinities are at odds, and from them life or death results.

What appears in the trials at the end of his life is only the logical conclusion of what his life had been. "His death cannot be understood without his life, and his life cannot be understood without the one for whom he lived—that is, his God and Father—and without what he lived for—that is, the gospel of the kingdom of the poor."[59]

What we have said about Jesus' death, therefore, harks back to his life and its theo-logical dimension, which is expressed in the interaction of an "invocation of God" and "service to the kingdom of God." What is typical of Jesus' invocation of God cannot be formulated and handed down over the centuries. He adopts an action pattern in which decisions are made on concrete and real-life matters, in a way that is distinct and viable in the given milieu. The newness of the God of Jesus does not lie in the formulation of Jesus' invocations, or even in the invocation "Father," but rather, "it is in action that Jesus wills that the invocation of the Father is to achieve a new form."[60]

When the image of God is studied in the activity of Jesus, his doctrine on God can be outlined in terms of the divine mediations that Jesus came to serve. And it is from within that service that he invoked God. This is why God appeared so conflictual to him, demanding the choice of an alternative. "Jesus does not say that God is the Father, which would not have been original; but he says that God is the destroyer of all oppression, including that inflicted by religion, and that I invoke God as the Father in his leveling of concrete instances of oppression."[61] This is why the different concepts of God symbolically present in the death-sentence scenes appear in their concrete reality in his confrontation with the most diverse of parties and factions.

If Jesus' death had its causes in his concrete life, then conflict and adherence to an alternative must also be sought there. Hence, putting aside all pietistic or merely symbolic qualities, his life cannot be understood apart from "the battle between God and the gods—that is, between the God whom Jesus preached as his Father and the god of the law, as interpreted by the guardians of the law, and the political gods of the Roman occupation forces."[62]

THE MEANING OF GOD TO JESUS

The paschal mystery throws light on the divinity alternative. The gods of oppression kill Jesus and the true God resurrects him, restores him to life—to life in abundance. But this, of course, is grasped only by those who, after the life of Jesus, believe in him. Jesus' historical life ended with the paradox that the one who defends the God of life dies, and yet Jesus was faithful to that God to the end.

What I should like to consider briefly now is the importance to Jesus during his life of the reality of God, not only the conviction that God is a God of life, but also the importance of the fact that Jesus invoked God, explaining his life in relationship to God—to put it briefly, Jesus' understanding of God, and what experiences he converted into mediations of the experience of God.

In order to clarify this point, we must retrieve a concept that has understandably been neglected because of its frequent manipulation, but is necessary in order to penetrate to the ultimate origin of Jesus' life: "mystery."[63] From what has been said earlier, the reader will readily understand that to turn to mystery now does not mean to abandon history, or to search out a place parallel to the historical process, or much less to turn away from the historical process. To refer to mystery means to refer to the ultimate quality of life and, in its ultimacy, to refer to God as the one who makes life something ultimate, not something temporary.[64]

The fact that life is something ultimate is evident to Jesus when it is seen as the mediation of God, something that is holy and that must not be manipulated, something that must be served and not used for one's own service, something that is the gift most radically given and yet most authentically one's own, something that is most concrete and real, and yet, to be properly understood, can be conceived only as open and limitless.

Life appears to Jesus as something that is given and is to be given: as a gift and a task. In this way, Jesus elaborates a notion of God in association with life, and an experience of God in association with the giving of life—in the end, with the giving of one's own life.[65]

In what follows, I shall summarize briefly and systematically what appears to be the core of Jesus' vision and experience of God—that is, what is really a mystery to Jesus, and how that mystery affected his life.[66]

Thesis 8: *To Jesus, the ultimate mystery of life transcends concrete life. God is always greater because the reality of God is—precisely—love. God is at the same time lesser because hidden in smallness and poverty. God's yes to the poor and no to poverty, the result of sin makes it intrinsically possible for Jesus' understanding of God to carry transcendence within itself.*

When Jesus inherited the various traditions concerning God from the Old Testament, he also inherited the various notions of the transcendence of God, explained in different ways in the exodist, prophetic, sapiential, and apocalyptic traditions. God is greater than nature and history, although Jesus does not use the systematic terms employed here. God is the creator (Mark 10:6, 13:19) and sovereign (Matt. 19:23–25, 10:28). The human being is God's servant (Luke 17:7–10; Matt. 6:24; Luke 16:13). God is incomprehensible (Matt. 11:25), and to God all things are possible (Matt. 19:26).

These are only examples of how Jesus formulated the transcendence of God. But the most typical aspect of Jesus' understanding of God is that God is greater because God is love and that this greater love of God is also partial— that is, it takes sides. Although it has been reiterated so often, we must remember that, unlike other religious teachers of his time, Jesus announced the coming of God's kingdom in grace, not in vengeful justice. God comes to save and to give life, not to take it away. The fact of God's being greater appears especially when the impossibility of life ceases to be impossible. In this regard, although it was not typical of Jesus to call God "Father,"[67] that Jesus does so does not betoken only his special relationship with God, but also the love-charged essence of Jesus' understanding of God. And hence, although it may not be new from a historical standpoint, Jesus' concentration on love as a form of relating to God is, indeed, of paramount importance.[68]

The fact of God's being greater is shown to Jesus in God's loving intentions for the world, but the historical and credible reality of that love appears to him in God's partiality toward the lowly. To Jesus, God is love because God loves those for whom no one else loves, because God is concerned about those for whom no one else has any concern. The previously quoted passages from the prophetic traditions—showing that God comes to the defense of the weak—the declaration of the poor as the privileged members of the kingdom to come, and Luke's moving parables on the forgiveness of sinners show how Jesus understood that God is love.

Jesus had the inner conviction that love exists in the ultimate depths of reality, that it is in relation to that love that human beings truly live, and that their life is truly life when they give life to others, when they love them. In this core of love, Jesus sees the reality of God, and from this core he judges the concrete events of history and views his own future. It is the concrete way that Jesus has (certainly not a conceptual way) of asserting that the reality of God is transcendent.

But, in addition, because the reality of God is seen to be partial toward the poor, love is not greater only on the basis of its own reality, but also in its historical materialization as love for the poor. In fact, if God's preferential love for the poor and the denunciation made by God of the poverty inflicted on the poor are considered together, love appears in the historical tension between yes and no, a tension that, by its own objective nature, generates history. And the history that is generated when one attempts to live according to God's love transcends itself and is therefore a mediation of God's transcendence. Love, therefore, is greater not only on the basis of its own reality, apart from anything else, but also on the basis of the history that it necessarily gives birth to and the history that emerges from it dialectically. Thus, one cannot establish the notion of God as love in an idealistic or scientific manner, but as a notion that, in order to endure as such, must repeatedly arise from the new history of love.[69]

The absolute yes that Jesus gives to love for human beings, and the maintenance of that yes throughout history, even in the presence of the negation of love, is the mediation of the understanding of God as love—a God who becomes manifest as lesser in hiddenness among the lowly and the poor, and who becomes manifest as greater and transcendent in the condemnation of poverty.

Thesis 9: *To that understanding of God there corresponds in Jesus a series of historical experiences that are mediations to him of the God who is greater. Those experiences are of two types: the celebration of what already exists of true life, and the constant search for what is the will of God.*

The understanding of God as a God who is love, and therefore greater, and who is partial to the lowly, is neither idealistic nor merely conceptual or poetic.

That understanding is reflected in Jesus' own experience, as we can infer from his words and his deeds.

When a systematic reconstruction is made of that experience, it is clear that Jesus was utterly convinced that living means living for others and serving others. Thus it corresponds to the reality of his vision of God. His historical service to others appears throughout the gospels, and is summarized in the phrase, "he went about doing good"; or in the famous saying of Bonhoeffer that Jesus is "the man for others." His orientation to the mystery of God certainly makes his life an ex-istence—a life not centered upon itself, but directed to someone else who gives it meaning. Precisely because his orientation is to a particular God, and not to just any divinity, his ex-istence is pro-existence. Existing for others and the conviction that one is thereby related to God is Jesus' fundamental experience.

That pro-existence is what Jesus celebrates and what Jesus seeks and in it are mediations of the experience of God. Jesus' meals with the poor and with sinners and the prayer of thanksgiving because the kingdom has been revealed to the lowly show the historical meaning that emerges in living for others. When that "living for" is converted to "being with" others, then love becomes clear, not only as an ethical requirement of praxis, but also as a reality with meaning and fulfillment, as a mediation of the fact that love is really the ultimate thing and, as such, fulfilling, and hence God's mediation.

There are obscure periods in history beyond which one cannot go at this or that specific time.[70] But, throughout history, one can and should go beyond any particular moment, because one must always search out the true forms of pro-existence. This is a profound experience that Jesus had throughout his life. Jesus' temptations, his ignorance of God's plans, and his prayer seeking God's will are manifestations not only of what is truly human, and hence limited, in his serving experience, but also of the conditions that make possible the experience of God as God.[71]

The fact that Jesus' life is marked not only by the decision to serve others, and thus relate to God, but is also marked by *how* to serve, is the manifestation of a radical orientation toward what is absolute, a radical attitude of respect for, and nonmanipulation of, what is ultimate. Although it still sounds rather shocking to some christologies, the fact of not possessing God is what causes Jesus to really possess God, to the extent to which this can be done in history. The fact that Jesus went through different theo-logical phases during his life; the fact that he went through a "conversion" process, not as a choice between good and evil, but as a choice between the good that must be done and the manner in which it must be done; the fact that Jesus did not know everything and that, not knowing, he sought how to know so as to serve better and sought to serve so as to know better—all of this shows that Jesus' experience of God was not one of definitive possession, but one of a search whereby he allowed God to be God far more effectively than through mere verbal declarations of God's transcendence.

Thesis 10: *To Jesus, accepting the mystery of God means treasuring it throughout his life, never manipulating it. His experience of God is radically historical. His faith grows into fidelity.*

Jesus, like many others, has the fundamental experience of the truth that one relates to the God of life by giving life to others, and this happens historically when he gives his own life. Like many others, he also has the fundamental experience of the truth that often life does not seem to flourish for the one who fosters it and even goes badly for that person. In other words, Jesus experiences the truth that sin appears to have more force than does love.

From a strictly theo-logical standpoint, this truth appears in all its harshness in the death on the cross. From that God whom he called Father, whose closeness was so real to him, and whose coming he expected soon, Jesus heard only silence.[72] The God of life abandoned him to the death of his physical person, certainly, and apparently abandoned his cause as well.

The vacuous atmosphere in which the final phase of his life took place is unmistakable, although his last entry into Jerusalem may have revived his hopes. The important thing to note is that Jesus did not succumb to the temptation that might seem inevitable to us in such a situation, nor did he seek a logic for his experience of God that would preclude or soften the tragedy. Jesus did not succumb to resignation, skepticism, or cynicism, which would have been understandable attitudes toward the historical failure of the praxis of love. Nor did he assume the attitude of "eat, drink, and be merry, for tomorrow we die," or its Epicurean version, or the more subtle one of finding meaning for one's own life (including the suffering in it and death) in dissociation from the meaning of life for others. The problem for Jesus did not consist in the fact that his death might not have the meaning of a martyr's death, but rather in the noninauguration of the kingdom of God.[73]

In this situation, it would be understandable if Jesus abandoned the concept of the God of life. But Jesus kept it to the end. His faith in the mystery of God became fidelity to that mystery. Described in human terms and from a negative point of view, Jesus gave signs that he could not be or act any other way. Although injustice triumphed, he was faithful to the practice of love; although the kingdom of God did not arrive, he retained his hope.

To be sure, it is difficult, if not impossible, for us to know what Jesus' concrete experience was, especially at the end of his life. However, the first Christian theologians were successful in working out the fundamental structure of his theological experience. The author of the Letter to the Hebrews is perhaps the one who best reproduced it.

Jesus' entire life is described in terms of dedication to the life of human beings. Jesus "stands for us all" (Heb. 2:9), giving us deliverance (2:10). He carries out that program of life historically, by "learning obedience" (5:8), experiencing contradiction (12:3), with prayers and supplication, and with a great outcry and tears to the one who could save him from death (5:7). Jesus remains faithful to that task, despite the contradictions. Hence he is described as one who lived the faith originally and fully (12:2) and as the faithful witness to the one who appointed him (3:2).

Hebrews admirably summarizes how Jesus exercised historical fidelity from within history to the praxis of love for human beings and fidelity to the mystery of God. His fidelity to history makes his fidelity to God credible; and his fidelity to God, to the one who appointed him, engenders his fidelity to history, to living "on behalf of others." Jesus is faithful to the deep conviction that the mystery of and for human life is really what is ultimate and what cannot be brought into question, despite all contrary appearances. He knows that herein lies the mediation of God and that God can be invoked from within its course. He also knows that when that invocation really is to God, it is so radical that one must remain faithful to life even in the presence of death and against death.

Divine Radicalization of the Historical

In the New Testament, of course, Jesus' experience of God is not expressed against the background of atheism, taken literally; it is expressed objectively against the background of idolatry. Hence, what I have said about the meaning of God to Jesus does not demonstrate the existence of God to secularized milieux. I have merely sought to point out that the radical life and praxis of Jesus are based on his radical conviction that at the heart of created reality there is something ultimate, which is for the sake of human beings, and that it must be maintained at any cost. In this sense, God, for Jesus, is not *added* to historical life, much less opposed to historical life. Jesus invokes God to radicalize what is historical and to maintain what the realm of history discloses about an inexhaustible mystery that cannot be manipulated.

In essence, Jesus, in his reality as a human being, does not define or demarcate God, nor does he make God comprehensible either to himself or to us. But neither does he allow history to be incomprehensible and life a total mystery. To Jesus, "allowing God to be God" essentially lacks a verifiable meaning. But to Jesus, not allowing God to be God, in the most crass or in the most subtle way, is the fundamental failure because it entails manipulation, impoverishment, ignorance, and the suppression of life. The ultimate mystery is the guarantee of the integrity of the penultimate. Even though daily life and history, bereft of ultimate mystery, may *conceptually* (in an atheistic ideology) attain a radical quality, they lose it from a practical, historical standpoint. When human beings set themselves up as absolute judges of the ultimate, they dehumanize other human beings.

At the beginning of this essay it was clear that for Jesus there could be no *gloria Dei* without *vivens homo*. I now wish to point out that no *vivens homo* can exist without *gloria Dei*. According to Jesus, the human being is humanized more and better with God than without God, although there is always the temptation to create divinities in order to dehumanize the human being. With a God who, in the beginning, established the criteria of being human, who offers a future to all humankind, who holds human beings responsible for history, who keeps silence on the cross so that we humans will not manipulate what is absurd, tragic, and failed in existence, and who denounces any type of oppression of humans by their fellow human beings—with this God, Jesus believes that the humanization of human beings and of history is not only better explained but better assured than without this God.[74] And, although these comments may seem banal, I cannot find a better way of asserting the importance of seeking the glory of God so that humans may truly live.

This is, briefly and systematically described, the meaning of God to Jesus. What Jesus offers us are not formulations of the reality of God, or even the formulation of "Father," but rather the structure for relating to the ultimate mystery, a relationship formulated as "affiliation."

The Letter to the Hebrews asserts this clearly. Jesus remained faithful to the one who appointed him (3:2); and he did so "as a son, set over his household" (3:6). The letter goes on to say that "we are that household of his" (3:6), not once and for all, or in a merely declaratory manner, but rather with the clearly understood condition that our history enter into the complexity that we have previously described, and with fidelity to the history that is lived in accordance with the mystery of God: "if only we are fearless and keep our hope high" (3:6).

PART III

JESUS AND THE CHRISTIAN LIFE

5

Following Jesus as Discernment

By Christian discernment I understand the particular quest for the will of God, not only to understand it but also to carry it out. Discernment is therefore to be understood not only literally but as a process in which the will of God carried out verifies the will of God thought.

I shall develop the theme from the basis of christology since traditional ecclesiology does not seem to offer an adequate response to the radical challenge posed to Christian life conceived as discernment in the sense I have applied it. While the traditional structures of ecclesial existence seemed to offer a sufficiently Christian channel for the will of God to be known and practiced on the basis of the inertia of living in this channel, the present-day church—at least in many parts of the world—is looking for a real incarnation and particular mediations of Christian life that cannot be deduced from the inertia of the old structures. The urgency of the task requires not vague determinations of what is good or bad but the quest for the particular act that truth requires to be performed. Insistence on the eschatological reserve, which is necessary in its way, is not sufficient to incarnate the Christian in the world today; it has its dangerous side, since the problem of discernment does not end with de-absolutizing the particular historical context, but in meeting the particular context of what has to be done according to Paul's requirement of a love that moves us on.

This setting of the question means that we have to overcome the simply ethical understanding of Christianity based on doing good and avoiding evil and progress to a serious theological questioning of the meaning of the Christian task. With the problem posed in this way, the sense of the title of this chapter should be clear, although on this point—as on other points—many christologies have not made it so. If being Christian means becoming sons and

This article originally appeared in *Discernment of the Spirit and of Spirits*, edited by Casiano Floristán and Christian Duquoc (*Concilium*, vol. 119 [1978]:14–24, New York: Seabury Press). Paul Burns translated the article for *Concilium*. The text has been edited for inclusion in the present volume.

daughters in the Son, then Christian discernment must have a structure similar to the discernment of Jesus, which can only be achieved by following him. The only thing that needs clarification and not presupposition is in what Jesus' discernment consisted, so that our following of him can be discernment in truth.

The title of the chapter would not be clear, however, if it implied a mechanical imitation of the process Jesus went through, since this—besides being impossible—would be a denial of the need for discernment at the present time. This is the moment to call on the Spirit of Jesus in whom we have to carry on our discernment. The only thing that needs clarifying is that this Spirit should be in truth the Spirit of Jesus, and not presupposed as already existing institutionalized in ecclesial structures or spontaneously in the various versions of pentecostalism and the charismatic movement. This has to be verified starting from Jesus, not declared a priori as the possession of an institution or a gift to particular groups. If we pose the problem of Christian discernment in the tension between the history of Jesus and the history unfolded by his Spirit, we shall not be able to offer simple recipes even starting from Jesus. What I am trying to put forward is the *structure* of Jesus' discernment, which should be re-created throughout history according to the Spirit of Jesus. This can only be done by starting from a trinitarian reality as opposed to a mere concept of the trinity.

THE FATHER OF JESUS AS REQUIREMENT AND POSSIBILITY OF DISCERNMENT FOR JESUS

Speaking of the trinitarian reality which Christian discernment requires means approaching it from the real history of Jesus.[1] In this sense, the first and basic statement to be made is that not just any understanding of the divinity requires us to discern in order to "correspond" to it. If the Father of Jesus had been the pure rationality of creation or its intrinsic morality, an absolute hypostasized as reason, power, or love, then Jesus would not have needed to discern. For Jesus, discerning the will of God meant at first simply and precisely clarifying for himself who God really is. This process of clarification gradually made clear to Jesus both the reality of God and the need to discern. We can call this first relationship between Jesus and God the first discernment on the basis of which the structure and contents of his particular discernments will become understandable.

We know, because we can deduce it from the gospels, that Jesus began his activity with the consciousness of a Jew who had received the best traditions concerning God, stemming from the history of his people. Jesus appeared to sum up these traditions in the tradition that called God the God of the kingdom, and it was to be in the quest for the particular will of God concerning this kingdom that God was to appear to him in the first place as an *always greater God*.

In his proclamation and inauguration of the kingdom of God, Jesus came to realize that the received tradition, including that of the will of God as expressed in the Old Testament, is neither absolute nor definitive. Despite his previous knowledge of God, Jesus came to feel that no tradition of God nor any of the possible structures of the kingdom were final and definitive, providing an unequivocal channel for finding the will of God. The temptations in the desert, the crisis in Galilee, the prayer in the garden and his death on the cross, all provide examples of this growing experience in discernment.

Jesus always saw the need to examine the will of God concerning the kingdom and indirectly concerning himself—a will that went beyond the limits of what was already known as good and was posited as something particular and new that he had to be and to do. From this point of view, the story of the temptations of Jesus, to which the evangelists attached so much importance, is nothing but the story of the dialogue between Jesus and his Father on how to do the right thing with his novel and sovereign liberty and in this way also with the very reality of God.

In the history of the real consciousness of Jesus, the God of the Jewish traditions then appeared to him with a formality that Jesus took absolutely seriously: God is always greater. But this transcendence of God does not appear basically in God's distancing the divinity from creation. It appears basically in questioning creation and through creation. The primary need to discern was seen by Jesus along with his discovery of the greater being of God. The objective reality of an always greater God is matched by Jesus' subjective attitude of allowing God to be God. "Discerning" and "the greater God" then become corresponding realities that are clarified in their mutual interaction.[2]

Thus the formality of God appeared to Jesus in God's always being greater. The content of this reality is that God is love and *partial love*. Jesus found the prime setting for discernment in his radical openness to this greater God; this setting is love of us, and in this sense the *greater* God appears as the *lesser* God. While the sovereign will of God would seem on principle to admit all natural and historical mediations, the setting for discernment became particularized for Jesus in love of his neighbor. The classic passages in which Jesus' discerning consciousness are embodied are: the Sabbath is made for the human being; the commandment of love for one's neighbor: no one has greater love than the one who lays down one's life for one's friend. All have to be read from this theological and not merely ethical perspective. This provides a surprising "making himself lesser" by God—a surprisingly "lessened" mediation of the primary will of God through love of one's neighbor.[3]

This appearance of the will of God in small things becomes even clearer to Jesus when the mediation of love appears partial and consciously partialized. The first setting for acting in accordance with the will of God is the service of love to the poor, the little, the oppressed. They are the privileged face of God in history and they are those who understand the kingdom. This is why they are, without doubt, the primary and irreplaceable setting for finding the will of God.

These simple observations—which obviously need development in all their complexity—are intended to show that for Jesus the problem of the first and basic discernment was simply the quest for the very reality of God and the place where this quest could mean finding God. Jesus' particular discernments came, then, at least logically after this one great discernment, although historically this first discernment went on developing through all the particular choices he made. This observation seems important if we are not to make the discernment of Jesus and our own discernment a matter of regional theology, a mere spiritual theology or religious psychology; since however simple it seems, what has been said here underlies all Christian discernment: the genuineness of particular discernments will arise from the conviction, not from routine repetition of the fact, that God is greater, and partial love.

So the original experience that Jesus had of God has to be taken in complete seriousness. This experience has recently been summarized as "God is always greater (and, if one likes, is by virtue of this fact also lesser) than culture, science, the Church, the Pope and everything institutional" (Karl Rahner); and, "the question is not whether someone is looking for God or not, but whether he is looking for him where he himself said he was" (Porfirio Miranda).

THE DISCERNMENT OF JESUS AS A PROTOTYPE OF THE STRUCTURE OF EVERY CHRISTIAN DISCERNMENT

Before analyzing the structure of the discernment of Jesus, I should like to make two preliminary observations. The first is that the title of this section is properly a statement of christological faith. Accepting that the discernment of Jesus provides the *prototype* of every Christian discernment is a reformulation of christological orthodoxy that cannot be analyzed further. It is another way of stating the finalness of Jesus as the believer by antonomasia, "he who has lived the faith in fullness and from the beginning" (Heb. 12:2), in whom the basic way of corresponding to God is revealed. The second observation is that I am concentrating on the *structure* of the discernment of Jesus, which is what we should in fact pursue, while the particular solutions to our discernments cannot and should not be identical to those of Jesus. From Jesus we learn not so much the solutions to our discernments as, more basically, how to learn to discern. We learn this not so much by analyzing the internal psychology of Jesus in his process of discernment, but on the basis of the choices and historical commitments that Jesus made. This *effected* discernment of Jesus supposes a *channel* of discernment that is the one we should pursue ourselves.

If we turn now to analyzing the particular structure of Jesus' discernment, we can say that along with his first appreciation of a God who is partial love for the poor, Jesus saw the love of God unconditionally placed between a "yes" and a "no." The unconditional "no" was directed at sin against the kingdom of God: that is, against everything that dehumanizes human beings, that brings them death as human beings that threatens, impedes, or annuls the human communion of sisters and brothers expressed in the *Our* Father. However difficult it may seem to discern what has to be done in particular situations, there was at least a clear criterion of discernment for Jesus. "The will of God is not a mystery, at least insofar as it applies to the brother and concerns love."[4] The first step toward discernment is therefore hearing the clear "no" given by God to the world of sin that dehumanizes human beings and has nothing mysterious about it, and above all, *carrying on* this "no" throughout history without trying to stifle or soften this voice in any way whatsoever, not even—as is frequently done—with apparently orthodox theodicies. The second corresponding step is hearing God's "yes" to a world that has to be reconciled, and above all, *carrying on* the Utopia of this "yes" as a task never to be abandoned even when history questions it in a radical way. We shall therefore be exercising discernment as long as we keep this consciousness alive and do not give way to the skepticisms, realisms, and even cynicisms that history offers us as more sensible solutions; we shall exercise discernment by remaining radically open to the praxis of love and the overcoming of sin objectivized in history. It is therefore not so much a question of purifying our *intention* with regard to love, nor of reconciling the sinner in his or her *innerness*. Even though this is also necessary, Jesus' discernment was directed primarily to corresponding to the objectivity *in* history of God's "yes" and "no" *to* history.

The history of Jesus provides us a posteriori with criteria for a praxis of love that discerns which praxis and criteria should become for us the channel along which we should discern in our turn. The first criterion is *partial incarnation* in history.

For Jesus becoming incarnate did not mean setting himself in the totality of history so as to correspond to the totality of God from there; it meant rather choosing that particular spot in history that was capable of leading him to the totality of God. This spot is none other than the poor and the oppressed. Conscious of this partiality, which reached him as an alternative to other partialities based on power, or to an innocuous universalism that always means collaboration with power, Jesus from the beginning understood his mission as addressed to the poor; he unfolded his incarnation historically in solidarity with the poor and in the parable of the final judgment—declared the poor and the oppressed to be the setting from which the praxis of love can be discerned.

The second criterion is an *effective praxis* of love. Jesus sought the will of God by seeking particular and effective solutions. Jesus sought not only to announce good news but to bring it about. He sought to convert the *good news* into a *good reality*. The whole of his public life, his miracles, his forgiveness, his controversies, bear witness to this, and an important part of the effectiveness he sought consisted in giving particular historical names to what constitutes sin and what constitutes love. Although Jesus obviously lacked modern techniques of analysis deriving from the social sciences, the gospels show his definite tendency to call things by their name. His giving particular names to the sin of the rich, the powerful, the priests and the governors, or his telling, for example, the rich young man what he had to do, are—in rudimentary form—

expressions of the need for particular mediations if love is to be historically effective and transforming.

The third criterion is a *praxis of socio/political love,* that is, a love that becomes justice. Love already extends on principle to any type of relationships created between persons (on the matrimonial, family, friendship, or professional level). The history of Jesus bears clear witness to the fact that the efficacy of love must be applied to the configuration of the whole of society, and the gospels, furthermore, show that, in fact and historically, Jesus gave this type of love the first place in his own praxis. The basic reason for this is that the God of Jesus is the God of the kingdom who seeks to re-create the whole human being and all human beings, and the form of love that we call justice corresponds to this type of social totality. The other forms of love, applying to other areas of human life, will be kept up and will take on new forms from the basis of the justice of the kingdom of God.

The fourth criterion is openness to a *conflictive love* precisely because this love has to be partial, effective, and sociopolitical. Conflict is intrinsic to the love of Jesus from the moment when he conceived his universality from the particular standpoint of the oppressed. While the love of Jesus is *for* all, its particular embodiment was seen by him to be in the first instance *with* the oppressed and *against* the oppressors precisely in order to humanize them all, to make them all brothers and sisters in history and in fact. This intrinsic conflict explains the extrinsic conflict that overtook the practice of Jesus' love in the form of polemic, rejection, persecution, and death, as all of the gospels witness. The *gratuitous* dimension of Jesus' love is also shown historically in this way—a dimension not opposed to efficacy, but one that arises when the power of the world tilts against an effective love and this holds firm even though its efficacy cannot be clearly felt.

This specific praxis of love, with these characteristics, shows the discernment practiced by Jesus in his quest for the will of a God who is "partialized love," and *through* this praxis we can also glimpse some formal characteristics of this discernment that converge with the reality of the greater God.

From this formal point of view, Jesus did not come to exercise his discernment only at a given moment, nor were his momentary judgments the most important, but his discernment had a *historical development.* The fact that God is greater did not come to Jesus from some momentary consideration of God's transcendence, but through the process and praxis of love. This is why his life went through not only different chronological stages but also through different theological stages, and why we should speak of a "conversion" of Jesus, since he did not absolutize or validate forever the particular form of building the kingdom and responding to God that he saw in the first stage of his life. This historicity of Jesus' discernment also includes its openness to risk, to making a choice in darkness, since he knew that it was more dangerous to interrupt this process of discernment than to risk falling into error.

The formality of Jesus' discernment was responsible for presenting his quest for the will of God in a *radical* form precisely because God is greater. One way in which this radicality clearly appears is Jesus' manner of presenting discernment in the form of alternatives rather than as complementary: one cannot serve two masters, one cannot serve both God and mammon, one cannot guide the plough and look behind, one cannot win life and keep it. By presenting the formal structure of discernment in this way, Jesus deprived it of ingenuousness. Discernment is the exercise not of ingenuous good will but of a critical will, one that explicitly recognizes rationalizations even when they are disguised as good in order to achieve what really has to be done. Jesus exercised discernment when faced with alternatives presented as supposedly neutral, or even good—as power, riches, and honor could appear to be. The radical nature of his discernment appears in his unmasking of his other options, which he shows to be not complementary but derogatory of the true reality of God.

The final characteristic of the form taken by Jesus' discernment is its *openness to verification*. One must therefore progress from a good clear conscience before discerning to a good objective conscience after having discerned. Jesus' history and his statements on true discipleship offer some criteria for verifying if this is the case: if discernment ends with a true praxis of the kingdom and not mere orthodox declarations; if this praxis has been produced through sacrifice; if this praxis results in the poor and the oppressed "hearing" the kingdom; if the power of sin has felt truly threatened and has reacted by way of rejection and persecution; if the one who discerns models himself or herself on the ideal of the Sermon on the Mount; if the historical and conflictive struggle to install the kingdom makes Christians pass from their first, generic faith, hope, and charity to a faith that is proof against incredulity, hope that is proof against despair and justice that is proof against oppression. The importance of these observations for the process of discernment is that through objective verification, the setting of discernment is transposed from pure intention to historical objectivity, and that these objective criteria prepare the discerning subject better for successive discernments. The terrifying lucidity of the final "may thy will be done" of Jesus' prayer in the garden was really prepared by the objective verifications of earlier discernments.

DISCERNMENT IN THE SPIRIT OF JESUS

Since his resurrection, Jesus has been present through his Spirit but physically absent; the first Christians began to build the kingdom of God, but this kingdom has not yet reached its fullness; the channel for the following of Jesus has been definitively approved by God, but the Spirit compels us to continue our discernment in history. The dialectical alternatives in these antithetical statements produce an objective difficulty with respect to discernment. The formal solution is clear: "Discernment is required in order to recognize the actions in which this Spirit ought to be manifested ever more mightily. But it does not show a basic way of life."[5] Christology makes it difficult to see what the actual content of this discernment is to be. Christology, like Jesus himself, becomes modest. It offers a way of discernment, not a new law. The elder brother makes way for his brothers and sisters so that they can carry on the building of history according to the ideal of the kingdom of God. Therefore, and on principle, one cannot speak a priori and in the abstract of what discernment should be today, since this would be setting limits to the activity of the Spirit and denying the greater being of God for our own history. So, to end this study I would rather bring forward some meaningful examples of discernment from the church in Latin America, examples that show the novelty of the Spirit moving—as I believe and hope—within the channel that Jesus showed us.

The first discernment, parallel to Jesus' case, is that of the real divinity of God. Faced with a history that shows us a God basically provident in history and eschatological beyond history, we find the truth of this God when God hears the clamor of the oppressed, demands justice, and announces liberation, leaving the ultimate fullness of history to the divine loving mystery. The achievement of this discernment has come about in distinction from and opposition to the idea of God handed on by so-called Western civilization and the culture of Christendom. It has been produced by denying the reality of a God of power, a God who historically is shown to be an oppressor, either subtly, as has often happened through religious and ecclesiastical traditions, or crudely in the image of the divinity hidden in the ruling systems, whether they call themselves Capitalism, National Security, Multinationals or Trilateralism. I believe that this discernment has been achieved by the Spirit placing Christians not at the power center but on the periphery, in poverty.

This brings me to the basic discernment that I see as having been achieved in Latin America: today the Spirit is very much alive in the midst of an oppressed people. In their particular tribulations and desires, we see what the Spirit of Jesus wants here and now, what must undoubtedly be done and what particular sin must be removed, even if it seems as small and particular as that hope expressed in the Old Testament: "They will build houses and live in them, they will plant vines and eat their fruit, they will not build for others to live, they will not plant for others to eat" (Isa. 65:21–22). This Spirit of Jesus and the will of God appear through these hopes and fears however apparently disproportionately small they may be in comparison with the reality of a greater God.

In meeting the Spirit in the poor today, the church is also beginning to become a church of the poor,[6] thereby putting into practice—that is, discerning—what Vatican II stated truly but generically on the subject of the church as the people of God. It will be a church in which each supports the other, but in this support, the poor have the privileged function of converting the others, of helping them to their faith.

As the church of the poor, the church is the sacrament of liberation. It is not the reality of the kingdom of God but is at the service of this kingdom. But again, it will be the poor who will be responsible for making this generic truth—which can be automatically repeated from other points of view—produce, that is discern, particular consequences. The church does not monopolize the service of the kingdom of God, but welcomes all persons of good will in this task and seeks to collaborate with them. It allows for various charisms—even of those who are outside it. It judges between true and false prophets not according to a priori, ecclesial criteria, but according to whether or not they are building the kingdom for the poor.[7] The church has discerned that the important thing is for the kingdom to become reality, not for it to monopolize the understanding and the praxis of this kingdom, even though it will always offer everyone the channel Jesus provided to bring it about in truth.

The meaning of Christian love for the poor has also been discerned. Charity has its own history. It has been helpful and promotional. It is now seen to be structural. This is a discernment of maximal importance, not because it outdates the other forms of charity, but because the Spirit has forced the poor to appreciate that charity must be structural. From this it also follows that charity is discerned as having to be a political love if it is to be effective, and that the secular mediations of the social, economic, and political structures that most clearly serve the poor have also been discerned.[8]

These discernments, which I see as having been brought about recently in Latin America, obviously go beyond the particular contents of the discernment of Jesus, but they have been effected—I believe—through following the channel Jesus provided. This is why they are self-evidently right even though they remain subject to the criteria of verification I have set forth and are open to the final eschatological reserve. Here we come to the root of the need expressed at the beginning of this article to set Christian discernment within the trinitarian reality of God. As Christians we exercise our discernment within the channel of following Jesus, with particular values, criteria, and verification. Within this channel, we listen to the requirements of the Spirit given to us to enable us to go on making history, following Jesus, and initiating the kingdom of God in particular situations. The final verification of whether we are doing this consists in whether God continues to appear as the greater God and as that reality which is effective and "partial" love for the poor of the earth. When the day comes when it is no longer necessary to discern in this way, the kingdom of God will have arrived, and God will be all in all.

6

Jesus' Relationship with the Poor and Outcast: Importance for Basic Moral Theology

THE IMPORTANCE OF THE SUBJECT
FOR CHRISTIAN MORAL THEOLOGY

The gospel narratives clearly show Jesus surrounding himself with and favoring sinners, publicans, the sick, lepers, Samaritans, pagans, and women throughout his life. This is accepted as a basic characteristic of his praxis.[1] The usual conclusion drawn from it is—correctly—that if even these people were favored by Jesus—which means that God's love for them is made plain—then all human beings possess the dignity of children of God and all human beings are truly brothers and sisters.

This conclusion, however important it may be, is not enough to demonstrate the importance of the fact for moral theology. The lessons drawn from it have served, historically, to work out basic principles of Christian anthropology and to inspire codes of moral practice, such as the traditional duty to help those in need. But an understanding of the relationship between Jesus and the poor and outcast cannot achieve its *systematic* value without setting these actions of his in the context of his fundamental praxis and seeing this relationship as fundamental to his praxis.

We must ask what is the basic lesson of Christian morality as it appears in the gospels and see Jesus' relationship with the poor and outcast as the basic enactment of his moral praxis, rather than merely as one more aspect of this praxis, and therefore an aspect that, however constant and worthy, still bears only an arbitrary relationship to the essence of his praxis.

This article first appeared in *The Dignity of the Despised of the Earth*, edited by Jacques Pohier and Dietmar Mieth (*Concilium*, vol. 130 [1979]: 12–20, New York: Seabury Press). Paul Burns translated the article for *Concilium*. The text has been edited for inclusion in the present volume.

The basic moral question can be put in these words: What do we have to do in order to bring about the kingdom of God in history?[2] Here two points must be stressed: first, we must determine the notion of what is to form the object of a praxis, in this case the kingdom of God; second, we must decide the Christian form of that praxis that will ensure that the kingdom of God comes about. When we come to analyze the relationship of Jesus to the poor and outcast we need to see what this relationship implies for the notion of the kingdom of God, the *bonum morale* to be brought about, and the ethical form praxis must take, that is, the *virtus* that will make the praxis Christian. We then have to see whether what we learn from the relationship is really essential to the constitution of the notion of the kingdom of God and to the Christian constitution of a praxis capable of bringing this kingdom into being.

THREE INITIAL POINTS

In view of the importance of the poor and outcast for practical morality, three points are worth making at the outset in order to set Jesus' relationship with them in their historical and existential context.

1. Today, as in Jesus' time, the poor and outcast make up the majority of the human race. This quantitative fact carries a qualitative charge. If Christianity is characterized by its universal claims, whether made on the basis of creation or of the final consummation, what affects majorities should be a principle governing the degree of authenticity and historical verification of this universalism. A fundamental morality, including one originating in Jesus, should certainly possess a universal direction, but it should be processed through the historical universalism of majorities. Otherwise, the universality it claims will be a euphemism, an irony, or a mythified ideologization. The "*misereor super turbas*" attributed to Jesus (Mark 6:34) should be a foregoing but necessary focus for determining fundamental morality, not only because of the subjective merciful approach it demonstrates, but equally because the object of the mercy is the majority.

2. These majorities are not only the sum total of individuals who are poor and outcast as individuals, but also collectivities made up of social groups. As *groups*, they will require, and there will be required for them, a different code of moral practice from what would be required in the case of purely interpersonal relationships. Since these are *social* groups, moral practice will necessarily result, even if this is not the direct intention, from its setting within the totality of social reality, which is conflictive and antagonistic, and will therefore have direct repercussions on the whole of society. So the gospel stories of groups, with their antagonistic character—the poor, sinners, and so on, contrasted with the rich, the Pharisees, and so forth—will have to be evaluated apart from the scenes in which Jesus related to the individuals alone.

3. The problem for these majorities is not only, or even primarily, that they are declared to be or treated as those without dignity, those not explicitly recognized as children of God, or, more precisely, as persons who are subjects

(agents) with the rights of subjects. Their unworthiness has an earlier rooting in a social reality, whether on the level of a socioeconomic infrastructure or on that of a religious superstructure. In the gospel narratives, these groups of persons are described under the general heading of "the poor," suffering under the yoke of some form of material oppression, and of "outcasts," because of their religious affiliations, or because they exercise professions held to be immoral. Jesus' actions were designed not only to declare their dignity in the sight of God, but also to mount a radical assault on the causes of their social indignity—the material conditions of their existence and the religious concepts of their time. The importance of this observation for basic ethics lies in showing that mere declarations of the dignity before God of the lowliest are insufficient unless they lead to an unmasking and transforming of the roots of their lowliness.

THE KINGDOM OF GOD IS FOR THE POOR AND OUTCAST

If a morality stemming from Jesus concerns itself with bringing about the kingdom of God, it is obviously important at the outset to decide what constitutes this kingdom. Yet Jesus himself, who is represented as using the term "kingdom of God" so often, did not precisely describe what he meant by it.[3] He declares that the kingdom is coming and that it is "good news" (Mark 1:15; Matt. 4:23; Luke 4:43). It might be possible to try to analyze the various concepts of the kingdom of God prevalent in Jesus' time and to decide which of them, or what synthesis of them, might have influenced his proclamation of it, but this would not seem to be a very fruitful approach. The statement that "the specific content of the kingdom stems from his ministry and actions, viewed as a whole"[4] seems to offer a better approach. And this is the approach in which his relations with the poor and outcast take on such fundamental importance.

Jesus proclaimed the kingdom as good news to the poor (Luke 4:18, cf. 7:22; Matt. 11:5) and declared that it was made up of the poor (Luke 6:20; cf. Matt. 5:3). This establishes a basic correlation between the good news and its principal (or only[5]) recipients, and indirectly shows of what this good news consists. If this kingdom is for the poor, if salvation comes not to the just but to sinners, if publicans and prostitutes will enter the kingdom before the pious, then the very situation of those for whom the kingdom is destined must demonstrate— though initially *sub specie contrarii*—the central content of the good news. In that case, the kingdom of God must be not a universal symbol of utopian hope, interchangeable with any other utopia, but more specifically the hope of those groups who suffer under some kind of material and social oppression.[6] The good news must then be, firstly and directly, what today is called liberation, whose biblical antecedents are to be found more in the line of the prophets than in the apocalyptic view of universal history.

Before prematurely spiritualizing the poor and universalistically extrapolating the notion of the kingdom, it will be well to remember that those for whom the kingdom is destined are those who are most deprived of life at its basic levels. In the passage where Jesus replies to the envoys from John the Baptist, the poor are described as the blind, the lame, the deaf, and so on. Joachim Jeremias interprets this passage not in any spiritualized sense, but in the sense that "according to the thinking of the time, the situation of such men was no longer worth calling life: in effect, they were dead."[7] The good news is then the bringing of life to those who have been denied it and deprived of it in the secular sphere.

The kingdom of God, that which is to be built, is therefore the antithesis of the situation of those who are most deprived of life. So, to gain a working idea of the content of the kingdom of God, we must adopt the viewpoint of those who lack life, power, and dignity, and not pretend there can be another and better viewpoint than theirs. In this way the idea of the kingdom will not be paralyzed by the abstract universalism of its content or by a precipitate imposition of the eschatological reserve on it.[8] The poor, sinners, and the despised are the necessary, though not absolutely sufficient,[9] starting point for an understanding of what is meant by the good news of the kingdom. The ultimate theo-logical reason for this is simply that God loves them and protects them and wishes them to have life.[10]

Besides this correlation between the kingdom of God and the poor, what the kingdom of God consists of can be discovered by considering Jesus' actions as actions in the service of the kingdom. His specific behavior toward the poor and outcast gives no gnostic revelation of what the kingdom is, but does reveal how the kingdom operates in practice. When his actions are praxis—that is, designed to operate on his surrounding historical circumstances in order to change them in a specific direction—he indirectly but nonetheless effectively shows with what the kingdom of God is concerned. There is therefore a correlation between Jesus' historical service and what the kingdom is to be, provided this service is understood as being for and from the poor and outcast. Jesus' actions in this respect operate on various levels, and I shall only briefly touch on them here.

First, there is the action of his words. The positive announcement of the good news is partly in the nature of a proclamation, in that it is an expression of the revelation of the gratuitous mystery of God and—unlike the proclamation of John the Baptist, for instance—of the supremacy of God's love over God's judgment and of the "partiality," or partisan "sides-taking" character of this love. But it is also in the nature of praxis in that it is conducive to the formation of a historical consciousness in the poor and outcast and in that it is also in fact a vehicle for ideological struggle through its polemical proclamation of the "partiality" of God.

Thus Jesus' words are a proclamation in which the mystery of God is expressed and also a praxis operating on surrounding historical reality.

With the positive announcement goes the practice of denunciation. The various anathemas condemn not only sinful conduct in itself, but also the sinful behavior of one social group toward another. Sin is condemned in the name of the good news not only as the personal failure of the person in his or her relationship with God, but also as something preventing the kingdom of

God from becoming a reality for the poor. The rich are told that their riches are an injustice and that they themselves are the oppressors of the poor (Luke 16:9; 19:1 ff.); the Pharisees that they do not practice justice and are blind leading the blind (Luke 11:42; Matt. 23:16, 24); the lawyers that they load intolerable burdens on others, burdens that they themselves do not move a finger to lift, that they have taken away the key of knowledge, preventing others from going in who wanted to (Luke 11:46, 52; Mark 12:38ff.); the priests that they have turned the temple into a robbers' den (Mark 11:55ff.); rulers that they lord it over their people (Mark 10:42).

The typical structure of Jesus' indictments and anathemas consists in condemning not only what is intrinsically sinful in the conduct of these social groups, but also the added hypocrisy of attempting to justify such behavior in the name of religion. Sinfulness has to have an object: these people are oppressors of the poor. So Jesus' condemnations are a defense of the poor; they also have a social implication, since they are directed against one group and in favor of another, condemning established relationships and thereby affecting them. This is the practice of proclamation from the reverse: denunciation.

Alongside the action of words in proclamation and denunciation, the gospels show particular actions of Jesus that can be summed up in the words "He has done all things well" (Mark 7:37) and are at their most characteristic in his cures and his dealings with sinners. They are normally described as happening in particular situations and addressed to individuals, but the type of person to whom they are addressed, as well as their content, shed light on the meaning of the kingdom.

If Jesus refused to perform miracles for his own justification, if the miracles are never described for the sake of their "miraculousness" but as works (*erga*), acts of power (*dunameis*), signs (*sēmeia*), then they can only be acts that demonstrate the sovereignty of God, that is, the reign of God (Luke 11:20) over those who are subjected to the sovereignty of evil. The same must be said of the forgiveness of sins. Even if the two scenes in which forgiveness is explicitly described (Mark 2:5; Luke 7:48) cannot be claimed to be historically accurate, it cannot be doubted that Jesus showed his solidarity with sinners, sitting at table with them (Mark 2:15–17; Luke 7:36–50) in order to show them God's love and so rescue them from their social isolation.

Jesus' specific actions in the service of the kingdom of God show, then, that this is the liberation of the poor and the outcast and that this liberation should not only be proclaimed as the will of God for the world, but should come about in history, should be brought to fruition.[11]

VOLUNTARY SOLIDARITY WITH THE POOR AND OUTCAST AS THE MANNER IN WHICH THE KINGDOM OF GOD IS ACTUALIZED

Jesus' relations with the poor and outcast show not only what the kingdom should be in action, but also how it is to be brought about. The means of doing so can be summed up as voluntary solidarity with the poor and outcast.

That this should be so does not stem from any a priori ratiocination, but follows the logic of the Old Testament witness of the Servant of Yahweh and the historical structure of Jesus' life on earth. The kingdom of God is announced and brought to the poor in a contrary and antagonistic world of sin. The good news is good not primarily because it adds to or goes beyond the positive element in a given situation, but because it goes against it. The theology of the Servant affirms that fullness passes through the moment of subsuming a negation and cannot be achieved from the inertia of the merely positive. In the first song the Servant is given the mission of spreading law and justice on earth (Isa. 42:1-9); in the fourth the Servant is burdened with the sin of the world so that this fullness can be brought to fruition (Isa. 52:13-53: 12).

This is the basic structure of Jesus' activity as he in fact performed it, independently of any possible view of himself as the Servant and of his first vision of how his mission was to be accomplished. Effective defense of the poor involves removing the real, objective sin that impoverishes them; this sin cannot be eradicated without taking on the condition of the poor; their dignity cannot be given back to them without taking on their humiliation.

This process is well illustrated on the theoretical level in the scene of the temptations, which should not be taken as one specific incident, and certainly not as happening at the outset of Jesus' ministry, but as an illustration of the climate and environment in which his life unfolded. They demonstrate his objective choice of service in the manner of the servant, without the power that—even used in the service of the powerless—would have removed him from the reality and consequence of poverty, humiliation, and persecution.

Jesus, in the specific historical reality of his life, conceived his mission in such a way that it had to follow a historical course leading inevitably to his being deprived of security, dignity, and life itself—the historical course of voluntary impoverishment. While it is difficult to point to particular incidents in the narratives that illustrate this process in action, the whole tenor of the gospels shows it at work, and Jesus' death on the cross proves it. Jesus was stripped of his dignity, as is shown by the insults hurled at him and in the theologized sense in which his adversaries seek to expel him from the synagogue and the temple, a real excommunication. He was stripped of security, as appears from the form of persecution mounted against him shortly before his death, which the gospels anticipate in the early part of his ministry (Mark 3:6; Luke 4:28-30) in order to stress the atmosphere of persecution in which he lived and functioned. Finally, Jesus was deprived of his own life, the true and final impoverishment.

What needs to be stressed in this objective process of impoverishment is that Jesus undertook it out of solidarity with the poor. The persecution he underwent can be understood in a personalist sense in view of the attacks he made on various social groups, but it will not be understood in depth without appreciating the element of defense of the poor contained in these attacks. The five controversies in Mark 2:1-3, 5 are based on a defense of the sick, sinners, and the hungry. When Jesus unmasked the hypocrisy of the Pharisees it was to show them avoiding duty to parents in need (Mark 7:1–13).[12] His impoverishment stems from something much deeper than asceticism. It stems from a voluntary solidarity with the poor and outcast.

The requirements Jesus laid on others show that same movement in the direction of basic impoverishment: the call to follow him in order to carry out a mission in poverty, to leave home and family, to take up the cross; these are not arbitrary requirements that he could just as well not have imposed, or in whose place he could just as well have imposed others. They are requirements in the direct line of impoverishment. The beatitudes show the same approach, from a different angle: the poor in material things are called to appreciate their poverty and live it as poverty in spirit, thereby participating actively in the movement of impoverishment.[13]

This active process of impoverishment that Jesus practiced in his life is simply the historical version of what was later theologized as his transcendent impoverishment: the incarnation and *kenōsis*. Note that this transcendent impoverishment took historical form not only through the assumption of human flesh, but also through the assumption of solidarity with the poor and outcast.

FUNDAMENTAL MORALITY AND THEO-LOGY

The actual relations between Jesus and the poor and outcast show both that the *bonum*, the bonum of fundamental Christian morality, lies in bringing the kingdom of God into being for the poor, and that the basic *way* in which this is to be brought about is voluntary impoverishment in solidarity with the poor. We need to ask at this stage whether these observations, though obviously important in the gospels, are really of basic importance, greater than any others, for Christian morality. To determine this we need to ask the further question of whether this interpretation of the kingdom gives the best idea of the ultimate reality of the God in whom Jesus believed and in whom Christians believe.

This interpretation involves both the revelation of God, and the approach to God through a faith that is specifically Christian. Unlike a basically *gnostic* conception, it is not a matter of merely knowing *about* God, but of knowing his will and how this will is put into effect. Hence the importance of approaching God through his mediation of the kingdom of God that we have to bring about. Unlike a directly *universalist* conception, this interpretation stresses the constitutive partiality of God toward those who have historically been most deprived of life, right, and justice. Unlike a purely *natural* conception of God, it lays emphasis on the scandalous element in God's own reality, what we call the *kenōsis*, the impoverishment and humiliation of the Son.

Such a *christianized* conception of God should be the ultimate basis for moral theology. Inversely, only the historical embodiment of this type of basic moral theology can provide an idea, beyond generic statements, of what God is really like.[14] The generically accepted correlation between God and the poor and outcast becomes both rewarding and challenging when seen from the standpoint of Jesus' actual dealings with them and when this relationship becomes the principle for both positing and resolving the basic question of morality.

7

"The Risen One Is the One Who Was Crucified": Jesus' Resurrection from among the World's Crucified

The resurrection of Jesus is the fundamental event and truth of the Christian faith. In this article I recall another truth, no less fundamental for the faith: The risen one is none other than "Jesus of Nazareth, the One who was crucified" (Mark 16:6). My motivation is no doloristic a priori, as if faith could hold no moment of joy and hope; nor any dialectical a priori conceptually necessary for theological reflection. Rather my motivation is a "double honesty"—honesty with the New Testament accounts and honesty with the reality of millions of men and women.

We must remember that the risen one is the crucified one for the simple reason that in this manner, and no other, Jesus' resurrection is presented in the New Testament. Nor is this merely a factual truth to notice—one more datum in the Paschal mystery. Rather it is a fundamental truth, in the sense that it is the foundation of the reality of the resurrection and therefore of any theological interpretation of the resurrection.

In the human race today—and certainly where I am writing—many women and men, indeed entire peoples, are crucified. This situation of so much of humanity makes the recollection of the one who was crucified something connatural and demands this recollection in order for Jesus' resurrection to be concrete, Christian good news and not abstract and idealistic good news. These crucified of history furnish the special lens through which we can grasp Jesus' resurrection "Christianly" and make a Christian presentation of it. This is what I seek to do in the pages that follow: "Christianly" concretize certain aspects of Jesus' resurrection from his reality as the crucified one, who in turn is better discovered from a point of departure in the crucified of history.

This article was originally published in *Sal Terrae,* March 1982, an issue entitled *La resurrección de Jesús.*

TRIUMPH OF GOD'S JUSTICE

Very quickly, through a believing process, what happened in Jesus' resurrection was *universalized*. Cross and resurrection began to function as universal symbols, of death as the lot of all human beings and of immortality as their aspiration and hope. God's power to raise from the dead was presented as the warranty of that hope, above and counter to the power of death.

All of this is meet and just, of course. But it would behoove us not to plunge headlong into this process of universalization. First we ought to plumb the concrete historicity of Jesus' mortal lot.

In the first Christian preaching, although we have it only in stereotypical form, Jesus' resurrection was presented in the following fashion: "You . . . made use of pagans to crucify and kill him. God freed him from death's pangs, however, and raised him up again" (Acts 2:23-24; cf. the same schema in Acts 3:13-15; 4:10; 5:30; 10:39; 13:28-30). In this proclamation, basic importance is ascribed to the fact that God has raised someone from the dead, yes; but no less importance is ascribed to the identification of *who* has been raised.

This person is none other than Jesus of Nazareth, the individual who, according to the gospels, had preached the coming of the kingdom of God to the poor, had denounced and unmasked the mighty, had been persecuted by them, condemned to death, and executed—maintaining, all the while, a radical fidelity to the will of God and a radical trust in the God he obeyed. He is identified in the first discourses as "the Holy and Just One" (Acts 3:14), and very shortly his mortal end is interpreted as the lot of the prophets (1 Thess. 2:15).

The importance of this identification does not, obviously, consist only in knowing the actual name of the one who has been the object of God's activity, but in understanding, through this identification, through the narrative and interpretation of the life of the crucified one, what Jesus' resurrection is all about.

One who lived thus, and therefore was crucified, has been raised from the dead by God. Jesus' resurrection is not only a symbol of God's omnipotence, then—as if God had decided arbitrarily and without any connection with Jesus' life and lot to show how powerful he was. Rather Jesus' resurrection is presented as God's response to the unjust, criminal action of human beings. Hence God's action in response is understood in conjunction with the human activity that provokes this response: the murder of the Just One. Pictured in this way, the resurrection of Jesus shows *in directo* the triumph of justice over injustice. It is the triumph not simply of God's omnipotence, but also of God's justice, although in order to manifest that justice God posits an act of power. Jesus' resurrection is thus transformed into good news, whose central content is that once and for all justice has triumphed over injustice, the victim over the executioner.

SCANDAL OF A DEATH-DEALING INJUSTICE

God's victorious act in Jesus' resurrection must not let us forget the supreme gravity of the action of human beings to which it is a response. The first Christian discourses repeat it tirelessly: "You killed him." To be sure, the tendency is to sweeten the accusation that the audience murdered Jesus! "Yet I know, my brothers, that you acted out of ignorance . . ." (Acts 3:17). But this phrase, calculated to console and move to conversion, by no manner of means attenuates the supreme gravity of the murder of the Just One. The resurrection is the prime affirmation of Paul's doctrine that where sin has abounded, grace is superabundant. But this superabundance of grace serves only to underscore the enormity of the sin of the murder of the Just One.

If we take seriously this dual, antagonistic presentation of the actions of God and human beings in Jesus' fate, then we can at least restate history's greatest scandal and what our response to it should be. A unilateral concentration on the activity of God in raising Jesus from the dead frequently means that the great scandal of history is, when all is said and done, one's own future death. What makes the resurrection of Jesus possible and necessary is the courage to hope for one's own personal survival. But if we do not shut out the repeated "You killed him," then what leaps out at us as scandalous is not simply death, but the murder of the Just One and the human possibility, a thousand times realized, of putting a just person to death. The question shouted in our face by the resurrection is whether we too do not participate in the scandal of putting the just one to death—whether we are on the side of the murderers or on the side of the life-giving God.

Jesus' resurrection not only presents us with the problem of how to deal with our own future death, it also recalls that we already have to deal with the death and life of others, that the tragedy of human beings and the scandal of history is not only that human beings must themselves die, but also that they can put other human beings to death. These reflections are not intended to minimize the universal problem of death or gloss over the unquestionable message of hope that appears in the resurrection of Jesus. They are only intended to emphasize that there exists, here and now, the immense scandal of the injustice that deals death in history and that the way to confront that scandal is the Christian way of confronting the scandal of one's own personal death. In other words, the Christian courage of one's own resurrection lives on the courage to overcome the historical scandal of injustice. The hope that is necessary in order to believe in Jesus' resurrection as the blessed future of one's own person passes by way of the practice of the historical love that gives life here and now to those who are dying in history.

For the hope of one's own resurrection, too, the universal evangelical formula is valid: One must forget oneself to gain oneself "Christianly." Someone for whom his or her own death would be the basic scandal, and the hope of his or her own survival the basic problem, would not have a Christian hope, would not have a hope sprung from Jesus' resurrection; such a one would have a hope centered in and for himself or herself—an understandable hope, but not a Christian hope. What de-centers our own hope to make it genuinely Christian hope is taking as absolutely scandalous the death of the crucified today, with which there can be no "deals," no compromise, and which must not be allowed ultimately to become something secondary in one's own interests in virtue of a hope in one's own resurrection. That historical scandal is the Christian mediation for the scandal of one's own death; and the determined, persevering struggle, truly a "hope against hope," for the lives of human beings is the Christian mediation for maintaining hope in our own resurrection.

HOPE FOR THE CRUCIFIED

Contemporary theology has done very well to transcend a doloristic conception of Christianity. In the face of so many other symbols of hope, at times in opposition to them (like those originating in Greek philosophy), theology has pointed out that its symbol of hope has a better "reputation"—enjoys more credibility—because it combines the corporeal, social, and even cosmic aspects of resurrection. Thereby it has recouped some basic aspects of the New Testament and has sought to come abreast of the demands of current anthropologies. Rightly it has sought to render the Christian symbol of the resurrection credible. But it has been too hasty in universalizing this symbol, its addressees, and the hermeneutic locus of its understanding. I would emend this precipitant universalization.

If we take seriously what has been said up to this point, we can only deduce—not through a fundamentalist reading of the texts, but by being deeply honest with them—that Jesus' resurrection is *first and foremost* hope for the crucified. God has raised a crucified one, and from this moment forward there is hope for the crucified of history. They can really see in the risen Jesus the first-born from among the dead, for they recognize him as their elder brother in reality and not merely intentionally. They can therefore have the courage to hope for their own resurrection and can even show their mettle in history—a "miracle" analogous to that of Jesus' resurrection.

The correlation between the resurrection and history's crucified, analogous to the correlation between the kingdom of God and the poor that Jesus preached, does not mean a de-universalization of the hope of humankind, but rather the discovery of the correct locus of this universalization. That locus, the world of the crucified, is not an exceptional or esoteric one. We must not forget that before being *the* cross—the language to which we are accustomed—Jesus' cross is *a* cross, one among so many carried before and after Jesus. We must not forget that there are millions of persons in the world who do not simply die, but, in various ways, die as Jesus died, at the hands of "pagans," at the hands of the modern idolaters of national security or of wealth. Many men and women really die, crucified, murdered, tortured to death, or "disappeared," for justice's sake. Many other millions die a slow crucifixion caused by structural injustice. Entire peoples today are transformed into trash and offal by the appetites of other men and women, peoples without face or comeliness, like the crucified one. Unfortunately this is not metaphor, but daily reality. From a quantitative viewpoint, what lends credibility to Jesus' resurrection today is that it can be the hope of the immense masses of humanity.

From a qualitative viewpoint, Jesus' resurrection is transformed into a universal symbol of hope to the extent that all men and women share in some form of crucifixion—in other words, to the extent that every human being's death has the quality of crucifixion. This is Christian death of antonomasia, and thus the type of death from which one may have the Christian hope of resurrection. One must share the crucifixion then, albeit analogously, in order to have Christian hope.

This is not the moment to engage in a systematic or phenomenological analysis of the analogy of the crucifixion. Suffice it to say that when one's own death is not the sole product of biological limitations or of the simple exhaustion of the energy necessary to maintain life, but is the product of surrender for love of others, especially helpless, poor, and defenseless others, when one's death is the product of injustice, then an analogy obtains between that life and death and the life and death of Jesus. Then—and only then, from a Christian viewpoint—one also shares in the hope of resurrection. Community in Jesus' life and lot bestows the hope that there will be realized in us what was realized in Jesus.

Apart from that community with the crucified one, however analogous and diversified this community be, Jesus' resurrection bespeaks only the possibility of survival. Survival after death, as the classic doctrine of the church testifies, is ambiguous: it can be salvation or condemnation. For there to be hope for one's survival and hope that this survival be salvific, one must share in the crucifixion. This is the starting point for the universalization of hope of resurrection and for the resurrection to become good news for all. For this universalization to be Christian, one must start out, as so often, from the scandalous Christian paradox: the good news is for the poor, and resurrection is for the crucified.

CREDIBILITY OF GOD'S POWER THROUGH THE CROSS

History's crucified await salvation. They know that power is necessary for this. At the same time they mistrust pure power, since this always shows itself unfavorable to them in history. They desire a power that will be genuinely credible. Simple promises, marvelous though they be, do not necessarily unleash hope. This happens only when promises are enunciated with credibility. It is no more important therefore to profess the omnipotence of God, "who restores the dead to life and calls into being those things which had not been" (Rom. 4:17), than it is to be assured of God's love. In other words, it is just as important to be sure that God's power is credible as it is to be sure that God has power at all. And so we must return again to the crucified one and acknowledge in him the presence of God, as Paul says, and the expression of the love of God, who delivers up the Son for love. Apart from these considerations, however threatened they may be by anthropomorphism, however unfathomable the mystery they express, the power of God in the resurrection is not simply and absolutely a piece of good news.

On Jesus' cross, in a first moment, God's impotence appeared. Of itself this impotence is not the cause of hope. But it lends credibility to the power of God that will be shown in the resurrection. The reason for this is that God's impotence, God's helplessness, is the expression of God's absolute nearness to the poor, sharing their lot to the end. God was on Jesus' cross. God shared the horrors of history. Therefore God's action in the resurrection is credible, at least for the one who has been crucified. God's silence on the cross, which causes natural reason and modern reason so much scandal, is not scandalous for the crucified. Their crucial concern is whether God was with Jesus on the cross. If the answer is yes, then God's nearness to human beings, initiated in the incarnation, proclaimed and rendered present by Jesus during his earthly life, is consummated. The cross says, in human language, that nothing in history has set limits to God's nearness to human beings. Without that nearness, God's power in the resurrection would remain pure otherness and therefore ambiguous, and for the crucified, historically threatening. But with that nearness, the crucified can really believe that God's power is good news, for it is love. Jesus' cross continues to be the most finished expression, in human language, of God's immense love for the crucified. Jesus' cross says, in credible fashion, that God loves human beings, that God pronounces a word of love and salvation, and that God personally utters and bestows the divinity itself as love and as salvation. Jesus' cross says that God has passed the test of love, and now we may believe in God's power as well.

Once God's loving presence on Jesus' cross has been grasped, God's presence in the resurrection is no longer pure power without love, pure otherness without nearness, a *deus ex machina* without history. The raising action of God and the hope of one's own resurrection continue, of course, to be the objects of faith and hope. God's presence in the crucified one does not render these realities more evident or more demonstrable. Those who ought to have the most difficulty with this faith and this hope are the crucified. But when they hear that God was on Jesus' cross, they comprehend something of supreme importance: that God's power is not oppressive but salvific; that it is not pure otherness with respect to themselves, but loving proximity. The resurrection of Jesus is transformed into "their" symbol of hope.

A resurrection rendered credible by God's nearness on the cross likewise confirms the deepest intuition of the crucified in the present, however this intuition may be constantly threatened by resignation, skepticism, or cynicism. At bottom, good is more real than evil, although the latter inundates us; grace is more real than sin, although it does not cease its death-dealing. There is more truth in the stubbornness of hope, in ever attempting the new, in ever seeking historical liberations, in refusing to strike any compact with what is limited and sinful in history—although both are omnipresent—than in the seeming wisdom of resignation.

The stubbornness of hope is what the resurrection ultimately says to the crucified; and it says this because it is the manifestation not only of God's power but also of God's love. Pure power does not necessarily generate hope. At best it generates calculated optimism. Love, however, transforms expectations into hope. It is the crucified God that makes the God who gives life to the dead credible, for it shows us a God of love, a God who is hope for the crucified.

JESUS' LORDSHIP IN THE PRESENT:
A NEW HUMAN BEING AND A NEW EARTH

Jesus' resurrection points to the absolute future, but it also points to the historical present. Jesus is already Lord, and believers are already the new men and women. Jesus' resurrection does not separate him from history, but introduces him into it in a new way, and believers in the risen one must now live as risen themselves in the conditions of history. Indeed, there is a correlation between both novelties: the present lordship of Jesus is shown in the fact that new men and women exist, and it is these new men and women who make it a reality *in actu* that Jesus be Lord in the here and now.

This great, consoling truth, however, sends us back to the one who was crucified. Apart from the active, effective recollection of the crucified one, the ideal of the new human being takes a dangerous, anti-Christian tack. It seeks an identification with the risen one *in directo,* with two destructive consequences. Either the new human being is equated with the individual who has taken leave of history and abandoned it to its fate (here we have all manner of enthusiastic movements, Pentecostal, and so on, whatever may be their intentions) or, worse, the new human being is equated with the individual who regards history from "on high," pretending thus to imitate the activity of the risen one (here we have the church's frequent authoritarianism and dogmatism where human beings are concerned).

This perversion of the understanding and practice of the new human being has its origins in what we might call a "docetist" understanding of Jesus' resurrection. It does not deny Jesus' flesh, as classical docetism did; but it makes his life, and especially his death, something provisional, which for all intents and purposes disappears when the resurrection occurs. Thus we have a risen one without a cross, an end without a process, a transcendence without history, a lordship without service.

We cannot dwell here on the pernicious concrete historical consequences of the danger that we have abstractly formulated. We can only underscore the urgency of keeping in mind "the one who was crucified" lest, negatively, we succumb to the danger of anything like direct identification with the one who was raised, and positively, in order to show how new human beings can live as risen in the here and now of history.

The path to the new human being is none other than Jesus' road to resurrection. It is said of him that he was made Lord in virtue of his abasement (Phil. 2:8–9; cf. Acts 2:36). This implies two things. First, Jesus underwent a process of coming to be Lord; second that process was a process of fidelity to the concrete history that produced that abasement. Nor is there any other route for the new human being. It would be a serious mistake to think that incarnation and fidelity to history were necessary only for Jesus, as if we were to be spared what he was not spared. To put it graphically, it would be a serious mistake to fixate on Jesus' resurrection in its last stage without retracing the same historical steps Jesus traced. The life of the new human being is still essentially a process.

The content of this process, described as a process of abasement, is only too familiar: one must become incarnate in the world of the poor, proclaim to the poor the good news, come forward in their defense, denounce and unmask the mighty, take on the lot of the poor, and the ultimate consequence of that solidarity, the cross.

This is what it means to live as risen in the here and now. In the expresssion of Ephesians it means being "predestined . . . through Jesus Christ to be his adopted sons" (Eph. 1:5). In more historical phraseology, it is the *following of Jesus*. To live *already* as risen men and women is to retrace Jesus' route; it does not mean direct identification with the risen one. It means retracing, in fidelity to history, the way of the cross.

The present lordship of believers is nothing other than service to the history in which they must take flesh; further, this is how they make it really true for Christ to be Lord of history in the here and now. This lordship is not exercised simply in that he is acknowledged as Lord by believers. It is exercised in their being servants *in actu*. In speaking of the kingdom of Christ in the present, nothing could be further from the truth than to say that Christ now seeks to be served, to have the whole world as his fiefdom. The truth is very different. The kingdom of Christ becomes real in the measure that there are servants as he was servant.

This is surely the great Christian paradox, abundantly repeated but so difficult to assimilate: to be lord is to serve. Jesus' resurrection has not eliminated this paradox. It has definitively sanctioned it.

Christ's lordship, then, is manifested in the note of service attaching to the lives of believers and in the efficacy of that service for the world. The former means that the new human being is none other than the servant human being, the one who actually does believe that it is more blessed to give than to receive, that those who most humble themselves in order to serve are greatest. The latter means that their service is for the salvation of the world.

The New Testament asserts that Jesus already exercises a "cosmic" lordship. The language produces vertigo, but it is easy to understand if it is historicized from a point of departure in another kind of New Testament language, such as that of "new heavens and a new earth" (Rev. 21:1) or "the kingdom of God." The believer is lord of history in toil for the establishment of that kingdom, in the struggle for justice and integral liberation, in the transformation of unjust structures into other, more human and humane ones. In the language of resurrection we could say that Christ's lordship is exercised by his followers in the repetition in history of God's deed in the raising of Jesus; it is exercised in giving life to history's crucified, in giving life to those whose lives are threatened. This transformation of the world and history in conformity with God's will is what gives actual form to Jesus' lordship—and incidentally, what renders it verifiable. Those who devote themselves to this live as risen in history.

The following of Jesus, service, and work for the kingdom are realities demanded by the historical Jesus, to be sure. But why call these things "ways of living as already risen"? What does Jesus' resurrection add to these demands?

With respect to content, it adds nothing. We know from the historical Jesus how we have to live in history. What the resurrection "adds" is that this life is the true life and that it is the "new" life, not because it transcends history, but because it overcomes history's sin. The resurrection does add the ongoing presence of Jesus among us, and thereby makes possible two modalities— without any new content—of living his following and discipleship historically.

The New Testament stresses that the new human being is the free human being and appeals to the resurrection as proof. For "the Lord is the Spirit, and where the Spirit of the Lord is, there is freedom" (2 Cor. 3:17). This liberty, of course, has nothing to do with license, with taking leave of history. Nor should this freedom be appealed to in a first moment for one's own benefit within the church, which happens in a certain theology of liberalism and enlightenment— although liberalism and enlightenment may be legitimate elsewhere. This is not where we find the basic freedom produced by the presence of the risen one. This presence consists rather in not being enslaved to history, to fear, in not being paralyzed by the risks and prudence of the world. Positively, this presence consists in the maximal freedom of love for service, without any limits being placed on service by anything at all. At bottom, it consists in the attitude of Jesus himself, who gives his life freely, without anyone's taking it from him.

A life radically free to serve brings its own joy amid the very horrors of history. This joy betrays the presence of the risen one. In the midst of history, one hears the words "Don't be afraid" and "I shall always be with you." Paul repeats, exultantly, that nothing will separate us from Christ's love. Despite all, and against all odds, the following of the one who was crucified produces its own gladness.

This freedom and this joy are the expression of the life we already live as new human beings, risen in history. They are the historical expression among us of the element of triumph in Jesus' resurrection. They distinguish the following of Jesus from compliance with a purely ethical demand that stands on its own: they brand Jesus' discipleship with its own truth and meaning. But—let us recall one more time—neither freedom, nor joy, nor any other expression of Jesus' resurrection, is "Christianly possible" apart from or counter to the following of Jesus crucified. There is no other road for the new human being, for the woman or man who wishes to share in Jesus' lordship here and now;

along this road, however, is the risen life of the lords of history in truth and deed.

A FINAL WORD TO THE CHURCH

It is frequently difficult for the church to proclaim Jesus' resurrection. The root of the difficulty lies in the church's wishing to proclaim it *in directo*—without the crucified one. When this occurs, the proclamation of the resurrection becomes routine, a symbol of universal hope, which can unleash emotions in a liturgical celebration but has little effectiveness for historical life. It can even happen that the church has to listen to its hearers say what the Athenians told Paul: "We're not interested." And it would be no wonder, for the proclamation of Jesus' resurrection is a revelation of God culminating a history of revelation. Those who come in at the end will not understand the whole story.

But those who have followed Jesus' route from the beginning, those who have made his path their own, with all of the insanity and scandal of the cross, will perhaps be able to hear from without—when the resurrection of Jesus is proclaimed—the word that leads within: that Jesus' life was the true life and that this is why Jesus abides forever; that life is mightier than death; that justice is mightier than injustice; that hope is more real than resignation. Fidelity to history in conformity with Jesus' discipleship will give them hope in a last beatitude, for themselves and for others, without telling them exactly how or when, but giving them the growing, unshakable conviction that God is drawing this history of horrors to the divinity itself.

Therefore the first question addressed to the church, precisely when it seeks to proclaim Jesus' resurrection, is whether the church is indeed united to the cross and to the numberless other crosses of current history. There is no other "place to stand" in order to speak in a Christian manner of resurrection of Jesus. When the answer has to be no, a feeling of powerlessness to speak of the resurrection comes over one. All manner of theoretical and practical roadblocks spring up when it comes to telling men and women something as simple as that they can live as risen right now and how to do it. The precipitant language of "mystery" and "faith" makes its appearance—precipitant not because the resurrection does not have to be expressed in this language, but because there is not enough history to lend lucidity to this language.

When the church is joined to the Crucified and to the crucified, however, it knows how to speak of the Risen One. It knows how to stir up hope, and how to bring Christians to live as risen persons in history's here and now. The words used may be the same as we hear elsewhere. But here they have a different meaning. The Christian hears them and they unleash a Christian life. We need no further example than the words of Archbishop Romero about the risen Jesus.

This is simply because in the crucified of history Jesus becomes present, as we hear in Matthew 25. In them, Jesus has returned—showing his wounds more than his glory, to be sure, but really there, in the poor.

All this may seem either insanity—"foolishness"—or else the height of some refined dialectic. I am well aware that the situation in El Salvador and throughout Central America is much more a replica of Good Friday than of Easter Sunday and that my theologizing may therefore seem to be making an Easter virtue of a Good Friday necessity, so to speak. Despite all, however, I end where I began: The resurrection of the one who was crucified is *true*. Let it be foolishness, as it was for the Corinthians. But without this foolishness, because it is true—or without this truth, because it is foolish—the resurrection of Jesus will only be one more symbol of hope in survival after death that human beings have designed in their religions or philosophies. It will not be the Christian symbol of hope.

This *truth* is still being historically repeated. An emphasis on the crucified one is not at the service of a conceptual dialectic. It issues from an observation of the historical reality of the crucified. When a pastoral minister in a base community in El Salvador, one suffering extreme hardship in the form of repression, was asked what his community was doing as church, he answered simply, "Keeping up the hope of the suffering. How? We read the prophets, and the Passion of Jesus. So we hope for the resurrection."

No one hopes for the resurrection like the crucified do. They sustain their hope by recalling the life and death of Jesus, seeking to reproduce them actively, or by suffering passively the lot that likens them to Jesus as the disfigured servant of Yahweh. Paradoxically, this gives them hope.

From the midst of history's crucified—without any compact or compromise with their crosses—Jesus' resurrection must be proclaimed. In those crucified, Jesus is present today. In service to them, the lordship of Jesus becomes present today. In the stubborn refusal to strike a pact with their crosses, and in the stubborn, persistent quest for liberation from these crosses, unshakable hope becomes present *in actu,* becomes present historically.

Now we understand a little better what it means to speak of Jesus' resurrection. Our understanding will enable us to correspond, in history, to the reality of the risen one.

8

A Crucified People's Faith in the Son of God

This article will attempt to show the reality and meaning of faith in Christ *from the standpoint of oppression*. So it makes no direct attempt at dogmatic christological formulations nor at working out the question of what is meant by Jesus' sonship in fundamental theological terms. Without denying the importance of either, I shall concentrate on the relationship between faith in Jesus and oppression: a relationship that can still, indirectly but effectively, shed light on both basic questions.

Oppression is not just one of many hermeneutical situations from which to approach faith in the Son of God. It is the situation that is *de facto* the most apt for the Third World today, and *de jure* the one that appears throughout Scripture for understanding the message of salvation. Any Christian theology that is biblical, and therefore historical, must take full account of the signs of the times in its reflection. These are many, but one recurs throughout history: "This sign is always the people crucified in history, uniting an ever-varying form of crucifixion with its continued existence. This crucified people is the historical continuation of the servant of Yahweh, who is stripped of everything by the sin of the world, even of his life, and above all of his life."[1]

THE SERVANT OF YAHWEH AND THE CRUCIFIED PEOPLE

It would be a historical and theological error to understand oppression only *"doloristically"* as an exaltation of sorrow and an apotheosis of suffering, or *ascetically* as the ideal setting for the practice of virtue. If oppression has become a sign of the times, and if it is to be recognized as such and experienced in a Christian fashion, this is because it has been accompanied by the hope and practice of liberation, which are central to the Christian faith.[2]

This article originally appeared in *Jesus, Son of God?,* edited by Edward Schillebeeckx and Johannes-Baptist Metz (*Concilium,* vol. 153 [1982]: 23–28, New York: Seabury Press). Paul Burns translated the article for *Concilium.* The text has been edited for inclusion in the present volume.

But it is equally fatal to faith, as well as offensive to the oppressed, to concentrate on liberation without plunging into the abyss of oppression, which, far from disappearing, is increasing to the limits of horror in countries such as El Salvador and Guatemala. This is repeating the perennial temptation facing Christian faith and theology to exalt the risen Christ without appreciating the horrors of the cross on the historical level.

From the standpoint of oppression, faith in the Son of God comes about in the first instance through the *likeness* that exists between a crucified people and the Son of God who took on the condition of a slave. Faith in the *huios Theou* is mediated above all through his resemblance to the *pais Theou* spoken of in the New Testament (see Matt. 12:13; Acts 3:13, 26; 4:27; 30), which translated the *ebed Jahvē,* as Isaiah presents him in the songs of the servant.

Theologically, this resemblance cannot be turned into pure identity, and we need to analyze of what precisely the resemblance consists. There is the familiar exegetical problem of whether the servant of Yahweh refers to an individual, a group—the remnant of Israel—or the whole collectivity of the people. But whatever the latest position on these details, the fact that there is a resemblance cannot be denied, as Archbishop Romero expressed it on a pastoral level:

> In Christ we meet the type of the liberator, the man who is so identified with the people that biblical exegetes can no longer distinguish whether the Servant of Yahweh proclaimed by Isaiah is the suffering people or Christ come to redeem us.[3]

The real nature of this *pais Theou,* who by virtue of being this is *the* Son of God and not just any son of any god, can be deduced from Isaiah's description of him. His basic features are these:

1. The servant's mission is saving, a salvation that is expressed in the liberating line of the Old Testament, as "Faithfully he brings true justice;/he will neither waver, nor be crushed/until true justice is established on earth" (42:3–4). He is presented in a partisan and polemical spirit, since his mission is directed to the oppressed and is "to open the eyes of the blind,/to free captives from prison,/and those who live in darkness from the dungeon" (42:7).

2. The servant is chosen, but his election is not only a manifestation of the sovereign freedom of God, which could be arbitrary, but of a scandalous will on God's part, since he has chosen to save "him whose life is despised, whom the nations loath,/ . . . the slaves of despots" (49:7); the chosen one is nothing in the eyes of the world and still more one who is crushed by the powers of the world. Inversely, the servant trusts in this scandalous God, who chooses scandalously, that "all the while my cause was with Yahweh,/my reward with my God" (49:4).

3. The servant in the end appears destroyed by men in history, so that he "seemed no longer human" (52:14ff.; 53:2ff.), abandoned, with no one to come to his defense or plead his cause (53:8). He is even shown as sharing the lot of sinners, being taken for one of them (53:12), being given a tomb with the

wicked (53:9), regarded as an outcast, someone punished, struck down by God (53:4).

4. This destiny was produced by the sins of humankind. The servant dies for these sins and these sins lead him to death The historical correlation between sin and producing death is affirmed, elevated to a universal drama (53:5, 8, 12).

5. The great paradox and scandal is that in the death that comes about through bearing the sins of many, there is salvation (53:5, 11). And it is suggested, inversely, that salvation comes about *only* by his bearing these sins.

6. This servant has triumphed through being a servant (53:10-12). His condition of a slave not only produces salvation for others, but exaltation for himself. In the New Testament, it is claimed that this *pais Theou* is the *Kyrios,* the Lord (Phil. 2:8-11); that he is the Son of God, constituted as Son precisely through obedience, but without forgetting that "this obedience is for the servant specifically translated into taking upon himself the sins of mankind."[4]

These characteristics of the servant of Yahweh, of the crucified Son of God, have been rediscovered in Latin America not through mere exegetical curiosity, not just through apologetic concern to support a soteriological theory which affirms that —at the end of the day—life comes out of death. This would be to mock those who are truly oppressed, an a priori dialectical, but not necessarily Christian, theodicy. If *these* characteristics of the Son of God have been rediscovered, it is because they have common ground, affinity, likeness with the situation there.

It is not easy to decide exactly how a crucified people can today be the continuation of the servant of Yahweh, a question that Ignacio Ellacuría has examined in depth.[5] But there is no doubt that many people in Latin America reproduce one or more of his characteristics, either simultaneously or complementarily. These are peoples who no longer appear human, as Puebla reminded us, who are deprived of all justice, their basic rights violated, and in particular their right to life threatened by sudden arrest, torture, assassination, and mass murder. They are also peoples who, like the servant, try to bring right and justice, who struggle for liberation, this being understood not only as liberation of the group that fights for it, but as liberation of the whole people of the poor. Then they are peoples who not only express oppression in the facts of their own existence, but who are actively repressed and persecuted when, like the servant, they try to establish right and justice. Finally, they are peoples who know that they have been chosen as a vehicle of salvation and who interpret their own oppression and repression as the road to liberation. Taken as a whole, many peoples in Latin America are the expression and product of the historical sin of humankind. They bear this sin, they struggle against it, while the power of historical sin is turned against them, bringing them death.

Exactly who constitutes this crucified people and how exactly they reproduce the features of the servant needs further analysis. But, structurally speaking, there can be no doubt that this people is not to be found among the powerful of the earth, not in the wealthy nations; nor can it simply be said to be found in the church, except in that church that has been persecuted for its option for the poor and has shared the fate of the crucified people. This people is made up of the poor majorities who die slowly as a result of oppression and structural injustice, or quickly as a result of repression by the forces of institutionalized violence. Taken as a whole, this people is what "makes up all that still has to be undergone by Christ" (Col. 1:24). So Archbishop Romero could say, with pastoral foresight, in his Corpus Christi address: "It is most opportune to pay homage to the Body and Blood of the Son of Man while there are so many outrages to his body and blood among us. I should like to join this homage of our faith to the presence of the Body and Blood of Christ, which we have shed, with all the blood shed, and the corpses piled up, here in our own land and throughout the world."[6]

This first but basic resemblance to the servant makes something basic possible for faith in the Son of God: A people that suffers in this way, that is so disfigured, tortured, and murdered, has no need of processes of demythologization or sophisticated hermeneutics to find in this Son, in the first place, a close brother. Through looking at Christ crucified, they come to know themselves better, and through looking at themselves, they come to know Christ crucified better. What the Letter to the Hebrews states then becomes a spontaneous reality: "For the one who sanctifies, and the ones who are sanctified, are of the same stock; that is why he openly calls them *brothers*" (2:11). It may seem that being able to call Christ "brother" does not mean a great advance in faith. But it is an advance compared to those—the rich in material goods, those who exercise an authority that is not one of service, whose science is their god—who cannot openly call Christ "brother."

FOLLOWING CHRIST AND BECOMING CHILDREN OF GOD

This first likeness to the servant produces an advance in faith to the extent that a crucified people conceives and lives its condition, its cause and its destiny as the following of Jesus. This is the form of believing in the Son of God from a point of oppression and exercised in praxis, but it is a real belief. The degree to which faith really comes about in this way cannot, in the final analysis, be quantified, since this is part of the mystery of the human being before God. But speaking about following Jesus means speaking about the basic structure of a real act of faith and a historical principle of verifying this faith.

The first element of this following is incarnation. This is clear on the basis of Christ's taking flesh. It is not, however, a question of taking any sort of flesh, but of taking on all that is weak and little in the flesh of history. We are dealing with a consciously partisan incarnation. To become incarnate in this way is to place oneself in the correct position for enabling oneself, through one's very reality, to go on making a Christian choice when faced with the alternatives that confront everyone in the course of life: riches or poverty, vainglory or humiliation, power or service.

A crucified people is already materially in this incarnation, and only needs to adopt it consciously in faith—whatever the degree of consciousness involved on the psychological level. Those who do not belong to this crucified people sociologically have to achieve this belonging through consciously lowering themselves, integrating themselves in the people in various ways, making common cause with the crucified people, taking on their struggle and their destiny. This type of partisan incarnation is itself an expression of faith in Christ.

The second element in this following is the practice of liberation, understood as the liberation brought by Jesus, as proclamation of the kingdom of God to the poor and as the various forms of service to make this announcement become reality. By its own historical condition, a crucified people already carries out various aspects of Jesus' service to the kingdom *in actu*. Its own existence, once it is aware of it, becomes a word that unmasks false gods—political and economic—in whose name oppression is ideologically justified. But beyond this, its practice formally becomes following or discipleship through maintaining two essential points.

The first is the maintaining of the hope, not merely the announcement, of the coming of the kingdom. Faced with the delays and rejections of the kingdom in history, maintaining faith in its coming is itself a sign of indestructible hope in the God of the kingdom: a hope that becomes the driving force of the practice of liberation. The second is maintaining love as the formal motivation behind the practice of liberation. Latin American theology has analyzed at length[7] the fact that love needs historical mediations. This fact is also a requirement of faith in the Holy Spirit, which renews the face of the earth. In its just struggle to move from *infra-existence* to *existence,* the crucified people should maintain its *pro-existence*—that the element of salvation of "the other" should not be lost sight of in the struggle for one's own liberation. This "other" is in the first place the totality of the world of the oppressed, for whose liberation the individual or group involved in the process of liberation should struggle; but it is also the oppressor, whose salvation is sought in the process of liberation. Although this process generates serious conflicts, its basic dynamism comes from love of other people, not from hatred or vengeance.

The third element is Jesus' aim, set out programmatically in the Beatitudes, particularly the version in Luke, which shows them concerned with material conditions of poverty, hunger, and affliction. But they are also concerned with the spirit in which these material realities should be lived and this is what sets the aim of those who follow Jesus. This spirit is utopian on account of the historical difficulty of achieving it fully and of combining it with other demands of the following of Jesus, such as clear denunciation and unmasking, with the conflict and antagonisms they generate and with the effectiveness that must be sought in the process of liberation. But it is a spirit that must always be sought, as it is Jesus' will, and because, furthermore, it lends its own efficacy to the practice of historical liberation.[8]

This means that the followers of Jesus must always keep a spirit of mercy in their hearts in the midst of the struggle necessary to achieve justice. They must keep a clear eye open to God's truth. God does not trivialize the struggle of the oppressed by reducing them all to equal value but judges them by what they can produce. They must work for peace, make the ideal of peace an ingredient in the struggle for justice, even though this struggle, however justly and even nobly undertaken, always involves some degree of violence, which in extreme cases can even include legitimate armed insurrection.[9] They must above all be ready to face persecution, to bear themselves with fortitude in persecution, even to the point of giving their lives, a sign of the greatest love that one can have and proof that following Jesus is really pro-existence.

A crucified people resembles Jesus by the mere fact of what it is and is loved preferentially by God because of what it is. But if it takes on the outward condition of the following of Jesus, then it knows him "from within" and grasps him not only as close brother, but as elder brother, as the first-born. Then what Paul said becomes a historical reality: "They are the ones he chose specially long ago and intended to become true images of his Son, so that his Son might be the elders of many brothers" (Rom. 8:29). The reality of the act of faith in Christ comes about in this reproducing of his features, in this becoming daughters and sons in the Son.

FAITH IN THE SON OF GOD

I have no doubt that in Latin America today this following of Jesus, and therefore this faith in Christ, exists in large measure. I shall conclude with a brief reflection on what the foregoing means in terms of the reality of a Christ believed in under the title of Son of God.

In my view, the very existence of a crucified people brings out, and in its most radical form, a seeking for ultimate reality and for the reality of the divine. We would be misunderstanding the whole question if we were to think that basically theological reflections merely served to justify political and socioeconomic choices. They certainly do this, and it is important that they should do so in order to show that faith works in history. But the inverse proposition is equally true. The very historical reality of a crucified people is clamoring for God, even before this clamor is consciously expressed. If anywhere, it is here that the "problem" of God is posed. Faced with the alternatives of life or death, liberation or oppression, salvation or condemnation, grace or sin, the transcendent quest for God appears in historical form.

A crucified people that also persists in following Jesus has already given a Christian answer to the problem, by transforming it into a "mystery." If it holds firm to its process of liberation, if it stands firm in hope, if it believes that the kingdom of God is coming, and yet believes it has to bear the sin of the world and that this bearing of sin is saving, then it is saying, wordlessly something extremely important about God, just as Pauline theology did in its day in words. It is saying that God is salvation, that God raises Jesus and "calls into being what does not exist" (Rom. 4:17). At the same time, the cross is a portent of God: "God's foolishness is wiser than human wisdom, and God's weakness is stronger than human strength" (1 Cor. 1:25). This is the mystery of God and the final word on reality. God draws history to the Trinity, submerging the Godhead in the horrors of that history. A crucified people that at one and the same time upholds the liberator God of the exodus and the God of the cross is stating that it believes in God and what it means by that God in whom it believes.

This shows what is meant by the "God" of whom Jesus is "the Son." If we believe in Jesus as the Son it is because in him the truth and love of the mystery of God have been shown in an unrepeatable form, and been shown in a way that is totally convincing to a crucified peope who have no problem in accepting Jesus' unrepeatable relationship with God so that they can confess him to be in truth the Son of God.

The formulation "Son"—a human word and therefore never totally adequate for describing Jesus—is a good vehicle for expressing the obedience, trust, and faithfulness to God that Jesus showed in his life on earth; it also well describes the experience that a crucified people has of God: trust in liberation, obedience to the service of liberation, and faithfulness in this service, whatever the consequences. What is implied in the metaphor "Son" can be deduced from the reality of being Jesus' "brother."

Formulations of belief in Christ are important, but their importance is secondary compared to what is actually believed. In Latin America he is called *the* Liberator. Of course theologians can and must examine these formulations to show their equivalence with those of the New Testament and the magisterium. But what matters ultimately is how this faith is expressed in practice. As Karl Rahner has said, if Jesus "really makes such a compelling impression on a person that they find the courage to commit themselves unconditionally to this Jesus in life and death and therefore to believe in the God of Jesus," then that person really and fully believes in Jesus as the Son of God.[10]

This is really happening for many Christians who are giving themselves in life and death to Jesus, who believe in him and in the God he called Father. What I have tried to show here is that this happens *from within* oppression, and, historically, *because* oppression has been taken on in a consciously Christian manner.

Notes

Note: *Throughout the present volume quotations from the Medellín General Conference of the Latin American Bishops are taken from* The Gospel of Peace and Justice, *ed. Joseph Gremillion (Maryknoll, N.Y.: Orbis Books, 1976). Quotations from the Puebla General Assembly of the Latin American Bishops are taken from* Puebla and Beyond, *ed. John Eagleson and Philip Scharper (Maryknoll, N.Y.: Orbis Books, 1979).*

FOREWORD

1. The reference is to Sobrino's *Christology at the Crossroads,* trans. John Drury (Maryknoll, N.Y.: Orbis, 1978).

2. See the Puebla Final Document, nos. 170–81, in *Puebla and Beyond: Documentation and Commentary,* ed. John Eagleson and Philip Scharper (Maryknoll, N.Y.: Orbis, 1979).

3. In Walter M. Abbott, ed., *The Documents of Vatican II* (New York: Herder & Herder, 1966), pp. 112, 113; cf. p. 123.

4. In Joseph Gremillion, ed., *The Gospel of Peace and Justice: Catholic Social Teaching Since Pope John* (Maryknoll, N.Y.: Orbis, 1976), p. 396.

CHAPTER 1. THE TRUTH ABOUT JESUS CHRIST

1. Of the numerous systematic christologies to have appeared in recent years, I cite those that seem to have been more influential and to which I have had access: Karl Rahner, *Theological Investigations* (London: Darton, Longman & Todd; New York: Seabury, 1974–83); idem, *Ich glaube an Jesus Christus* (Einsiedeln: Benziger, 1968); idem, *Foundations of Christian Faith: An Introduction to the Idea of Christianity,* trans. William V. Dych (New York: Seabury, 1978), pp. 176–321; Karl Rahner and Wilhelm Thüsing, *A New Christology,* trans. David Smith and Verdant Green (New York: Seabury, 1980); Karl Rahner and Karl-Heinz Weger, *Our Christian Faith: Answers for the Future,* trans. Francis McDonagh (New York: Crossroad, 1981), pp. 85–123, 159–79; Walter Kasper, *Jesus the Christ,* trans. V. Green (London: Burns & Oates; New York: Paulist, 1977); Christian Duquoc, *Christologie: Essai dogmatique* (Paris: Cerf, 1968); idem, *Jésus, homme libre* (Paris: Cerf, 1974); Olegario G. de Cardenal, *Jesús de Nazaret* (Madrid: Católica, 1975); José Ignacio González Faus, *La humanidad nueva,* 2 vols. (Madrid: Eapsa; Mensajero; Sal Terrae, 1974); idem, *Acceso a Jesús* (Salamanca: Sígueme, 1979); José-Ramón Guerrero, *El otro Jesús: para un anuncio de*

Jesús de Nazaret, hoy (Salamanca: Sígueme, 1976); Hans Küng, *On Being a Christian,* trans. Edward Quinn (London: Collins, 1977); Edward Schillebeeckx, *Christ, the Sacrament of the Encounter with God,* trans. Paul Barrett (London: Sheed & Ward, 1977); idem, *Jesus: An Experiment in Christology,* trans. Hubert Hoskins (New York: Crossroad, 1979); Piet Schoonenberg, *The Christ: A Study of the God-Man Relationship in the Whole of Creation and in Jesus Christ,* trans. Della Couling (New York: Herder & Herder, 1971), pp. 105–75; D. Wiederkehr, "Esbozo de cristología sistemática," in *Mysterium Salutis* (Madrid: Cristiandad, 1971), 3/1:505–670 (original: Johannes Feiner and Magnus Löhrer, eds., *Mysterium Salutis: Grundriss heilsgeschichtlicher Dogmatik* [Einsiedeln: Benziger, 1965]); Hermann Dembowski, *Grundfragen der Christologie: Erörtert am Problem der Herrschaft Jesu Christi* (Munich: Kaiser, 1971); Wolfhart Pannenberg, *Jesus, God and Man,* trans. Lewis L. Wilkins and Duane A. Priebe (Philadelphia: Westminster, 1977); Jürgen Moltmann, *The Crucified God: The Cross of Christ as the Foundation and Criticism of Christian Theology,* trans. R. A. Wilson and John Bowden, 2nd ed. (New York, Evanston, San Francisco, London: Harper & Row, 1973); idem, *Theology of Hope: On the Ground and the Implications of a Christian Eschatology,* trans. James W. Leicht, 5th ed. (New York and Evanston: Harper & Row, 1967).

2. "Quaestiones Selectae de Christologia," *Gregorianum* 61 (1980): 609–32.

3. Ibid., p. 609.

4. Ibid., p. 619.

5. I use the terms "Latin American christology" and "christology of liberation" not in any technical sense but simply descriptively, referring to the approaches and content of authors such as Leonardo Boff, Ignacio Ellacuría, Segundo Galilea, Gustavo Gutiérrez, and myself.

6. For an examination of the various christological viewpoints of Puebla by a European author, see Jacques van Nieuwenhove, *Church and Theology in Puebla: Thoughts on the Latin-American Bishops' Message to the Universal Church* (Puebla, Mexico: Prospective International, 1980), pp. 31–39. See also Sobrino, *Puebla: serena afirmación de Medellín: Cristología* (Puebla: Conferencia General del Episcopado Latinoamericano, 1979), pp. 41–59: "Reflexiones sobre el documento de cristología en Puebla."

7. The term "christology" as used in Latin American books and articles may arouse expectations of something different from what is actually forthcoming, since Latin American liberation christology is not a complete christology in the traditional sense. That is, it does not treat all of the themes treated in the classic christologies. Liberation christology generally proceeds from a point of departure in the historical Jesus and only then moves to the various New Testament, conciliar, and traditional christologies (without going too far afield in any analysis of this last).

8. Accordingly, I shall frequently refer to what I have written elsewhere.

9. "Las 'élites' latinoamericanas: Problemática humana y cristiana ante el cambio social," in *Fe cristiana y cambio social en América Latina: Encuentro de El Escorial* (Salamanca: Sígueme, 1973), p. 209.

10. *Christology at the Crossroads: A Latin American Approach,* trans. John Drury (Maryknoll, N.Y.: Orbis, 1978), p. 82.

11. Schillebeeckx has set forth the mutual relationship of the two meanings of "good news" in his *Jesus: An Experiment in Christology,* pp. 107–14.

12. See Gustavo Gutiérrez, "Movimientos de liberación y teología," *Concilium* 93 (1974): 451.

13. See Gutiérrez, *The Power of the Poor in History: Selected Writings,* trans. Robert R. Barr (Maryknoll, N.Y.: Orbis, 1983), p. 219, n. 66.

14. There can be no doubt that it was Leonardo Boff, in his *Jesus Christ Liberator: A Critical Christology for Our Time* (trans. Patrick Hughes [Maryknoll, N.Y.: Orbis, 1978], originally published in Portuguese in 1972), who gave this title its currency. Most importantly, Boff indicates in this work that Jesus Christ is the yardstick of liberation and not vice versa.

15. See Juan Luís Segundo, *The Liberation of Theology,* trans. John Drury (Maryknoll, N.Y.: Orbis, 1976).

16. See Leonardo Boff, "Jesucristo liberador: Una visión cristológica desde Latinoamérica oprimida," in *Jesucristo en la historia y en la fe,* ed. Antonio Vargas-Machuca (Salamanca: Sígueme, 1977), pp. 178ff.

17. "Today, in the faith experience of so many Christians of Latin America, Jesus is seen and loved as the Liberator" (Leonardo Boff, "Salvación en Jesucristo y proceso de liberación," *Concilium* 96 [1974]: 375).

18. Leonardo Boff, *Jesus Christ Liberator,* p. 182.

19. Gustavo Gutiérrez, *A Theology of Liberation: History, Politics and Salvation,* trans. Caridad Inda and John Eagleson (Maryknoll, N.Y.: Orbis, 1973), pp. 145-87; Hugo Assmann, *Theology for a Nomad Church,* trans. Paul Burns (Maryknoll, N.Y.: Orbis, 1976), p. 67; Rubem Alves, *Cristianismo: ¿opio o liberación?* (Salamanca: Sígueme, 1973), pp. 187-91; Leonardo Boff, *Jesus Christ Liberator;* idem, "Salvación en Jesucristo y liberación," *Concilium* 96 (1974): 375-88; idem, *Teología desde el cautiverio* (Bogotá, 1975), pp. 145-71; idem, in *Theology in the Americas,* ed. Sergio Torres and John Eagleson (Maryknoll, N.Y.: Orbis, 1976), pp. 294-98; idem, *Pasión de Cristo, pasión del mundo,* 2nd ed. (Santander: Sal Terrae, 1982); idem, "Jesucristo Liberador," pp. 175-99; Raúl Vidales, "¿Como hablar de Cristo hoy?" *Spes* (January 1974): 7ff.; idem, "La práctica de Jesús," *Christus* (Mexico City) 40 (1975): 43-55; Segundo Galilea, "Jesús y la liberación de su pueblo," in *Panorama de la Teología Latinoamericana II* (Salamanca: Sígueme, 1975), pp. 33-44; Segundo Galilea and Raúl Vidales, *Cristología y pastoral popular,* 2nd ed. (Bogotá: Paulinas, 1976); José Porfirio Miranda, *Being and the Messiah: The Message of Saint John,* trans. John Eagleson (Maryknoll, N.Y.: Orbis, 1976); José Comblin, *Jesus of Nazareth: Meditations on His Humanity,* trans. Karl Kabat (Maryknoll, N.Y.: Orbis, 1976); Ignacio Ellacuría, *Freedom Made Flesh: The Mission of Christ and His Church,* trans. John Drury (Maryknoll, N.Y.: Orbis, 1976), pp. 23-51; idem, "Tesis sobre posibilidad y sentido de una teología latinoamericana," in *Teología y mundo contemporáneo: Homenaje a Karl Rahner en su 70 cumpleaños,* ed. Antonio Vargas-Machuca (Madrid: Cristiandad, 1975), pp. 325-50; idem, "¿Por qué muere Jesús y por qué le matan?" *IDOC Internationale* (1979): 105-12; A. Castillo, "Confesar a Cristo y seguir a Jesús," *Estudios Centroamericanos,* 322/323 (1975): 512-31; J. Delgado, "Lectura latinoamericana del Evangelio de San Marcos," ibid.: 532-54; Jon Sobrino, "Following Jesus as Discernment," "Jesus' Relationship with the Poor and Outcast: Importance for Basic Moral Theology," "Jesus and the Kingdom of God: Significance and Ultimate Objectives of His Life and Mission," and "The Epiphany of the God of Life in Jesus of Nazareth" elsewhere in this book.

20. See Jon Sobrino, *Christology at the Crossroads,* pp. 1-16; idem, "The Importance of the Historical Jesus in Latin American Christology," chap. 2 in this book.

21. See Jon Sobrino, *Christology at the Crossroads,* pp. 41-46; see also chap. 3, "Jesus and the Kingdom of God."

22. "We learn what the kingdom basically was for Jesus not only from what might be extracted from his notion of the kingdom, but from *Jesus' actual life in the service of the kingdom"* (see p. 85).

23. The magisterium of the church has been putting more and more stress on Jesus' special relationship with the poor. See *Lumen Gentium,* no. 8; Medellín, *Poverty of the Church,* no. 7 (in *Gospel of Peace and Justice,* ed. Joseph Gremillion, p. 473); *Evangelii Nuntiandi,* nos. 6, 12; Puebla Final Document, nos. 190, 1141.

24. See Jon Sobrino, *Christology at the Crossroads,* pp. 79–178.

25. See Ignacio Ellacuría, "Las bienaventuranzas como carta fundacional de la Iglesia de los pobres," in *Iglesia de los pobres y organizaciones populares,* Oscar A. Romero et al. (San Salvador: UCA, 1978), pp. 105–18.

26. On this much debated question see G. Marchesi, "Gesù de Nazareth: tu chi sei?" *Civiltà Cattolica* 3137 (March 1981): 429–43.

27. "It is no longer a matter of following someone who is proclaiming a kingdom of which his followers have a more or less accurate idea in their minds already. It is no longer a matter of cooperating in a project that stands in continuity with their own legitimate aspirations as human beings and Jews. Rather than following something pretty much in line with Jewish orthodoxy, they must follow something which will call that very orthodoxy into question. Their discipleship is now typified by Jesus in all his historical concreteness" (Jon Sobrino, *Christology at the Crossroads,* p. 58).

28. See Ignacio Ellacuría, "¿Por qué muere Jesús?"

29. See Jon Sobrino, *Christology at the Crossroads,* pp. 259–72.

30. See *Christology at the Crossroads,* pp. 41–61, 158–76, 217–35; chap. 4, "Epiphany of the God of Life"; and chap. 5, "Following Jesus as Discernment."

31. This is a rare subject in christological tractates. It is acquiring crucial importance today, however, in function of discipleship, as well as of the passage from Matthew 25. See Karl Rahner, *Ich glaube an Jesus Christus;* idem, *Foundations of Christian Faith,* pp. 305–11; Olegario G. de Cardenal, *Jesús de Nazaret,* pp. 580–603.

32. See Karl Rahner, *Foundations of Christian Faith,* p. 295.

33. See Gustavo Gutiérrez, *A Theology of Liberation,* pp. 189–96.

34. This is the basic thesis of Jürgen Moltmann's *The Crucified God* and *Man: Christian Anthropology in the Conflicts of the Present* (trans. John Sturdy [Philadelphia: Fortress], 1974), which has influenced liberation christology on this point.

35. See Jon Sobrino, *The True Church and the Poor* (Maryknoll, N.Y.: Orbis, 1984), pp. 84–124.

36. See n. 20, above, and my remarks below concerning dogmatic formulations.

37. Karl Rahner and Karl-Heinz Weger, *Our Christian Faith,* p. 90.

38. See Walter Kasper, *Jesus the Christ,* pp. 164ff.; Wolfhart Pannenberg, *Jesus, God and Man,* pp. 133–58.

39. Walter Kasper, *Jesus the Christ,* p. 163.

40. Among the many studies of New Testament christology, see Oscar Cullmann, *The Christology of the New Testament,* trans. Shirley C. Guthrie and Charles A. M. Hall (London: SCM, 1968); R. Schnackenburg, "Cristología del Nuevo Testamento," in *Mysterium Salutis* (Madrid: Cristiandad, 1971), 3/1:245–414 (translation of *Mysterium Salutis: Grundriss heilsgeschichtlicher Dogmatik,* ed. Johannes Feiner and Magnus Löhrer, as cited in n. 1, above); Ferdinand Hahn, *Christologische Hoheitstiteln* (Göttingen: Vandenhoeck & Ruprecht, 1963); Josef Ernst, *Anfänge der Christologie* (Stuttgart: KBW, 1972); Martin Hengel, *The Son of God: The Origin of Christology and the History of Jewish-Hellenistic Religion,* trans. John Bowden (London: SCM,

1976); Walter Kasper, *Jesus the Christ,* pp. 163–96; José Ignacio González Faus, *La humanidad nueva,* 1:339–66. For a contemporary systematic explanation of the title, see González Faus, *Este es el hombre,* 2nd ed. (Santander: Sal Terrae, 1981), pp. 21–47.

41. I take no account here of what is said to be the "most ancient" christology, in which, it is claimed, the first christological reflection took two simultaneous directions: Jesus is considered as Son of God, exalted in the resurrection, and as Son of Man, expected at the end of time. See R. Schnackenburg, "Cristología del Nuevo Testamento," pp. 268–76.

42. Walter Kasper, *Jesus the Christ,* p. 166.

43. For the christology of the councils and tradition, see P. Smulders, "Desarrollo de la cristología en la historia de los dogmas y en el magisterio eclesiástico," in *Mysterium Salutis,* 3/1:417–503; José Ignacio González Faus, *La humanidad nueva,* 2:375–517; Alois Grillmeier, *Christ in Christian Tradition,* trans. John Bowden (New York: Sheed & Ward, 1965); idem, *Jesus der Christus im Glauben der Kirche* (Freiburg: Herder, 1979).

44. "Jesus is identified as 'son of God' not in virtue of a preestablished principle, as if we possessed, a priori and instinctively, a yardstick for what is divine, but on the basis of his word (the promise of the kingdom of God), his activity (the signs that anticipate that kingdom), his attitude (his creative freedom), his resurrection (his victory over death, which ratifies his prophetic struggle)" (Christian Duquoc, *Jesús, hombre libre* [Salamanca: Sígueme, 1975], p. 114 [original: *Jésus, homme libre,* as cited in n. 1, above]). "The concrete, historical interpretation of the Son of God predicate means that Jesus' divine sonship is understood, not as supra-historical essence, but as reality which becomes effective in and through the history and fate of Jesus" (Walter Kasper, *Jesus the Christ,* p. 164).

45. Walter Kasper, *Jesus the Christ,* p. 176.

46. *Contra Arianos,* 2, 70 (*PG* 26:296C).

47. By setting two terms in contiguity—God and suffering—the Council of Nicaea situates us between the two most crucial questions of history and human life. And in giving an affirmative response to the question of whether the two are coupled, it sets the heart of Christian faith in high relief: the unimaginable, unexpected inburst of a faith that refuses to be boxed in by human explanatory capacities or human desires, a faith that, on the contrary, is the judgment and condemnation of these" (José Ignacio González Faus, *La humanidad nueva,* 2:487–88).

48. Karl Rahner and Karl-Heinz Weger, *Our Christian Faith,* pp. 93–94.

49. See Jon Sobrino, *Christology at the Crossroads,* pp. 91–95.

50. On the importance of the difference between God's "mediation" and "mediator," see Sobrino, *True Church and the Poor,* pp. 41–42.

51. Karl Rahner and Karl-Heinz Weger, *Our Christian Faith,* pp. 96–97.

52. For the relationship between the act and the object of cognition where Christ is concerned, see Karl Rahner, *Ich glaube an Jesus Christus,* and Rahner's general statement of the question on pp. 11–15.

53. *Dei Verbum* describes faith as the surrender of the whole human being to God (no. 5). Here we examine the totality of this surrender in Jesus himself.

54. I have considered the historical manifestation of transcendence in "Monseñor Romero y la Iglesia salvadoreña: un año después," *Estudios Centroamericanos* (March 1981): 146–50; and "Dios y los procesos revolucionarios," *Diakonia* (April 1981): 53ff.

55. See the Puebla Final Document, nos. 92, 265, 668, 1138. For a systematic treatment, see Jon Sobrino, *The True Church and the Poor,* pp. 160–93, 228–52.

56. Both Leonardo Boff (*Jesus Christ Liberator,* pp. 119–20) and Jon Sobrino

(*Christology at the Crossroads,* pp. 221–22) attribute the greatest christological importance to the intuition expressed by Bonhoeffer here. See also various authors, *Teología de la cruz* (Salamanca: Sígueme, 1976).

57. This profound truth has been systematically developed by Karl Rahner, *Theological Investigations* (London: Darton, Longman & Todd; New York: Seabury, 1974–83), 4:107–12.

58. Of the innumerable exegetical works on Jesus' life, the following may be consulted, which—from various viewpoints, to be sure—study Jesus' life as a whole: Josef Blank, *Jesus von Nazareth: Geschichte und Relevanz* (Freiburg: Herder, 1977); Herbert Braun, *Jesus of Nazareth: The Man and His Time,* trans. Everett R. Kalin (Philadelphia: Fortress, 1979); Günther Bornkamm, *Jesus of Nazareth,* trans. Irene and Fraser McLuskey (New York: Harper & Row, 1975); C. H. Dodd, *The Founder of Christianity* (London: Collins, 1973); Etienne Trocmé, *Jesus as Seen by His Contemporaries* (Philadelphia: Westminster, 1973); Norman Perrin, *Understanding the Teaching of Jesus* (New York: Seabury, 1983); Joachim Jeremias, *New Testament Theology: The Proclamation of Jesus,* trans. John Bowden (New York: Scribner's, 1971); C. Schuetz, "Los misterios de la vida y actividad pública de Jesús," in *Mysterium Salutis,* 3/2:72–141.

59. Walter Kasper, *Jesus the Christ,* p. 197.

60. Ibid., p. 198.

61. On the councils and tradition, see n. 43, above.

62. International Theological Commission, article cited in n. 2, above: "Quaestiones Selectae de Christologia" p. 619; José Ignacio González Faus, *La humanidad nueva,* 2:512ff.

63. González Faus, *La humanidad nueva,* 2:474–80.

64. "Quaestiones Selectae de Christologia," p. 619. The citations in nn. 1, 19, 58 above demonstrate the need to return to Jesus' humanity and a theological consideration of the same.

65. "Quaestiones Selectae de Christologia," p. 619. In 1973, Ignacio Ellacuría wrote: "Today it would be absolutely ridiculous to try to fashion a christology in which the historical realization of Jesus' life did not play a decisive role. The 'mysteries of Jesus' life,' which once were treated peripherally as part of ascetics, must be given their full import—provided, of course, that we explore exegetically and historically what the life of Jesus really was" (*Freedom Made Flesh,* p. 26).

66. See chapter 2, "The Importance of the Historical Jesus in Latin American Christology." This historical view of Jesus in no way contradicts the other view, expressed in categories of nature; but it is richer than that other and capable of including it, while the reverse is not necessarily true. "If history is a more solidly metaphysical entity than nature, then our reflections on history should be more profound than our reflections on nature and hence more operational" (Ignacio Ellacuría, *Freedom Made Flesh,* p. 26).

67. See chapter 2, and José Ignacio González Faus, *Acceso a Jesús,* pp. 44–58.

68. E. Schweitzer, "Die theologische Leistung des Markus," *Evangelische Theologie* 24 (1964):337–55.

69. "Quaestiones Selectae de Christologia," p. 623.

70. In my opinion, a directly sociopolitical hermeneutical principle would yield an inadequate rereading of Jesus. But if the hermeneutical principle is Jesus' partiality towards the poor, then justice is done to the gospel—the gospel is allowed to "speak"—and the sociopolitical consequences of Jesus' life are set forth in an adequate light.

71. Karl Rahner, *Theological Investigations,* 4:116.

72. "Quaestiones Selectae de Christologia," p. 622.

73. See Walter Kasper, *Jesus the Christ,* pp. 206–8; Carlos Escudero Freire, *Devolver el Evangelio a los pobres* (Salamanca: Sígueme, 1978). Obviously liberation christology accepts this notion of salvation as liberation, and Medellín and Puebla have employed it repeatedly. Paul VI, in *Evangelii Nuntiandi,* made liberation a key concept for evangelization (see nos. 30–38), while emphasizing that it must be understood integrally and spared any reductionism.

74. Cf. Joachim Jeremias, *New Testament Theology,* p. 104.

75. See "Quaestiones Selectae de Christologia," p. 627. For an appraisal of the christology of liberation in terms of the soteriological models of the New Testament and church tradition, see Leonardo Boff, *Pasión de Cristo, pasión del mundo,* pp. 153–217.

76. See Karl Rahner, "Salvation: Theology," in *Sacramentum Mundi: An Encyclopedia of Theology,* ed. Karl Rahner et al. (New York: Herder and Herder; London: Burns & Oates, 1968–70), 5:425–33, 435–38.

77. See Joachim Jeremias, *New Testament Theology,* pp. 116–17.

78. See José Ignacio González Faus, *Acceso a Jesús,* pp. 173–77.

79. See "Quaestiones Selectae de Christologia," pp. 631–32.

80. Ibid., p. 632.

81. Ibid., p. 618.

82. Christian Duquoc, *Cristología* (Salamanca: Sígueme, 1971–72), 1:267 (translation of *Christologie,* as cited in n. 1).

83. Karl Rahner, *Theological Investigations,* 1:181–82.

84. Karl Rahner, *Theological Investigations,* 3:31. See also Bernhard Welte, *Auf der Spur des Ewigen* (Freiburg: Herder, 1965), pp. 424–58.

85. Karl Rahner, *Theological Investigations,* 4:107.

86. Christian Duquoc, *Cristología,* 1:268.

87. Ibid., 1:272.

88. Besides the works of Rahner cited in n. 1, see Walter Kasper, *Jesus the Christ,* pp. 240–52; Christian Duquoc, *Cristología,* 1:266–72; Olegario G. De Cardenal, *Jesús de Nazaret,* pp. 276–301, 307–29; José Ignacio González Faus, *La humanidad nueva,* 2:485–517, 625–59; Piet J. A. M. Schoonenberg, *The Christ,* pp. 66–104; Wolfhart Pannenberg, *Jesus, God and Man,* pp. 283–364.

89. Karl Rahner and Karl-Heinz Weger, *Our Christian Faith,* p. 98; see also Karl Rahner, *Foundations of Christian Faith,* pp. 290–91; idem, *The Love of Jesus and the Love of Neighbor,* trans. Robert Barr (New York: Crossroad, 1983), p. 30.

90. For an elucidation of dogmatic statements as doxological, see Jon Sobrino, *Christology at the Crossroads,* pp. 321–28; Wolfhart Pannenberg, *Jesus, God and Man,* pp. 183–87; *Basic Questions in Theology,* trans. George H. Kehm (Philadelphia: Fortress, 1970–71), 1:202–5, 211–38; E. Schlink, "Die Struktur der dogmatischen Aussage als ökumenisches Problem," *Kerygma und Dogma* 3 (1957): 251ff.

91. See Jon Sobrino, *True Church and the Poor,* pp. 156–59.

92. "The Hypostatic Union does not differ from our grace by what is pledged in it, for this is grace in both cases (even in the case of Jesus). But it differs from our grace by the fact that Jesus is our pledge, and we ourselves are not the pledge but the recipients of God's pledge to us" (Karl Rahner, *Theological Investigations,* 5:183).

93. Karl Rahner (*Theological Investigations,* 4:65–67) has stressed the relationship between the two mysteries in the strict sense of the word, *ad extra* of God, the incarnation and grace.

94. Karl Rahner and Karl-Heinz Weger, *Our Christian Faith,* p. 99.

95. Ibid.

96. Ibid., pp. 99–100.

97. See Jon Sobrino, *Christology at the Crossroads,* pp. 3–4.

98. *Acceso a Jesús,* p. 207.

99. D. Wiederkehr, "Esbozo de cristología sistemática," pp. 517–26; Piet J. A. M. Schoonenberg, *The Christ,* pp. 51–66; Wolfhart Pannenberg, *Jesus, God and Man,* pp. 287–94; Karl Rahner and Wilhelm Thüsing, *A New Christology,* pp. 15–17; José Ignacio González Faus, *La humanidad nueva,* 2:509–12; Olegario G. de Cardenal, *Jesús de Nazaret,* pp. 303–29.

100. D. Wiederkehr, "Esbozo de cristología sistemática," p. 519.

101. *Jesús de Nazaret,* pp. 308–9.

102. Walter Kasper, *Jesus the Christ,* p. 230.

103. See Jon Sobrino, *Christology at the Crossroads,* pp. 338–40.

104. See ibid.

105. D. Wiederkehr, "Esbozo de cristología sistemática," p. 581.

106. See chap. 8, "A Crucified People's Faith in the Son of God."

107. See Sobrino, *Christology at the Crossroads,* pp. 105, 338.

108. Walter Kasper, *Jesus the Christ,* p. 165.

109. Ibid.

110. See Sobrino, *Christology at the Crossroads,* pp. 105–6, 339–40.

111. See Christian Duquoc, *Jesús, hombre libre,* p. 116.

112. Ibid., p. 117.

113. Karl Rahner has stressed the systematic importance of this basic truth. See *Theological Investigations,* 4:77–102; idem, in *Mysterium Salutis* (Span.), 2/1:360–445.

114. "The unity of the man Jesus with the *Logos* is expressed in the New Testament only indirectly as the inner ground of the unity between the Father and Jesus" (Walter Kasper, *Jesus the Christ,* p. 233); see also Wolfhart Pannenberg, *Jesus, God and Man,* p. 334; D. Wiederkehr, "Esbozo de cristología sistemática," pp. 506–7.

115. On the distinction between christological "concentration" and christological reduction, see Sobrino, *True Church and the Poor,* pp. 41–43. Karl Rahner, who is likewise engaged in a christological concentration (see *Theological Investigations,* 1:123–25), enjoins the greatest caution in order to avoid a christological reduction (*Foundations of Christian Faith,* p. 13).

116. Christian Duquoc, *Jesús, hombre libre,* p. 117.

117. Walter Kasper, *Jesus the Christ,* p. 233.

118. See Sobrino, *Christology at the Crossroads,* pp. 105–7, 338–340.

119. See ibid., p. 226.

120. See the works of Rahner cited in n. 113 above.

121. See Karl Rahner, *Theological Investigations,* 4:112–20.

122. In Joseph Gremillion, ed., *Gospel of Peace and Justice.* José Ignacio González Faus *(Acceso a Jesús)* quotes this text in his treatment of the recapitulation of all things in Christ and subjoins a celebrated passage from Karl Barth, which may shed light on what we seek to show: "In Jesus Christ is not merely one man, but the *humanum* of all men, which is posited and exalted as such to unity with God" (Karl Barth, *Church Dogmatics,* vol. 4, *The Doctrine of Reconciliation,* trans. G. W. Bromiley [Edinburgh: T. & T. Clark, 1958], part 2, p. 49). Clearly, the intent here is to demonstrate the possibility of humanity's elevation to the divine level. Now, if this is not to remain pure metaphor, it will necessarily imply God's assumption, in the incarnation, of all that is human, as such.

123. In Walter M. Abbott, ed., *Documents of Vatican II,* p. 22.

CHAPTER 2. THE IMPORTANCE OF THE HISTORICAL JESUS IN LATIN AMERICAN CHRISTOLOGY

1. See chap. 1, n. 19.

2. See chap. 1, n. 1.

3. Karl Rahner, "Current Problems in Christology," in *Theological Investigations* (London: Darton, Longman & Todd; New York: Seabury, 1974–83), 1:149–200; "On the Theology of the Incarnation," ibid., 4:105–20.

4. Karl Rahner, "The Eternal Significance of the Humanity of Jesus for Our Relationship with God," ibid., 3:35–46.

5. See "Thoughts on the Possibility of Belief Today," ibid., 5:3–22.

6. See D. Wiederkehr, "Esbozo de cristología sistemática," in *Mysterium Salutis* (Madrid: Cristiandad, 1971), 3/1:558 (original: Johannes Feiner and Magnus Löhrer, eds. *Mysterium Salutis: Grundriss heilsgeschichtlicher Dogmatik* [Einsiedeln: Benziger, 1965]).

7. That Jesus preached not himself but the kingdom of God is commonly accepted in systematic christologies today (see Rahner, Schillebeeckx, Kasper, Küng, and so on). However, insufficient emphasis is laid on the fact that Jesus' relationship is to the kingdom of God in its quality precisely as *kingdom*.

8. This point has been vigorously underscored by Edward Schillebeeckx in *Jesus: An Experiment in Christology* (trans. Hubert Hoskins [New York: Crossroad, 1979], pp. 43–57), as well as by Walter Kasper in *Jesus the Christ* (trans. Verdant Green [London: Burns & Oates; New York: Paulist, 1977], pp. 26–28).

9. Herein lies the positive pastoral intent as well as the limitation, of the christologies of Pannenberg, Schillebeeckx, Kasper, and Küng. It should be noted, however, that Schillebeeckx has recently expressed the wish that christology orient itself more along the lines of Latin American christology and profit from its profound inspiration—so that we must doubtless conclude that he seeks to transcend his own christological focus: "Befreiungstheologien zwischen Medellín und Puebla," *Orientierung,* 42nd year, no. 1, pp. 6–10; 43rd year, no. 1, pp. 17–21.

10. See Leonardo Boff, "Jesucristo Liberador: una visión cristológica desde Latinoamérica oprimida," in *Jesucristo en la historia y en la fe,* ed. Antonio Vargas-Machuca (Salamanca: Sígueme, 1977), pp. 178ff.

11. See José Porfirio Miranda, *Being and the Messiah: The Message of Saint John,* trans. John Eagleson (Maryknoll, N.Y.: Orbis, 1977), p. ix.

12. See Ignacio Ellacuría, *Freedom Made Flesh: The Mission of Christ and His Church,* trans. John Drury (Maryknoll, N.Y.: Orbis, 1976), pp. 23–25, 3–19.

13. Gustavo Gutiérrez, *The Power of the Poor in History: Selected Writings,* trans. Robert R. Barr (Maryknoll, N.Y.: Orbis, 1983), p. 209.

14. This thinking is analogous to that of Christian Duquoc ("El Dios de Jesús y la crisis de Dios en nuestro tiempo," in *Jesucristo en la historia y en la fe,* ed. Antonio Vargas-Machuca [Salamanca: Sígueme, 1977], p. 49) on Jesus' own invocation of God: "In action, Jesus decides that the invocation of the Father reaches a new form."

15. Here we note the different sense of the ecclesiality of faith as compared with that, for instance, of Walter Kasper (*Jesus the Christ,* p. 27).

16. See Ignacio Ellacuría, "La Iglesia de los pobres, sacramento histórico de liberación," *Estudios Centroamericanos* 348/349 (1977): 707–22; Gustavo Gutiérrez et al., *Cruz y Resurrección: Presencia y anuncio de una iglesia nueva* (Mexico City: CRT-

Servir, 1978); Oscar A. Romero et al., *Iglesia de los pobres y organizaciones populares* (San Salvador: UCA, 1978); Ellacuría, "Una buena noticia: La Iglesia nace del pueblo latinoamericano," *Estudios Centroamericanos* 353 (1978): 161–73.

17. Gustavo Gutiérrez has emphasized that a liberative ecclesial praxis has the perspective of the poor, whose liberation is precisely at issue (*Power of the Poor in History,* pp. 210–14) and that in this praxis, implemented from a point of departure in the poor, the poor evangelize us (ibid., p. 105). Thus, the circle to which I have referred: from encountering Jesus in the gospels, to evangelizing the poor, to encountering Jesus in the poor.

18. See Walter Kasper, *Jesus the Christ,* pp. 27–28.

19. Ignacio Ellacuría, "Discernir el 'signo' de los tiempos," *Diakonía* 17 (April 1981): 58.

20. Hugo Assmann, *Theology for a Nomad Church,* p. 54.

21. Ibid.; italics added.

22. Hugo Assmann ("Tecnología y poder en la perspectiva de la teología de la liberación," in *Tecnología y necesidades básicas,* Asociación de Economistas del Tercer Mundo [San José, Costa Rica: CPID / Consejo Mundial de Iglesias, 1979], pp. 31–32) has once again emphasized the primacy for theological thought of Latin American reality and its demand for transformation. "Liberation theology says that the crucial experience of this nonsatisfaction of basic needs is the 'prime consideration,' and that in this 'prime consideration' is included the struggle for the just satisfaction of these needs. This struggle is just, real, and normal. It needs no sort of ulterior justification. 'Theology' as 'second act' and critical reflection upon praxis can be useful for 'dislodging resistance,' but it neither is nor pretends to be the legitimation of this struggle. On the contrary, theology is itself liberated, as theology—that is, as a possible valid and relevant discourse upon the 'Word of Life' (see 1 John 1)—in virtue of its logically required acceptance of this struggle on the part of the people against anti-life."

23. Ignacio Ellacuría, "Hacia una fundamentación filosófica del método teológico latinoamericano," *Estudios Centroamericanos* 322/323 (1975): 419.

24. How cognition of reality develops concretely from a determinate social location is something that calls for a detailed analysis. But at all events two forms of social consciousness, arising from the same social location, are to be distinguished: one is the product of an intuitive, sapiential cognition; the other is articulated by way of analysis. The first is necessary, surely, but the second is also required for christo-*log*-ical reflection. See Leonardo Boff, "Jesucristo Liberador," pp. 178–87.

25. Albert Schweitzer, *Geschichte der Leben-Jesu-Forschung* (Munich and Hamburg: Siebenstern Taschenbuch, 1966), p. 47. Others posit the horizon of the movement of Jesus' life in the defeat of a Hegelian idealism rather than of the authoritarianism of dogma. See Carlos Palacio, *Jesucristo: historia e interpretación* (Madrid: Cristiandad, 1978), pp. 51–52.

26. See Wolfhart Pannenberg, *Jesus, God and Man,* pp. 53–114: "Jesus' Resurrection as the Ground of His Unity with God."

27. See Carlos Palacio, *Jesucristo: Historia e interpretación,* pp. 36–51.

28. Walter Kasper, *Jesus the Christ,* p. 20.

29. Edward Schillebeeckx, *Jesus: An Experiment in Christology,* p. 28.

30. Ibid., p. 30.

31. *Theology of Hope: On the Ground and the Implications of a Christian Eschatology,* trans. James W. Leicht (New York and Evanston: Harper & Row, 1967), pp. 240–41.

32. This is the radical differential between Latin American theology and the hermeneutics of Rahner, Bultmann, Fuchs, Ebeling, Gadamer, and Pannenberg, who seek continuity between the past of sacred history and the present of the believer in a common horizon of understanding, against which the past and the contemporary believer, despite the distance between the two, would strike a mutual relationship. This common horizon is bestowed, in the case of Christian faith, by Christ.

33. See Ignacio Ellacuría, "La teología como momento ideológico de la praxis eclesial," *Estudios Eclesiásticos* 53 (1978): 467ff.

34. See Fernando Belo, *A Materialist Reading of the Gospel of Mark* (Maryknoll, N.Y.: Orbis, 1981); Michel Clévenot, *Lectura materialista de la Biblia* (Salamanca: Sígueme, 1978; Engl. trans. *Materialist Approaches to the Bible,* trans. William J. Nottingham, Maryknoll, N.Y.: Orbis, 1985), pp. 109–212. What Latin American christology values in these studies is their presentation of Jesus' life as the story of a practice, but without, as so often happens, bracketing the "practicer"—without prescinding from the person of Jesus.

35. Willi Marxsen, *The Resurrection of Jesus of Nazareth,* trans. Margaret Kohl (Philadelphia: Fortress, 1970), p. 141: "The cause of Jesus continues. . . ." Cf. ibid., p. 78.

36. Thus Latin American christology does not ignore the problematic of the believer's meaning—the meaning of faith in Christ and faith in general. But it does reposition the locus of the seizure of meaning. I have explicitly reflected on this subject elsewhere, with respect to both the problem of the meaning of Jesus and that of the meaning of the believer. See *Christology at the Crossroads,* trans. John Drury (Maryknoll, N.Y.: Orbis, 1978), pp. 79–102, 146–78; and "La promoción de la justicia como exigencia esencial del mensaje evangélico," *Estudios Centroamericanos* 371 (1979).

37. "The concrete content of [the kingdom] emerges from [Jesus'] ministry and activity as a whole" (Edward Schillebeeckx, *Jesus: An Experiment in Christology,* p. 143).

38. Carlos Palacio, *Jesucristo: Historia e interpretación,* p. 50.

39. It is interesting that wherever the situation is seen to be in continuity with that of Jesus, the faithful return spontaneously to the historical Jesus, even outside Latin America. See the book by Indian theologian Sebastian Kappen, *Jesus and Freedom* (Maryknoll, N.Y.: Orbis, 1977), and the above-mentioned christologies from Spain developed from a viewpoint analogous to that of liberation, especially the excellent book by José Ignacio González Faus, *Acceso a Jesús* (Salamanca: Sígueme, 1979), and his articles "En defensa de las cristologías sudamericanas" (*Sal Terrae* [January 1979]: 45–51); "Diccionario de términos discutidos en Puebla" (*Sal Terrae* [March 1979]: 206–7, 211–12).

40. See José Ignacio González Faus, *Acceso a Jesús,* p. 45.

41. See *Jesus: An Experiment in Christology,* pp. 81–102.

CHAPTER 3: JESUS AND THE KINGDOM OF GOD

1. Karl Rahner and Wilhelm Thüsing, *A New Christology,* trans. David Smith and Verdant Green (New York: Seabury, 1980); Hans Küng, *On Being a Christian,* trans. Edward Quinn (Garden City, N.Y.: Doubleday, 1976), p. 214; Leonardo Boff, *Jesus Christ Liberator: A Critical Christology for Our Time* (Maryknoll, N.Y.: Orbis, 1978), p. 63; Jon Sobrino, *Christology at the Crossroads: A Latin American Approach,* trans. John Drury (Maryknoll, N.Y.: Orbis, 1978), p. 41.

2. See Wilhelm Thüsing, "La imagen de Dios en el Nuevo Testamento," in *Dios*

como problema, ed. Joseph Ratzinger (Madrid: Cristiandad, 1973), pp. 80–120.

3. See Rahner and Thüsing, *A New Christology,* p. 8.

4. Walter Kasper, *Jesus the Christ,* trans. Verdant Green (London: Burns & Oates; New York: Paulist, 1977), p. 72.

5. See Sobrino, *Christology at the Crossroads,* pp. 151–76.

6. By way of contrast with the insistence of so many first-world theologies on the eschatological reserve imposed by the absolute character of the kingdom, in Latin America the insistence is on the "mediating concretions of the kingdom," inasmuch as the latter "is not given in its totality, but in historical mediations, and is realized at all levels of political, economic, social, and religious reality" (Leonardo Boff, "Salvación en Jesucristo y proceso de liberación," *Concilium* 96 [1974]: 385–87).

7. See Jürgen Becker, *Johannes der Täufer und Jesus von Nazareth* (Neukirchen/Vluyn: Neukirchener, 1972), pp. 12–15.

8. Wolfhart Pannenberg, "The Revelation of God in Jesus," in *Theology as History,* ed. James M. Robinson and John B. Cobb, Jr., New Frontiers in Theology: Discussions among Continental and American Theologians, vol. 3 (New York, Evanston, and London: Harper & Row, 1967), pp. 101–33.

9. Walter Kasper, *Jesus the Christ,* p. 72.

10. Walter Kasper (*Jesus the Christ,* pp. 89–99) follows the same method, except that he does not sufficiently analyze Jesus' activity, especially in the aspect of its conflictuality, controversy, and praxis of efficacious, partisan, socio-political love. Kasper reduces the latter to a general love of God that in turn translates, likewise rather generically, into love, forgiveness, and mercy.

11. L. Armendáriz, "El 'Reino de Dios,' centro y mensaje de la vida de Jesús," *Sal Terrae* (May 1976): 364.

12. Ibid.

13. "Thus the reign of God is neither a spatial nor a static concept. It is a *dynamic* concept. It denotes the reign of God in action, in the first place as opposed to earthly monarchy, but then in contrast to all rule in heaven and on earth. Its chief characteristic is that God is realizing the ideal of the king of righteousness . . ." (Joachim Jeremias, *New Testament Theology: The Proclamation of Jesus,* trans. John Bowden [New York: Scribner's, 1971], p. 98; italics in original).

14. "Whatever political dreams or indeed whatever fantastic expectations of the destruction or rebirth of the world were bound up with the hopes of the Jews, it is a fundamental part of these hopes that the spirit of resignation which banishes God to a misty place beyond our ideals and which accepts the idea that no change is possible in this world, is totally strange to it" (Günther Bornkamm, *Jesus of Nazareth,* trans. Irene and Fraser McLuskey [New York, Evanston, and London: Harper & Row, 1960], p. 65).

15. To be sure, Jesus moved in an apocalyptic atmosphere as far as the expectation of the imminence of the end and the transformation of reality is concerned. But his categories of *content,* of how the kingdom of God *draws near* and how one corresponds to its approach, are those of prophecy. Hence I detail the latter, however sketchily.

16. See José Porfirio Miranda, *Marx and the Bible,* trans. John Eagleson (Maryknoll, N.Y.: Orbis, 1974), pp. 77–108; J. Alonso Díaz, "Términos bíblicos de Justicia Social y traducción de equivalencia dinámica," *Estudios Eclesiásticos* (January–March 1976): 95–128.

17. Thus the age-old dream of the peoples will come to realization, a dream of genuine justice—justice because it is partisan justice. "Kingly righteousness . . . was not primarily one of dispassionate adjudication, but of the protection which the king extends to the

helpless, the weak and the poor, widows and orphans" (Joachim Jeremias, *New Testament Theology,* p. 98).

"When in human history the function of judge or of what later came to be called judge was conceived, it was exclusively to help those who because of their weakness could not defend themselves; the others did not need it. . . . When the Bible speaks of Yahweh as "Judge" or of the Judgment whose subject is Yahweh, it has in mind precisely the meaning which we have seen for the root *špht:* to save the oppressed from injustice" (José Porfirio Miranda, *Marx and the Bible,* p. 114).

18. Although there is a discontinuity between the prophetical and apocalyptical traditions, a basic continuity obtains where the justice of God is concerned. " 'Resurrection of the dead' was not an anthropological or a soteriological symbol, but a way towards expressing belief in the righteousness of God. God is righteous. His righteousness will conquer" (Jürgen Moltmann, *The Crucified God: The Cross of Christ as the Foundation and Criticism of Christian Theology,* trans. R. A. Wilson and John Bowden, 2nd ed. [New York, Evanston, San Francisco, London: Harper & Row, 1973], p. 174).

19. This notion is characterized especially by formal determinations: the sudden irruption of the kingdom, its attribute of universal judgment, its concealment and mystery in the present. See Günther Bornkamm, *Jesus of Nazareth,* pp. 64–81. This is why it seems so important not to center the occurrences of the kingdom's approach on apocalyptic *thinking,* but on what Jesus says and does in this "meantime," this interim.

20. Joachim Jeremias, *New Testament Theology,* pp. 108, 116; italics in original.

21. Ibid., p. 112; italics in the original.

22. Ibid., p. 113.

23. This is the ultimate explanation for the allegation of blasphemy directed against Jesus, for which he is sentenced to death. See Jürgen Moltmann, *The Crucified God,* pp. 128–35; Jon Sobrino, *Christology at the Crossroads,* pp. 204–9.

24. Oscar Cullmann, *Jesus and the Revolutionaries,* trans. Gareth Putnam (New York: Harper & Row, 1970), p. 27.

25. See ibid., p. 25.

26. Joachim Jeremias, *New Testament Theology,* pp. 212–13.

27. Gustavo Gutiérrez, *A Theology of Liberation: History, Politics and Salvation,* trans. Caridad Inda and John Eagleson (Maryknoll, N.Y.: Orbis, 1980), p. 198.

28. This is the ultimate explanation for the allegation of subversion that occasions Jesus' death, for he subverts a political order based on oppressive power. See Jürgen Moltmann, *The Crucified God,* pp. 136–45; Jon Sobrino, *Christology at the Crossroads,* pp. 209–15.

29. I shall develop the theme of discernment in history after Jesus' resurrection in chap. 5, "Following Jesus as Discernment."

30. As discerned in history after the resurrection of Jesus. I have elaborated on this in "El seguimiento de Jesús como discernimiento cristiano" (*Concilium* [November 1978]: 521–29).

31. "Homilía con motivo de la expulsión del P. Mario Bernal" ("Homily on the Occasion of the Expulsion of Father Mario Bernal"), delivered in Apopa, February 13, 1977, as found in *Estudios Centroamericanos* 348–49 (1979): 859.

CHAPTER 4: THE EPIPHANY OF THE GOD OF LIFE

1. See, for example, Wolfhart Pannenberg, *Was ist der Mensch?* (Göttingen: Vanderhoek & Ruprecht, 1962, rev. 1964), pp. 5–31; Engl. trans., *What Is Man? Contem-*

porary Anthropology in Theological Perspective, trans. Duane A. Priebe (Philadelphia: Fortress, 1970), pp. 1–27. Freedom is conceived as "openness to the world" (p. 3). "The human being is completely directed into the 'open' " (p. 8). And "the word [God] can be used in a meaningful way only if it means the entity toward which the human being's boundless independence is directed" (p. 10). It is not that Pannenberg disregards the complexity of the human being's historical life, as is evident throughout the work cited, but in relating the human being to God methodologically, he does so by concentrating on the freedom of the human being. See also, on this topic, his work *Gottesgedanke und menschliche Freiheit* (Göttingen, 1972).

2. "Affirmations concerning the divine reality or divine action lend themselves to an examination of their implications for the understanding of finite reality" (Wolfhart Pannenberg, "Wie wahr ist das Reden von Gott?" in *Evangelische Kommentare* 4 [1971]: 631). Or, stated christologically, "As long as the whole of reality can be understood more deeply and more convincingly through Jesus than without him, it proves true in our everyday experience and personal knowledge that in Jesus the creative origin of all reality stands revealed" ("The Revelation of God in Jesus of Nazareth," *Theology as History,* New Frontiers in Theology, vol. 3, ed. J. M. Robinson and J. B. Cobb [New York: Harper & Row, 1976], p. 133).

3. See A. Deissler, "El Dios del Antiguo Testamento," in *Dios como problema,* ed. J. Ratzinger (Madrid, 1973), pp. 65–69.

4. See Carlos Escudero Freire, *Devolver el Evangelio a los pobres* (Salamanca, 1978), p. 9.

5. "One must be very careful when speaking of the 'notions of God' that Jesus had, for Jesus does not expound on notions of God that may be formulated and taught to others. Rather, he acts in such a way that the concrete decisions and practices that he adopts are different from those of his environment. He uses a parable or an image in such a way that one may sense from his manner of acting, together with his proclamation (which tells about an event), and from their mutual interaction, that God is such, or, more aptly, that God acts in such and such a way" (H. Kessler, *Erlösung als Befreiung* [Düsseldorf, 1972], pp. 77ff.). I have also used this way of approaching Jesus' understanding of God in "Jesús y el Reino de Dios," *Sal Terrae* (May 1978): 345–64.

6. See J. Ernst, *Anfänge der Christologie* (Stuttgart, 1972); Ernst Käsemann, *Der Ruf der Freiheit,* 3rd ed. rev. (Tübingen: Mohr, 1968), Engl. trans., *Jesus Means Freedom* (Philadelphia: Fortress, 1970), pp. 16–41; Christian Duquoc, *Christologie: Essai dogmatique sur l'homme Jésus* (Paris: Cerf, 1968), Span. trans., *Cristología* (Salamanca, 1972), pp. 109ff.; Jürgen Moltmann, *Der gekreuzigte Gott,* 2nd ed. (Munich: Kaiser, 1973), Engl. trans., *The Crucified God: The Cross of Christ as the Foundation and Criticism of Christian Theology,* trans. R.A. Wilson and John Bowden (New York: Harper & Row, 1974), pp. 136–45; Joachim Jeremias, *Neutestamentliche Theologie,* I: *Die Verkündigung Jesu* (Gütersloh: Mohn, 1971), Engl. trans., *New Testament Theology: The Proclamation of Jesus,* trans. John Bowden, (New York: Scribner's, 1971), pp. 250–56; Günther Bornkamm, *Jesus von Nazaret,* 3rd ed. (Stuttgart: Kohlhammer, 1959), Engl. trans., *Jesus of Nazareth* (New York: Harper; London: Hodder & Stoughton, 1960), pp. 96–100; Herbert Braun, *Jesus: Der Mann aus Nazaret und seine Zeit* (Stuttgart: Kreuz, 1969), pp. 72ff.; Leonardo Boff, *Jesucristo el Libertador: Ensaio de Cristología critica para o nosso tempo* (Petrópolis: Vozes, 1972), Engl. trans., *Jesus Christ Liberator: A Critical Christology for Our Time,* trans. Patrick Hughes (Maryknoll, N.Y.: Orbis, 1978), pp. 101–4; José Miranda, *Marx y la Biblia* (Salamanca: Sígueme, 1971), Engl. trans., *Marx and the Bible: A Critique of the*

Philosophy of Oppression, trans. John Eagleson (Maryknoll, N.Y.: Orbis, 1974). If I emphasize the fact that Jesus was a nonconformist, it is for the purpose of showing that European and Latin American theologians are in agreement with it. The problem will be to ascertain exactly in what respect and for what reason he was a nonconformist.

7. See I. Ellacuría, "El pueblo crucificado: Ensayo de soterología histórica," in *Cruz y Resurrección* (Mexico City, 1978).

8. This idea is repeated often, sometimes to insist, rightfully, that theology should not reduce human life to its purely sociopolitical dimensions; but sometimes to keep the notion of supernatural life apart from historical life, as noted in some official documents—for example, the Declaration on Human Advancement and Christian Salvation (International Theological Commission) or the Consultation Document (Puebla).

9. Here I am analyzing the confirmation and intensification that Jesus makes of the Decalogue. Later on, we shall see how he criticizes certain scriptural passages dealing with ritual regulations. In the latter sense, it may be said that "the scriptures themselves . . . had to submit to Jesus' criticism" (Bornkamm, *Jesus of Nazareth,* pp. 97-98).

10. Jeremias, *New Testament Theology,* p. 210.

11. Ibid., p. 208.

12. Käsemann, *Jesus Means Freedom,* p. 26.

13. See Leonardo Boff, *The Lord's Prayer* (Maryknoll, N.Y.: Orbis, 1983).

14. Jeremias, *New Testament Theology,* p. 200.

15. For the reconstruction of the most original traditions in this passage I am following Pierre Benoit and M. E. Boismard, *Sinopse des quatre Evangiles* (Paris, 1972), pp. 105f., 115-17.

16. Ibid., p. 116.

17. On the disputed historical and theological meaning of "the poor," see Ignacio Ellacuría, "Las Bienaventuras como Carta Fundacional de la Iglesia de los Pobres," in *Reino de Dios: Iglesia de los pobres y organizaciones populares,* Centro de Reflexión Teológica (San Salvador: UCA Ed., 1978).

18. See Carlos Escudero Freire, *Devolver el Evangelio,* pp. 259-77.

19. Ibid., p. 271.

20. Ibid., p. 270.

21. Ibid., p. 266.

22. Jeremias, *New Testament Theology,* p. 104.

23. Escudero Freire, *Devolver el Evangelio,* p. 273.

24. See Sobrino, "Jesús y el Reino de Dios," pp. 356ff.

25. See Jeremias, *New Testament Theology,* p. 109.

26. Ibid., p. 116.

27. St. Jerome is more categorical when he asserts: "Hence all riches derive from injustice, and unless one loses, the other cannot gain. Therefore it is clear to me that the familiar proverb is eminently true: 'The rich person is either unjust or an heir of an unjust person' " (*Letters, PL,* 22, 984).

28. Escudero Freire, *Devolver el Evangelio,* p. 273.

29. Ibid., p. 315.

30. *Synopse,* pp. 354-56.

31. Ibid., pp. 357ff.

32. Ibid., p. 335.

33. Jeremias, *New Testament Theology,* p. 145.

34. See Boismard, *Synopse,* pp. 105ff.

35. See H. Braun, *Jesus,* pp. 161ff.

36. Jeremias, *New Testament Theology,* p. 210.

37. Duquoc, *Cristología,* p. 110.

38. Bornkamm, *Jesus of Nazareth,* p. 97.

39. Käsemann, *Exegetische Versuche und Besinnungen,* vol. 1 (Göttingen, 1969), p. 207.

40. Braun, *Jesus,* p. 73.

41. Bornkamm, *Jesus of Nazareth,* p. 106.

42. See Ellacuría, "Fe y Justicia," *Christus* (October 1977): 23ff.

43. Bornkamm, *Jesus of Nazareth,* p. 100.

44. See Boismard, *Synopse,* pp. 349–52.

45. See C. Schutz, "Los misterios de la vida y actividad pública de Jesús," in *Mysterium salutis: Manual de teología como historia de la salvación* (Madrid: Ed. Cristiandad, 1969), III/II, p. 92. Internally, Jesus lives with the dilemma of true and false messianism, and that dilemma "existed as a real problem throughout his life" (Ellacuría, *Teología política* [San Salvador: Secretariado Social Interdiocesano, 1973], Engl. trans., *Freedom Made Flesh: The Mission of Christ and His Church,* trans. John Drury [Maryknoll, N.Y.: Orbis, 1976], p. 56).

46. See Bornkamm, *Jesus of Nazareth,* p. 157; C. H. Dodd, *The Founder of Christianity* (London: Macmillan, 1970), p. 137.

47. Bornkamm, *Jesus of Nazareth,* p. 153.

48. See Dodd, *Founder,* p. 127.

49. Ibid., pp. 128–29.

50. See Boismard, *Synopse,* p. 417; Bornkamm, *Jesus of Nazareth,* p. 164.

51. Bornkamm, *Jesus of Nazareth,* p. 164.

52. See Boismard, *Synopse,* p. 417.

53. Braun, *Jesus,* p. 51.

54. Moltmann, *The Crucified God,* p. 136.

55. See Braun, *Jesus,* pp. 49ff.; Bornkamm, *Jesus of Nazareth,* pp. 163–67.

56. Boismard, *Synopse,* p. 408.

57. See Joachim Jeremias, *Jerusalem zur Zeit Jesu* (Göttingen: Vandenhoek & Ruprecht, 1962, rev. 1967), Engl. trans., *Jerusalem in the Time of Jesus: An Investigation into Economic and Social Conditions during the New Testament Period,* trans. F. H. Cave and C. H. Cave (Philadelphia: Fortress, 1969); Fernando Belo, *Lecture matérialiste de l'évangile de Marc: Récit-Pratique-Idéologie,* 2nd ed. rev. (Paris: Du Cerf, 1975), Engl. trans., *A Materialist Reading of the Gospel of Mark,* trans. Matthew J. O'Connell (Maryknoll, N.Y.: Orbis, 1981).

58. See Moltmann, *The Crucified God,* pp. 128–30. Historically, those responsible for Jesus' death were those who were protecting the interests of the temple: "It may be reasonably thought that the architects of his death were primarily the members of the priestly caste, exasperated upon seeing Jesus appear as a religious reformer of the cultural practices that were in effect in his time" (Boismard, *Synopse,* p. 408).

59. Moltmann, *The Crucified God,* p. 127.

60. Christian Duquoc, "El Dios de Jesús y la crisis de Dios en nuestro tiempo," in *Jesucristo en la historia y en la fe,* ed. A. Vargas-Machuca (Salamanca, 1977), p. 49.

61. Ibid.

62. Moltmann, *The Crucified God,* p. 127.

63. See K. Rahner's analysis, in both its positive and expositive aspects, as a polemic of what "mystery" means theo-logically, *Theological Investigations,* vol. 4, trans. Kevin Smith (Baltimore: Helicon, 1966), pp. 36–73.

64. In essence, this is the ultimate problem of theodicy. It involves "justifying God," but on the basis of the supremacy of life. If death has the last word, then life is vain as a mediation of God, and the reality of God is vain; and reality itself and what takes place in it will be vain as well. M. Horkheimer, in *Die Sehnsucht nach dem ganz Anderen* (Hamburg, 1970), although he himself does not claim to be a believer in the conventional sense, has put it admirably: "[God] is important, because theology is present in any authentic human action. . . . A policy that does not preserve a theology within itself, even if only in a very unreflective way, will in the long run be nothing more than some form of 'business,' regardless of how well it is conducted" (p. 60). And although the author does not know how to identify the positive content of theology, and does not wish to do so, he defines it as the ultimate justification of life: "An expression of a desire, of a desire that the murderer may not be able to emerge victorious over the innocent victim" (p. 62).

65. The relationship of the mystery and its qualification as a mystery in experience itself is a transcendental relationship. "The whither of the experience of transcendence is always there in the nameless, the indefinable, the unattainable. For a name distinguishes and demarcates, pins down something by giving it a name chosen among many other names. But the infinite horizon, the whither of transcendence, cannot be so defined. We may reflect upon it, objectivate it, conceive of it so to speak as one object among others, and define it conceptually: but this set of concepts is only true, and a correct and intelligible expression of the content when this expression and description is once more conditioned by a transcendent act directed to the whither of this transcendence" (Rahner, *Theological Investigations,* vol. 4, p. 50).

66. Here I am of course referring to Jesus' experience as a human being, without treating of the eternal trinitarian relationship between the Son and the Father. Because I cannot go into greater detail here, I shall give a bibliography on the subject. Its size will also show that this consideration of Jesus' theo-logical experience is of great current interest and is not an invention of Latin American theology. Jeremias, *New Testament Theology,* pp. 61–68, 250–56; Bornkamm, *Jesus of Nazareth,* pp. 103–52; Braun, *Jesus,* pp. 159–70; Norman Perrin, *Rediscovering the Teaching of Jesus* (New York: Harper & Row, 1967), pp. 148–53; K. Niederwimmer, *Jesus* (Göttingen: Vandenhoek, 1968), pp. 53–70; Wolfhart Pannenberg, *Grundzüge der Christologie* (Gütersloh: Mohn, 1964), Engl. trans., *Jesus, God and Man,* trans. Lewis T. Wilkins and Duane A. Priebe (Philadelphia: Westminster, 1968), pp. 223–35; Moltmann, *The Crucified God,* pp. 112–53; Karl Rahner and Wilhelm Thüsing, *Christologie, systematisch und exegetisch* (Freiberg: Herder, 1972), Engl. trans., *A New Christology,* trans. David Smith and Verdant Green (New York: Crossroad, 1980), pp. 8–15, 161, 191–94; Leonardo Boff, *La experiencia de Dios* (Bogotá, 1975), pp. 54–68; idem, *Jesus Christ Liberator,* p. 145; W. Wiederkehr, "Esbozo de cristología sistemática," in *Mysterium salutis* III/I, pp. 649–52; Piet Schoonenberg, *Hij is ein God van Mensen* (The Hague: Momberg, 1969), Engl. trans., *The Christ: A Study of the God-Man Relationship in the Whole of Creation and in Jesus Christ,* trans. Della Coulton (New York: Herder & Herder, 1971), pp. 130–40; Duquoc, *Christología,* pp. 226–44; idem, "The Hope of Jesus," *Concilium* 59, *The Dimensions of Spirituality* (New York: Herder and Herder, 1970), pp. 21–30; G. I. Gonzalez Faus, *La humanidad nueva* (Madrid, 1974), pp. 114–22; Urs von Balthasar, "Fides Christi," *Verbum Caro: Skizzen zur Theologie,* 2 vols. (Einsiedeln: Johannes), Span. trans., *Ensayos teológicos* II (Madrid: Sponsa Verbi, 1964), pp. 51–96; E. Fuchs, "Jesus und der Glaúbe," *Zur Frage nach dem historischen Jesus* (Tübingen: Mohr, 1960), pp. 238–57; Christian Duquoc et al., "El Dios de Jesús y la crisis de Dios en nuestro tiempo," in *Jesucristo en la historia y en la fe* (Salamanca, 1977), pp. 21–85.

67. Jeremias has stressed the historical quality and originality of this invocation (*New Testament Theology,* pp. 63–68). Duquoc also accepts its genuineness, though he does not see its originality in the invocation itself, but in its inclusion within liberating action ("El Dios de Jesús y la crisis de Dios en nuestro tiempo," p. 49).

68. It is still important to remember that the first Christian theologians defined God as "love" (1 John 4:8, 16), and declared love for one's neighbor to be the fundamental commandment (1 John 4:11; John 13:34, 15:12, 17; Gal. 5:14; Rom. 13:8ff.).

69. Pannenberg has shown (in *Theology and the Kingdom of God,* ed. Richard J. Neuhaus [Philadelphia: Westminster, 1969], pp. 64–71) that, from a conceptual stand-point, the notions of God as creator, as power over everything, and as absolute future are reconcilable only if God's ultimate reality is love. But this analysis is conceptual, based on the coherence of these concepts. I am attempting rather, to show that history indicates that it *must* be so.

70. Jon Sobrino, *Cristología desde América Latina* (Mexico City: Centro de Reflexión Teológica, 1976), Engl. trans., *Christology at the Crossroads,* trans. John Drury (Maryknoll, N.Y.: Orbis, 1978), p. 126.

71. Ibid., pp. 96–99.

72. "Not until we understand his abandonment by the God and Father whose imminence and closeness he had proclaimed in a unique, gracious, and festive way, can we understand what was distinct about his death" (Moltmann, *The Crucified God,* p. 149).

73. Ernst Bloch (in *Das Prinzip Hoffnung,* 3 vols. [Frankfurt: Suhrkamp, 1959]) presents a keen analysis of the meaning of the martyr's death, in this instance that of the "red hero": "As soon as he confesses his cause leading to martyrdom, the cause for which he has lived, he goes clearly, dispassionately, and consciously toward the nothing-ness in which he has been taught to believe as a free spirit" (p. 1378). It is different for Jesus, not on the psychological level, but on the theo-logical one; to Jesus, what was at stake was not only the meaning of "his" life, but the reality of the kingdom of God. Nevertheless, Bloch himself, when he passes from psychological to metaphysical con-siderations, poses the problem of the survival of what is real as such, in the end—the supremacy of life: "Because the central moment in our existence has not yet occurred absolutely in the process of its objectivization, and, finally, in its fulfillment; and hence the hero cannot really succumb to what is perishable" (p. 1387). When it actually happens, death will be extraterritorial to him (p. 1391).

74. "As Bonhoeffer rightly said, the only credible God is the God of the mystics. But this is not a God unrelated to human history. On the contrary, if it is true, as we recalled above, that one must go through man to reach God, it is equally certain that the 'passing through' to that gratuitous God strips me, leaves me naked, universalizes my love for others, and makes it gratuitous. Both movements need each other dialectically and move toward a synthesis" (Gustavo Gutiérrez, *A Theology of Liberation* [Maryknoll, N.Y.: Orbis, 1973], p. 206).

CHAPTER 5: FOLLOWING JESUS AS DISCERNMENT

1. Many of the points in this article are dealt with at greater length in my *Christology at the Crossroads: A Latin American Approach* (Maryknoll, N.Y.: Orbis, 1978), pp. 79–178.

2. It should be said in passing that Jesus' ignorance, on the theological level, is the condition of his discernment: knowledge of a greater God is only possible from the

standpoint of not knowing. Of course, I am dealing throughout the article with the relationship between Jesus as creature and his Father, not the intra-trinitarian relationship between the first two persons of the Trinity.

3. For this "diminution of God," as we may call it, see *Christology at the Crossroads,* pp. 165–76.

4. Ernst Käsemann, *La llamada a la libertad* (Salamanca: Sígueme, 1975), p. 35. German original: *Der Ruf der Freiheit,* 4th ed. (Tübingen: Mohr, 1968).

5. Ignacio Ellacuría, "La Iglesia que nace del pueblo por el Espíritu," *Misión Abierta* 71 (1978): 155ff.

6. Idem, "La Iglesia de los pobres, sacramento histórico de liberación," *Estudios Centroamericanos* 348–49 (1977): 707–22.

7. See Enrique D. Dussel, "Differentiation of Charisms," *Concilium* 129 (1977).

8. This is the standpoint from which we may understand the extensive and weighty discussions on the relationship between the church and capitalism or socialism as a process of discernment of how to *bring about* the kingdom of God in practice. See Juan Luis Segundo, "Capitalism–Socialism: The Theological Crux," *Concilium* 96 (1974); Ellacuría, "Economic Theories and the Relationship between Christianity and Socialism," *Concilium* 125 (1977).

CHAPTER 6: JESUS' RELATIONSHIP WITH THE POOR AND OUTCAST

1. This study does not purport to be an exegesis of the various synoptic traditions and their contributions to the subject. I am not trying to discover what in their accounts of Jesus is genuinely historical as opposed to historicized in the early communities, but I am assuming that there exists a sufficient deposit of historicity related to the subject to enable the data to be ordered systematically.

2. See Ignacio Ellacuría, "La Iglesia de los pobres: Sacramento histórico de la liberación," *Estudios Centroamericanos* (October–November 1977): 710ff.

3. See Walter Kasper, *Jesus the Christ,* trans. Verdant Green (London: Burns & Oates, 1977), pp. 72–73; Edward Schillebeeckx, *Jesus: An Experiment in Christology,* trans. Hubert Hoskins (New York: Seabury, 1979), p. 143.

4. Schillebeeckx, *Jesus;* Jon Sobrino, "Jesús y el reino de Dios," *Sal Terrae* (May 1978): 350.

5. See Joachim Jeremias, *New Testament Theology: The Proclamation of Jesus,* trans. John Bowden (New York: Scribner's, 1971), pp. 116–17.

6. On this duality in the meaning and concept of "the poor," see ibid., pp. 109–13.

7. Ibid., p. 104.

8. This does not mean reducing the kingdom of God to the basic levels of life, but it does mean that these should be borne in mind lest we forget the basic requirement of the kingdom when speaking of more abundant life and eschatological fullness in accordance with the gospel.

9. The mere fact of poverty is important in determining the nature of the kingdom of God, but not all poverty is automatically efficacious for historical salvation. See Ellacuría, "Las bienaventuranzas como carta fundacional de la Iglesia de los pobres," in *Iglesia de los pobres y organizaciones populares,* by Oscar A. Romero et al. (San Salvador: UCA, 1978), p. 118.

10. As the Puebla Final Document recognized (no. 1142): "For this reason alone, the poor merit preferential attention, whatever may be the moral or personal situation in which they find themselves. . . . God takes on their defense and loves them (Matt. 5:45;

James 2:5)" (John Eagleson and Philip Scharper, eds., *Puebla and Beyond: Documentation and Commentary,* trans. John Drury [Maryknoll, N.Y.: Orbis, 1979], p. 265). See Gustavo Gutiérrez, "Pobres y liberación en Puebla, *Páginas,* (April 1979): 11ff.

11. See Carlos Escudero Freire, *Devolver el evangelio a los pobres: a propósito de Lc 1–2* (Salamanca: Sígueme, 1978), pp. 269ff.

12. See Pierre Benoit, M.-E. Benoit, and J. L. Malillos, *Sinopsis de los cuatro evangelios con paralelos de los apócrifos y de los padres* (Bilbao: Desclée de Brouwer, 1976), pp. 96–110, 215–17.

13. See Ellacuría, "La Iglesia de los pobres."

14. Otherwise such statements remain paradoxical, and without any practical effect. One might ask what real results the fine words of Karl Barth have had, written decades ago and quoted by Gutiérrez in "Pobres y liberación en Puebla," to the effect that God always takes the side of the poor, and only the side of the poor, absolutely and unconditionally—that God is always against the proud, those with rights and privileges, and always for those who are denied their rights (*Kirchliche Dogmatik* [Zürich: Evangelischer Verlag, 1940], 1:434).

CHAPTER 8: A CRUCIFIED PEOPLE'S FAITH

1. Ignacio Ellacuría, "Discernir 'el signo' de los tiempos," *Diakonia* 17 (April 1981): 58.

2. Medellín took pains to link the "injustice which cries to the heaven" (Justice, no. 1) with the "desire for total emancipation, for liberation from every form of slavery, for personal maturation and collective integration" (Introduction, no. 4). Both taken together constitute the signs of the times.

3. Homily of October 21, 1979, in J. Sobrino, I. Martín Baro, and R. Cardenal, *La voz de los sin voz* (San Salvador, 1980), p. 366.

4. Christian Duquoc, *Christologie: Essai dogmatique* (Paris: Cerf, 1973), p. 143.

5. See "El pueblo crucificado," in *Cruz y resurrección: Presencia y anuncio de una iglesia nueva* (Mexico City: CRT/Servir, 1978); "Las bienaventuranzas como carta fundamental de la Iglesia de los pobres," in Oscar A. Romero et al., *Iglesia de los pobres y organizaciones populares* (San Salvador: UCA, 1978), pp. 105–118; "El verdadero pueblo de Dios," *Estudios Centroamericanos* (June 1981): 529–54.

6. Homily of June 21, 1979, in Jon Sobrino, I. Martín Baro, and R. Cardenal, *La voz de los sin voz* (San Salvador, 1980), p. 337.

7. See chapter 5 above, "Following Jesus as Discernment."

8. Archbishop Romero gave us a remarkable example of how to combine the practice of effective liberation with the spirit of the Beatitudes. See my "La Iglesia en el actual proceso del pais," *Estudios Centroamericanos* 372–73 (1979): 918–20; and "Mons. Romero y la Iglesia salvadoreña, un año después," ibid. 389 (1981): 148–50.

9. See Archbishop Romero's third and fourth pastoral letters in Romero, *Voice of the Voiceless* (Maryknoll, N.Y.: Orbis, 1985), pp. 85–161; and the November 17, 1979, Pastoral Letter of the Nicaraguan Bishops.

10. Karl Rahner and Karl-Heinz Weger, *Our Christian Faith: Answers for the Future,* trans. Francis McDonagh (New York: Crossroad, 1981), pp. 93–94.

Index

Compiled by William E. Jerman

Also from Orbis . . .

CHRISTOLOGY AT THE CROSSROADS
Jon Sobrino
A landmark contribution to contemporary christological thought and action, rooted in the historical Jesus and in the Latin American experience of injustice and oppression.

"The most profound elaboration of a theological method from the perspective of Latin America." *Theological Studies*

"The most thorough study of Christ's nature based on Latin American liberation theology." *Time Magazine*

0-88344-076-8 **462pp.** **Paper**

THE TRUE CHURCH AND THE POOR
Jon Sobrino
This unusual scholarly venture into ecclesiology focuses on the poor as the channel through which God's spirit is manifesting itself today.

"Speaking with the struggling voices of Central America and relying upon the power and truth of the Gospel, Jon Sobrino continues forward from his *Christology at the Crossroads* to the type of church that the mission of Jesus Christ requires, namely, a church not only *for* the poor, but the true church *of* the poor." *Peter Schineller, S.J.*

0-88344-513-1 **384pp.** **Paper**

THEOLOGY OF CHRISTIAN SOLIDARITY
Jon Sobrino and Juan Hernández Pico
Two Jesuit theologians reflect on the theological significance of the growing Christian movement of solidarity with the suffering people of Latin America.

"This work's main agenda is a timely one, especially for progressive Christians in the First World: One cannot be *for* the poor without being *with* them." *Ken Sehested*

0-88344-452-6 **112pp.** **Paper**

JESUS OF NAZARETH YESTERDAY AND TODAY
Juan Luis Segundo

In this monumental five-volume series, one of this century's most prominent theologians places the person and message of Jesus directly before believer and non-believer alike. He argues for the extrication of Jesus from intricate theological categories, and attempts to shake off the christological dust of the centuries so all may hear the words Jesus spoke.

Volume I: FAITH AND IDEOLOGIES

Sets forth the methodology and defines the terms for a christology for today.

"Continues to develop the key concepts previously analyzed in *The Liberation of Theology*. A must for those exploring the frontiers of contemporary theology."

Alfred T. Hennely

0-88344-127-6   368pp.   **Paper**

Volume II: THE HISTORICAL JESUS OF THE SYNOPTICS

Explores the nature and implications of Jesus' parables and the proclamation of the kingdom of God as found in the synoptic gospels.

"A rigorous, coherent and insightful exegesis in conversation with contemporary biblical scholarship, identifying the anthropological, religious and ideological significance of Jesus."   *Newsletter, Currents in Contemporary Christology Group*
American Academy of Religion

0-88344-220-5   240pp.   **Paper**

Volume III: THE HUMANIST CHRISTOLOGY OF PAUL

Spanning both theology and exegesis, Segundo shows how Paul opens up a "humanizing political realm that no repression or control can render useless."

"Although an integral part of his five-volume work, this volume stands apart as a constructive hermeneutical study of Paul and a theological anthropological groundwork for liberation theology."   *Roger Haight, S.J.*

0-88344-221-3   256pp.   **Paper**

Volume IV: THE CHRIST OF THE IGNATIAN EXCERCISES

A detailed study of the christology imbedded in the *Spiritual Exercises* of Ignatius Loyola.   *(forthcoming)*

Volume V: AN EVOLUTIONARY APPROACH TO JESUS OF NAZARETH

Concludes the series addressing the questions of what it means to have faith in God and in Jesus.   *(forthcoming)*

JESUS BEFORE CHRISTIANITY
Albert Nolan

A challenging portrait of Jesus as he was before he became enshrined in doctrines, dogmas, and ritual. Here is a man deeply involved in the problems of his time—which turn out to be the problems of our time as well. Nolan shows us a surprisingly new way of understanding what is meant by Jesus' divinity.

"The book is full of arresting and challenging insights for the Christian of today. Nolan's ideas are stated with passionate conviction and he has read widely and judiciously among modern exegetes of varied schools." *Catholic Herald*

0-88344-230-2   160pp.   Paper

JESUS CHRIST LIBERATOR
A Critical Christology for Our Time
Leonardo Boff

A distinctive contribution to the contemporary quest for the meaning of Jesus.

"A book forged in unique circumstances of Latin American liberation theology, but the truth and power of its message could light fires anywhere." *Donald Senior, C.P.*

"An excellent introduction to the basics of contemporary liberation christology and thought, written from a position of deep faith." *The Christian Century*

0-88344-236-1   336pp.   Paper